THE HOLISTIC HAGGADAH

HOW WILL **YOU** BE DIFFERENT THIS PASSOVER NIGHT?

הגדה של פסח

Traditional Haggadah with Original Commentary by

Michael L. Kagan

With original translations of Hallel and
Blessings over the Meal by
Reb Zalman Schachter-Shalomi

Illustrations by Sandra Pond

URIM PUBLICATIONS
Jerusalem • New York

The Holistic Haggadah: How Will You Be Different This Passover Night?
by Michael L. Kagan

Printed at Hemed Press, Israel.
First Edition
ISBN 965-7108-49-7

Design and layout by Marek Lasman
Haggadah illustrations by Sandra Pond
Original photograph on cover of round, hand-made *shmurah* matzah by Ari Greenspan
Cover graphic and design by Shanie Cooper

Urim Publications, P.O. Box 52287, Jerusalem 91521 Israel

Lambda Publishers Inc.
3709 13th Avenue Brooklyn, New York 11218 USA
Tel: 718-972-5449 Fax: 718-972-6307
mh@ejudaica.com

www.UrimPublications.com

'05'

The Order of the Haggadah

Dedicated to my ancestors:

To those who died in serenity and

to those who died in violence.

May they all rest in peace.

Amen.

And specifically to the fond memories of

Uncle Harold

Uncle Jack

Aunty Ray

Uncle Harry

Each of whom contibuted to our Seder table in their own unique way.

I miss you all.

Personal Introduction

In 1989 my wife, Ruth, my eldest son Itamar, our new baby boy Ori and I were honored to be guests at the Seder table of Rabbi Meir and Anne Sendor in Sharon, Massachusetts. I was in Boston for postdoctoral research but that was just an excuse. I was really there to find a Teacher.

I had met Rabbi Meir a few months earlier and had started learning non-Ḥasidic Kabbalah with him. Now we were at his Seder table. There were about 15 adults and an equivalent number of children present. Rabbi Meir and Anne had the enviable skill of being able to throw out questions to the children that had the adults reeling. This "two world" learning experience fascinated me and I have been trying to replicate it ever since, albeit unsuccessfully. Then came the time for the eating of the matzah. Rabbi Meir introduced us to his eating meditation tradition that allowed for concentrated mindfulness during the eating of the matzah, the maror and the Hillel sandwich. I was seated next to him. I watched with amazement as he held the slice of matzah between his hands and slowly chewed. Tears poured down his cheeks, his face was luminous. I couldn't tell whether the light was shining down upon him from above or whether he was radiating it. I was awestruck. Something was happening that was deeper than I had imagined. The Seder table – no, all of Pesaḥ – suddenly took on a dimension that I had only tangentially touched upon in other non-Jewish contexts; it had become transformed into a vital personal spiritual experience. The historical dimension faded into the background as the immediate, present-time relevance sprung into the foreground. I began to realize that all of these rituals were serious, powerful and vital. That's not to say that I had previously underestimated their importance; after all, a mitzvah is a mitzvah. But now something had changed – I had changed. *Mah nishta-nah*? What is different? I was different.

My childhood memories of the Seder table are probably quite typical: an extended table decorated with the finest chinaware, my uncles and aunts (may those that have already passed-on rest in peace – they certainly didn't get much here) gathered together in the dusk, the lighting of the candles, the kiddush, the green stuff dipped into salt water, my siblings and I standing while singing the *Mah nishta-nah,* the proud faces of my mother and father, the nods of approval from my uncles and aunts

and then the mad rush of indecipherable incantations as my father and uncles raced through the next pages, slowing down just in time for the ten plagues and then on again, non-stop, until the eating of the matzah and the meal. In answer to my protestations over this annual mini-marathon my father would always say: "When the time will come for you to conduct your own Seder at your own table then you can do it in whichever way you want." For many years I took that remark as an insult and then later, as a challenge. Now I view it as a blessing. The re-Telling of the story is a personal affair. It must refract through the multi-faceted crystal of the life that is ours. We must diligently search the corners of our being for the face that is ours, for the Seder that is ours, for our unique connection to the past, to the future, to the Creator. May your journey be eventful and may God bless your every step.

User's Manual

Please read before operating. It is highly recommended that you read through the commentaries before the actual Seder night. Mark the ones that most speak to you and use them as seeds for discussion or meditation. In fact I would even recommend refraining from bringing this Haggadah to the Seder table because it might become too distracting. Rather use a simpler book that consists of the basic text alone.

The Holistic Haggadah is an accumulation of teachings that have been sown, and then watered and ripened by those tears of Rabbi Meir and which I have been harvesting ever since. The more I learn, the more I realize that the saying in the Talmud, that Moses heard all future teachings, is true. In my ignorance the teachings may seem novel – I have not attempted to deliberately ignore similar concepts from more respected sources. This is a very personal commentary and my goal is to encourage you to write your own.

There are four, even five, levels of text: the level of Doing, the level of Saying, the level of Being and the level of Deepening. Then there are the footnotes. This structure was not preconceived but rather emerged as construction began. It was immediately pointed out to me* that this construct parallels the Four Worlds of the Kabbalah:

* Thanks to Reb Tirzah Firestone.

Atzilut – the World of Emanation (Spirit),
Beriah – the World of Formation (Psychological, Intellectual),
Yetzirah – the World of Creativity (Emotion),
Assiyah – the World of Physicality (Doing).

This itself parallels the four letter Name of God: the י (*yod*) and the ה (*hey*) and the ו (*vav*) and the ה (*hey*). (The footnotes can either be considered as the hook on the *yod* or the foot on the lower *hey*.) While the Holistic Haggadah is not a kabbalistic Haggadah you will find some overt references to kabbalistic understandings. This is especially true of the commentary concerning the Four Cups. For this I have to thank my Teacher, Reb Zalman Schachter-Shalomi. The moment he knew that I was working on a Haggadah he insisted that I include his kabbalistic understanding of the order of the Four Cups.

The Level of Doing: This section concerns the practicalities of what to do at each juncture of the Haggadah. While I have tried to be accurate concerning halachic requirements, this book should not be considered halachically authoritative. There are many varied *minhagim* (traditions, styles) and I have followed the ones that I am most familiar with.

The Level of Saying: The text used in this section is the standard Ashkenazi version and appears in italics. The translation of the main text is my own. The translation of the Hallel Psalms, the Blessings over the Meal, the *Nishmat* (The Breath) prayer and the *Nirtzah* (Conclusion) prayer are by Reb Zalman. It is a great honor and opportunity for all of us that he has agreed to the inclusion of his translations. Whereas I have tried to extract meaning through exactitude, Reb Zalman has given multi-dimensional inspiration through poetry and poetic license. You will find that these translations are prayerful and actually fit the tempo and meter of the Hebrew; they can therefore be said or sung harmoniously in the two languages at the same time.

It should be noted that the word "Egypt" does not appear in the book. I have used the Hebrew term for that country – "Mitzraim" – and "Mitzrim" instead of "Egyptians." The reason for this is that the people of modern day Egypt live under a stigma for the role attributed to the ancient people who once lived in that land. Why perpetuate this? Furthermore, the word Egypt doesn't carry with it any metaphorical meaning, whereas the word Mitzraim – meaning "a Place of Constraints" – says it all.

I have followed the transliteration protocol for Hebrew into English:

the guttural letter "het" appears as "ḥ" So, for example, Pesach is written "Pesaḥ" and chametz is written "ḥametz." The guttural letter "kuf" appears as "kh". So baruch is written "barukh".

I have been made very well aware, by my children and many a guest, of my ability to stretch out a Seder night by my insistence on saying every word almost until the time for saying the morning *Shemah Yisrael* prayer. I have therefore indicated at various points when parts of the text can be skipped and they are printed slightly fainter than the regular text.

The Level of Being: This level of commentary lands somewhere between the historical and the here and now – usually on an intellectual level. It derives from teachings that I have given over for the last ten years as I've explored the holistic nature of Judaism and Jewish practice. Maimonides, amongst others, encourages us to find our own *Ta'amei Mitzvot* (lit. "taste for the commandments").* By this he does not imply that we should taste (i.e. try) each commandment to see which one suits us, but rather that we should taste each one and identify what the taste is like, what it does to us, what associations it conjures up, what it feels like and how it resonates within our souls. Metaphorically, a *mitzvah* can be seen as a key to a matching gate; but since each person's gates are totally unique, each key has to be specially crafted for its own gate. In this way the *mitzvah* can become integrated into each one of us in a personal and holistic manner.

The Level of Deepening: This level is more meditative in that it tries to provide material to feed the spiritual journey. Its purpose is to jolt us into going beyond the obvious or even metaphorical understandings of the ritual or text. It forces us to streeeeetch, to move beyond our comfort zones, to examine who we are and why we're doing all these strange things. It moves away from the historical level and digs deep into our psycho-spiritual worlds. Many times the commentary will be accompanied by a suggested exercise within the spirit of the festival that will help water the seeds of change, for it is in this level that the fertile soil exists that can catalyze the sinking of deep roots and the growing of tall trees.

Footnotes: In the footnotes I have tried to provide context for many of

---

* The Hebrew word "*mitzvah*" can be translated as "to join together," implying that God's intention is for us to become enjoined with our true Selves and the Source of all Life through the set of instructions called the *Mitzvot*. Traditionally there are 613 *mitzvot*, which are compared to the 613 limbs and sinews of the human body (see section 7.9 and the healing power of ḥaroset).

the quotations that appear in abbreviated form in the main text. I strongly recommend spending the time to familiarize oneself with the source of each quote, especially those appearing in the complex Midrashic section of the Telling. References are also given to websites, films and, where known, origins of ideas appearing in the commentaries.

I would be very appreciative for your feedback, suggestions, references and comments.

Acknowledgements

My recognition of certain close friends and teachers who have wittingly or unwittingly inspired me are sprinkled throughout the footnotes. I would especially like to acknowledge those who have helped me through my own deliverances from Mitzraim: Ruth Gan Kagan, my *ezer kenegdo* – my helper in spite of myself – through her love and commitment she has helped me face, fight and survive those parts of myself that have risen up to try and prevent my true Self from shining through. Rabbi Meir Sendor was there when I needed to vent my anger against "the system." He introduced me to the principles of Kabbalah and Jewish meditation. Matananda Ben Shmuel (formerly Hadassah Ben Yishai), who came into my life about eight years ago and permanently changed it for the Good through her teachings, guidance, clarity, humility and patience. She remains a true "Zen master," hitting me over the head whenever I fall asleep. Reb Shlomo Carlebach *z"l*, who I began to know just months before he left this world. I am still learning to appreciate the depth of his Torah. Reb Zalman Schachter-Shalomi, whose smile, warmth, laugh, song and immense Torah wisdom, understanding and knowledge fill me with the hope that old systems can renew themselves as they renew the world. Harold Lewy, who taught me how to live outside the box. Levi Ben Shmuel, a true friend and companion on the journey of Life who was with me when all this began and who is still there for me now. Ruth Seagull, who took the unenviable task of proofreading the original manuscript upon herself twice. Sandra Pond, who graciously provided the illustrations, Kim Mayroze who perfected the graphics, Azriel Cohen who drew the Chinese characters and Tzvi Mauer, the publisher of Urim, who courageously agreed to publish *The Holistic Haggadah*. My children, Itamar, Ori, Itai, Ayelet and Avital, who are constant reminders to me

of love, faith, innocence and Divine connectivity. Their questions and answers are endless sources of inspiration. My gratitude to all those who have trodden the path towards freedom with me, who have encouraged me to continue and who have trusted me to assist them.

Finally, to my parents; to my mother, who has given me the gift of being sensitive to the pain of the world and to my father, for giving me the wherewithal to do something about it.

The word "*inspire*" means to breathe in. As the Creator breathed the breath of life into every living creature, so I thank Her for breathing into me the inspiration behind every word and idea expressed in this work.

Hodu Le'YAH ki Tov,
ki LeOlam Ḥasdo

YAH* is good! Thank Him!
She** is kind to all the world's beings.

As you have entered in Peace may
The Compassionate One bless you to leave in Peace.
Bon Voyage.

M.L.K.
Boulder, Colorado
Jerusalem, Israel

* In his translations Reb Zalman prefers to use *YAH* rather than Lord or *HaShem* (The Name). I concur with his opinion that lordship is an unfamiliar concept in our times whereas *YAH*, as in *HalleluYAH* – *Praise God* – should always be on the tip of our tongues. Furthermore, *YAH* is the name associated with the Godly attribute of *Ḥokhmah* (wisdom), which is the level of greatest expansion and is thus fitting for the Pesaḥ theme of "*From the narrow straits I cried to YAH, from the great expansion YAH answered.*" (Psalm 118). To support this the Talmud states (Eruvin 18b) that: Since the Sanctuary was destroyed it is enough for the world to use only two letters [of the Tetragrammaton].

** To emphasize that God is above any gender classification, in spite of the limitations of language, I have rendered the Divine pronoun as sometimes "he" and sometimes "she" depending on context.

What is a Holistic Haggadah?

The cycle of the Jewish year can be viewed as and lived as a healing spiral or medicine wheel. Each festival interweaves with the one before and the one after it to create a truly holistic* journey that we tread throughout our lives. When appreciated in this manner, each festival and occasion takes on a dimension that goes far beyond the confines of the festival itself. As you will see as you pass through this Haggadah, there are continual references to other parts of the year, not because of some abstract association but because of its holistic nature. By this I mean that all parts of the cycle are somehow interconnected and relate to every other part. Thus the cycle forms an organic whole. Wholeness is a criterion for Holiness, and Holism bridges the gap between the two.**

To visualize this in two dimensions, let us contemplate the perfection of the circle. All points on the circumference are of equal distance from the center. Rebbe Naḥman of Bratzlav emphasizes the Holiness of the

* The term holistic was first coined by the statesman Jan Smuts (South African philosopher-statesman, Zionist, father of "Holism," 1870–1950) in *Holism and Evolution* (1926, republished in 1973). His contribution to philosophy was mostly forgotten until the 1980s when the holistic movement took hold in the west. Smuts was a Christian Zionist who took every occasion to promote the cause of the nascent Zionist movement. He once said: "Nothing in the whole bloody history of the human race compares with the history of the Jewish people."

** The word "holism" (and "holistic") comes from the Greek "holos" which means "whole." The word "holy" is also derived from the same Greek root, as is "health." In old and middle English "whole" was spelled "hol," and then "holle." The "w" was only added much later. In Hebrew the best translation would be "*shalem*," as in the verse: "And Jacob came *shalem* (whole) to the town of Shekhem." (Genesis 33:18 and Rashi *cit. loc.*). *Shalem* is related to the word "*shalom*," meaning "peace." From a holistic point of view health and peace are intimately connected – inner peace leads to a healthy body; outer peace leads to healthy relationships. *Shalom* is also one of the names of God and is therefore associated with Holiness. To become Holy is to become Whole. Smuts defines Holism as follows: "...in so far as the elements or parts cohere and coalesce into the structure or pattern of a whole, the whole must itself be an active factor or influence among them; otherwise it is impossible to understand how the unity of a new pattern arises from its elements. Whole and parts mutually and reciprocally influence and modify each other; the one is pliant to and molded by the other; the parts are molded and adjusted by the whole, just as the whole in turn depends on the cooperation of its parts." (*Encyclopedia Britannica*, 1927. For an introduction to the theory of holism and its spiritual implications see: www.isss.org/smuts.htm).

circle, especially during Hasidic ritual dance: moving in a circle; eyes towards the center; no leader, no follower; all leader, all follower; hand outstretched to the common locus; no one nearer, no one further; oneness exemplified; one point; one unending line with neither beginning nor end; harmony with the Divine Oneness; harmony with the Divine Oneness at the center; perfection. The Hebrew word for circle and dance is the same – *mahol.* Miriam, the Prophetess, danced with the women in a circle after the crossing of the Reed Sea.* During the festival of Succot we carry our Four Species – the *lulav* (palm branch), *hadas* (myrtle branches), *aravah* (willow branches) and *etrog* (species of citrus fruit) – and we encircle the Torah. These species represent our own being. They represent, are metaphors for, various parts of the physical body (spine, eyes, mouth and heart), as well as our emotional, psychic and spiritual bodies. They come together as one; we draw them in and draw them out with our breath. On the seventh day we circle seven times, encompassing the seven *Sefirot*** – the fractal image of the cosmos mirrored in our own bodies.

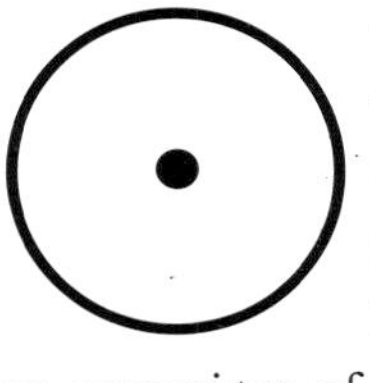

The letter *aleph* is the silent, first letter of the Hebrew alphabet. Its numerical value is therefore one. It represents Unity, undivided consciousness, Oneness.

The first letter, however, of the Torah is the *bet* – "*B'reishit – In the beginning of God's creation of the world of Spirit and the world of Material....*" It is the second letter of the alphabet and has a numerical value of two: bifurcation, binary, division, duality, dimensions, up/down, good/evil, male/female. A mystical understanding of this is that the black letters of the Torah are written on the white background of unified existence. As such, the first diagram becomes inverted with the dot at the center of the circle representing our physical "reality" and the area around it, behind it and in front of it becomes the God-field.*** Of course, the outer circle disappears in the infinitude of Divine existence. With the

---

* See the ceremony of Miriam's Cup at the end of the Maggid section.

** For an explanation of the *Sefirot* and the Tree of Life, see Section 9.

*** Field in Hebrew is *sadeh*, as in: "A man found him (Joseph) wondering in the field" (Genesis 37:15). Deepak Chopra (*Ageless Body – Timeless Mind*) has reinterpreted the classic Hindu word for field to mean a field as understood in physics, namely a continuum of influence such as an electromagnetic field in which there is interconnectivity between all the parts in time and space. According to Chopra, this field

four species mentioned above, we shake them in the six directions as we stand in the center of our cosmic sphere.

The Jewish calendar is a coupling of two, normally non-coupled, clocks, namely the sun and the moon. The sun is the clock of the earth, for it regulates the cycle of the seasons. The summer equinox is always in the summer and the winter equinox is always in the winter. Plant life responds to the amount of sunlight per day in determining the appropriate time to awaken after the winter hibernation. The winds are a function of sunlight warming and cooling the planetary atmosphere. The daily sleep/awake cycle (the circadian rhythm) is entrained to the spin of the planet on its axis vis-à-vis the sun. The annual rhythm of the seasons is determined by the angle of the earth to the sun. In short, the pulse of nature is sun-based. The moon, however, has very little effect on the earth apart from the tides. The amount of the surface of the moon that is facing the sun is constant; what changes is the angle between the sun, the moon and the earth. This results in the phases of the moon, which are independent of the seasons.

In a solar-based calendar the months are always fixed to their seasons and, for example, Christmas is always in the winter, whereas the months in a lunar-based calendar continuously regress in relationship to the seasons.* Thus, in the Muslim calendar, which is solely based upon the moon, the month of Ramadan can fall out in the summer one year, in the spring a few years later and in the winter a few years after that.

In many religions and cultures the sun is assigned a masculine identification or energy whereas the moon is assigned a feminine identification or energy. This designation is also Biblical. In Joseph's dream, he reports seeing the sun, the moon and eleven stars bowing down to him. His father, Jacob, rebukes him saying, "*Shall I and your*

---

of consciousness is the basis of the Ayurvedic healing practices. I suggest that the Hebrew use of the term *sadeh* be equally reinterpreted to mean the field of God-consciousness that pervades all of Creation.

* This regression is caused by the fact that the solar year cycle is approximately 365.25 days whereas the lunar year cycle is 354.372. Thus every solar year the lunar year shifts backwards by 11 days. For a fascinating article about neo-lithic awareness of these differences see: www.geocities.com/mythical_ireland/ancientsites/knowth/calendarstone.html.

mother and your brothers come to bow down to you upon the earth?"* So the father (male) is the sun and the mother (female) is the moon. That the moon is understood to be a female symbol is rather obvious considering the periodicity of the moon's phases is so closely aligned with the periodicity of a woman's fertility cycle.** The female energy of the moon influences the female cycle on earth as it does the rhythm of the tides. Coincidently, water is also seen as a female energy.***

Following this line of argument, in spiritual terms the sun – male – is associated with the world of physicality and the moon – female – is associated with the world of spirituality. So inherent within the Jewish calendar, the union of the solar seasonal cycle and the lunar monthly cycle, is the tension between male and female, between physical and spiritual, between Yang and Yin energies.

Pesaḥ is the pace-maker. "*And God spoke to Moses and Aaron in the Land of Mitzraim, saying: 'This month**** shall be the beginning of the months for you; it will be the first of the yearly cycle of months for you'*" (Exodus 12:1–2). And: "*The day that you are leaving (Mitzraim) is in the month of the spring*" (Exodus 13:4). So Pesaḥ, or more correctly, the New Moon of the month of Nisan, must forever be in the spring season. And here lieth the tension, since, left to its own devices, the month of Nisan would regress relative to the seasons until Pesaḥ would be celebrated in the middle of winter! In order to correct for this aberration a leap year*****

---

* Genesis 37:10. Interestingly enough, this dream is never actually fulfilled. Joseph manipulates his brothers into bowing down to him but stops himself before he can make his father do the same. In fact the dream could never have been literally fulfilled because Joseph's mother, Raḥel, had long been dead. Rashi suggests that it implies his adopted mother, Bilha.

** It is a known female experience that the menstruation cycles of groups of women in close contact begin to resonate together, similar to the physical phenomenon of resonance, such as pendulums swinging on a common frame. Anita Diamond in her book *The Red Tent* suggests not only that the 28–30 day fertility cycle is attuned to the lunar cycle but also that women in nomadic communities have cycles that coincide exactly with that of the moon such that menstruation always occured on the new moon.

*** See the end of the Maggid section for the connection between Pesaḥ, water and Miriam, the Prophetess.

**** The Hebrew word for month is "*ḥodesh*," which literally means "new," referring to the moon's renewal.

***** A leap year is referred to as a "pregnant year," thus maintaining the imagery of the male/female union.

is introduced by adding an extra month seven times every nineteen years.* This extra thirteenth month (Adar II) is squeezed into the calendar immediately preceding Nisan.

The Yin-Yang symbol that derives from the ancient Chinese Tao or I-Ching philosophy,** shows a circle divided equally into a light area and a dark area. Within the light area there is a dark circle and within the dark area there is a light circle. The symmetry is beautiful and profound. It is the symbol of dynamic harmony extending throughout the cosmos.*** It shows the duality of the Creation enclosed within the Oneness of the Creator. The Yin is the female principle (anima) and the Yang is the male principle (animus). Within the male there is the female element and within the female there is the male element. Earth is Yang; Spirit is Yin. Sun is Yang; moon is Yin. Opposites balance; harmony unites – holism.

Now, let the dark area of the Yin-Yang represent the winter months and the light area the summer months and let's map out the cycle of the Jewish year on its surface.**** What then is the white circle within the depth of winter? The festival of light – Ḥanukah! Conversely, the dark circle in the peak of summer? Tisha B'Av, the black hole of destruction and grief! Ḥanukah, the celebration of the rededication of the Temple and reestablishment of national autonomy; Tisha B'Av, the commemoration of the destruction of the Temple and the loss of national autonomy. Now look carefully at the tail of the summer period. This coincides with Tu B'Shvat, the 15th day of the month of Shvat, almost a month and a half

---

* See the reference to the Stone of Knowth on page 13.

** The Chinese characters of I-Ching are 易經. The second character means a book, a profound book. The first character means ease or change. Since I-Ching is easy, some people call it "The Book of Ease" or "The Book of Changes." The original Chinese character of 易 is , which is a symbol combining the sun (top) and moon (bottom). (Quoted from www.chinesefortunecalendar.com/YinYang.htm). The Yin-Yang symbol is constructed by tracing the shadow of the sun cast at a specific time by an 8-foot pole placed in the earth. The length of the shadow is shortest during the summer equinox and longest during the winter equinox. When the entire year of shadow-lengths are plotted radially the result is the Yin-Yang (ibid.).

*** From a Ḥasidic perspective it symbolizes the spark of Godliness (light) that exists even in the places of darkest shadow caused by the thickest husks (klipot). And on the contrary, that even in the greatest Tzaddik there must be a trace of darkness.

**** This mapping of the year cycle was first pointed out to me by my friend Jacob Spilman.

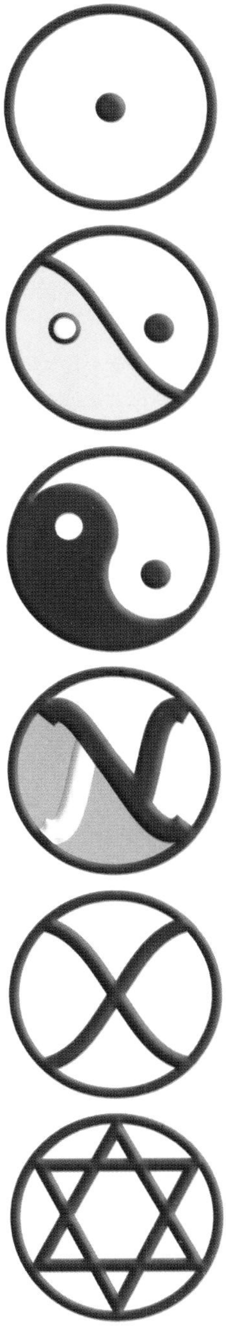

after Ḥanukah, and is the New Year* for trees. In the Judean Hills surrounding Jerusalem the almond trees are in full blossom. There may be snow on the ground, freezing winds blowing through the wadis, but there they are – the blossoming almond trees. Nature is stirring; the sap is once again rising; life returns after the dark night of the soul.

Ḥanukah is that time of our lives in which everything seems dark. We struggle so, but to no avail.** No hope visible. Depressed. The only thing to do is light a candle. A small act in order to remember the miracle of life, the fragility of life. Just hang in there and keep looking at the lights.

Tu B'Shvat is very different. The end is in sight. Even though it's still dark the first light is showing on the horizon. You know that you have past through the worst, that you are on the way up, beginning the journey of return.*** Nature calls.

After the month of Shvat comes Adar and on the full moon is the festival of Purim, which celebrates the victory over the destructive forces of Haman.**** The leitmotiv of Purim is "order out of chaos"; that in the world of duality there seems to be no Master, no rhyme or reason for the events that take place so chaotically around us. It just seems like a big coincidence. The Book of Esther is read, in which the name of God doesn't even appear. It describes a series of strange events whose interconnectiveness seems very thin at the least. And yet by the end of

---

* The first mishnah in tractate Rosh HaShannah states that there are four New Years: 1st of Tishrei – New year for years; 1st of Nisan – New Year for kings; 1st of Elul – New Year for animals; and 15th of Shvat (Beit Shammai says the 1st of Shvat) – New Year for trees.

** The necessity of experiencing the dark night of the soul is beautifully described by Caroline Myss in Spiritual Madness, available at www.myss.com.

*** In the vision of Ezekiel (1:14) the angelic creatures (the Living Ones) are seen flying towards and away from the Holy Throne ("ratzu v'shuv," lit. "running and returning"). This process is understood in Ḥasidism to describe the soul's relationship with the Divine. We can get close but then we have to go back. Many times this "going back" feels like going back to the same place or level that we came from and that can be very depressing. Rebbe Naḥman of Bratzlav assures us that even though it may feel like we're back at the beginning, we are in fact on a higher rung. And this is the way of learning. Reb Zalman of Boulder says in the name of Rav Barukh Ben Ashlag that when we're in the light we get blinded to our own faults and it is only when we return to the shade that we can see the work that still needs to be done.

**** Purim is a post-Biblical festival ordained by the Sages, although a hint of it can be found in Exodus 34:17: "Do not make gods out of your masks," followed immediately by, "You shall keep the feast of matzah...."

the story the Jews are victorious and the evil Haman is hung on the gallows intended for Mordeḥai. And Esther, the hidden Jewish queen, comes out and reveals her true origins and fulfills her life-purpose and the Divine plan. God's face is hidden, but God's hand is revealed.* *Here*

Exactly one month later, on the full moon of Nisan, is the Festival of Freedom. Why must Purim occur in the month immediately preceding Pesaḥ? Because we must recognize and acknowledge that there is an inherent order to the world, otherwise we might as well stay in Mitzraim. In fact the celebration on the first night of Pesaḥ** is called the Seder – the Order in the Darkness. *2019 Still Please help me Lord.*

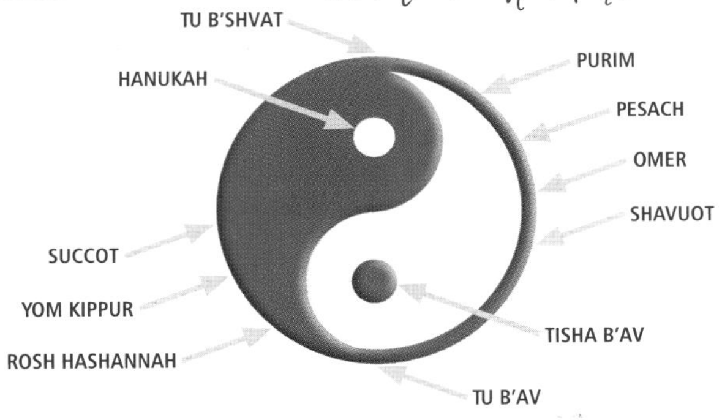

From the second day of Pesaḥ, the counting of the Omer*** begins. This is a 7x7+1 day count leading up to Shavuot. The commandment is to literally "count the days." From a kabbalistic point of view this time is essential for the integration of the self with the Self as we leave slavery behind and move towards ultimate freedom. Each of the seven weeks vibrates with the energy of another *sefirah* of the Tree of Life: Ḥesed, Gevurah, Tiferet, Netzaḥ, Hod, Yesod and Malkhut. Each day of each week vibrates with the energy of another *sefirah*. So the first day of the first *Because every day counts Bless G.L*

---

* Order out of chaos and *chaos* out of order have become important components of the "new" physics. See Chaos by James Glick, *Order out of Chaos* by Ilya Prigogine and *Dissipative Spatial Structures* by M. L. Kagan (Doctoral thesis, Hebrew University of Jerusalem, 1987).

** The Hebrew calendar contains devices that enable us to use the days of Pesaḥ to predict the day of the week upon which each of the year's festivals will fall. The code is aleph-taf, i.e., the first and last letters of the Hebrew alphabet – alef and taf – are paired; so are the second and the penultimate letters, bet and shin, and so on. The first day (aleph) of Pesaḥ will be the day on which **T**ishah (begins with the letter taf) B'Av will fall; **S**havuot (begins with letter shin) falls on the second day of Pesaḥ, and so on.

*** See the Counting of the Omer, Section 9

week is the energy of *Ḥesed* in *Ḥesed*; the second day of the first week is *Gevurah* in *Ḥesed*; the third day of the third week is *Tiferet* in *Tiferet*, and so on. Since each *sefirah* relates to the physical, emotional, psychological and spiritual worlds, then as each day is counted so the work of aligning, adjusting, awakening, arousing and attuning on all these levels can take place.* The purpose of all this is to arrive at a state of Oneness** when standing at the mountain receiving the Torah. And this is Shavuot.

Shavuot is a predominately female festival. It is celebrated through consumption of milk products, symbolizing the Great Mother aspect of the Divine. The Book of Ruth*** is read, which describes the exploits of Naomi and her daughter-in-law, and the synagogues are decorated with greenery as a reminder of the Garden of Eden.**** This festival should be the climax of the year. What more could there possibly be after God's descent on the mountain and the giving of the Torah? But something goes terribly wrong – the Golden Calf is built forty days later and the entire vessel cracks. We weren't ready to attain such heights. And the year goes tumbling down, through the 17th of Tammuz (the Golden Calf), down and down and down to the black hole of Tisha B'Av (the revolt of the spies in the desert and the destruction of the First and Second Temples).

The Ninth of Av (Tisha B'Av) is a Yang (male) energy day, for it literally means the ninth day of the month of the father (Av). It occurs in the middle of the summer when the sun (father – see above) burns the hottest, when the anger of the father strikes out and almost destroys his children. It is a time of deep grieving over the damaged relationship with the father figure of the family.***** But it is also a time of great healing,

---

* The totality of this work would be the equivalent of a Jewish Yoga practice.

** "And Israel camped as One," Rashi on Exodus 19:3. This is on a community level but is also understood to be on an individual level since the two are inseparable. This state of Oneness was a prerequisite for receiving the Torah. Two years later the same state was achieved as the people left the mountain en route for the Promised Land. This is hinted at in the identical gifts offered by the twelve princes in Numbers 7. Unfortunately, in both cases the fall occurred not long after: the Golden Calf and the complaining in the desert (Exodus 32 and Numbers 11:1 respectively).

*** In English the word "ruthless" means "one lacking in compassion." A lesser-used word is "ruthful," i.e., full of compassion. Compassion in Hebrew is raḥamim, which in the singular is reḥem, meaning "womb."

**** The Midrash on Genesis 1:31 ("**The** Sixth Day") suggests that the sixth day refers to **the** sixth day of Sivan – Shavuot – implying that the giving of the Torah is the completion of the Creation.

***** Sometimes the role of the father is taken on by the mother of the family ("Who wears

for it is said that the possibility of the Messiah is born on this day. Out of the flames the New arises. And six days following the making of peace with the masculine there is the celebration of Tu (15th) B'Av – the love festival where male and female are reconciled.

Out of the black hole we rise higher and higher, passing through the month of Elul up to Rosh HaShannah, higher still to Yom Kippur, higher still to Succot, eventually reaching the peak with the festival of joy – Simḥat Torah.

How does this stretch of the year work? Rosh HaShannah is the time, with the help of the *shofar*, to remember to "get back on track" – *Teshuvah* (lit. "to return") to the flow of our uniquely individual, God-given river. This is a male energy dominated period in which the moon is least visible and the King sits in judgment (*din*). By Yom Kippur we are expected to demonstrate that we have earnestly changed direction and ask for forgiveness for having gone off course.* By Succot we show our faith in God by leaving our "secure" homes to live under the Clouds of God's Glory. The male and female principles come together again as we shake the *lulav* in the enclosure of the *succah* and pray for rain and the fertility of the land. This is the time to bring the parts together for a complete healing and integration of the self, as symbolized by the *Ushpizin* – the Holy Guests.**

Finally we close the *succah*, put aside the *lulav* and simply dance with the Torah in ecstatic joy. This is Simḥat Torah – the Joy of the Torah.

If we now look back at the circle with the point in the middle we must admit that this is only a two dimensional representation of this healing cycle. In truth the point at the center is actually a line that acts to unwrap the circle into a spiral ladder, or Tree of Life, similar to the unfolding of the DNA helix. So that when we return to Pesaḥ year after year we are never in the same place. So this year – how will **you** be different?

---

the pants?").

* The word for sin in Hebrew (*ḥet*) literally means to miss the mark. Iniquity (*avon*) means to be off balance and transgression (*peshah*) means to go over the boundaries. So following the analogy from Zen archery, when the archer releases the arrow, if there is some inner imbalance within the archer's emotional and spiritual self then the arrow will miss the target and go out of bounds. See: *Zen in the Art of Archery*, E. Herrigel (Arkana, 1987).

** 1st night Avraham and Rivka, 2nd night Yitzḥac and Sarah, 3rd Yaacov and Ruth, 4th Moshe and Miriam, 5th night Aaron and Hannah, 6th night Yoseph and Tamar, 7th night David and Raḥel (see Section 9 for a different configuration)

The cycle of the year can be depicted in a linear manner in which the vertical axis represents spiritual "peakness" and the horizontal axis represents time.

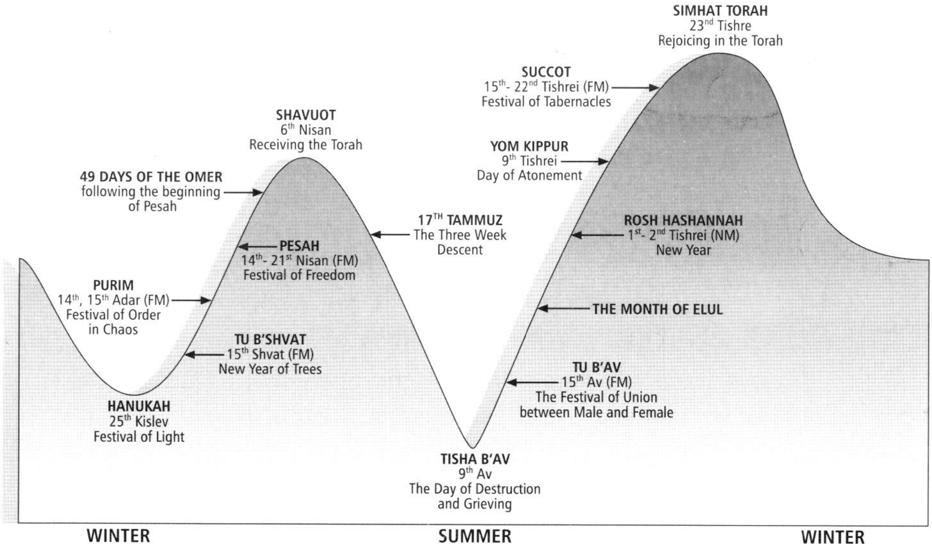

In the Beginning – Between Purim and Pesaḥ

The month between Purim and Pesaḥ can be juxtaposed with the month before Rosh HaShannah, six months away. That month of Elul is accompanied by an intense period of introspection and soul-searching, leading to a crying out for forgiveness. Now, before Pesaḥ, there's no time for such luxuries of the free for we are still deep in Mitzraim. The relevant question is not: "How well have I been living my life?" but rather, "Do I want to live? Am I ready to be brought out of Mitzraim – the place of the living dead?" The world has to be engaged on the physical level. There's work to be done, ḥametz to be removed, kitchens to be koshered. This is especially emphasized by the fact that from the first of Nisan confessional prayers are no longer said during the morning and afternoon prayer services. This is not the time to be asking for forgiveness. "Hurry up! It's time to leave!"

Pesaḥ must occur in the spring season (Exodus 12:1) because, as seedlings begin to penetrate out of the darkness of the soil towards the sun, so too do we move out of the darkness of our confinement towards the Light of God. Thus the rhythms of the natural world and the rhythms of the spiritual world coincide.

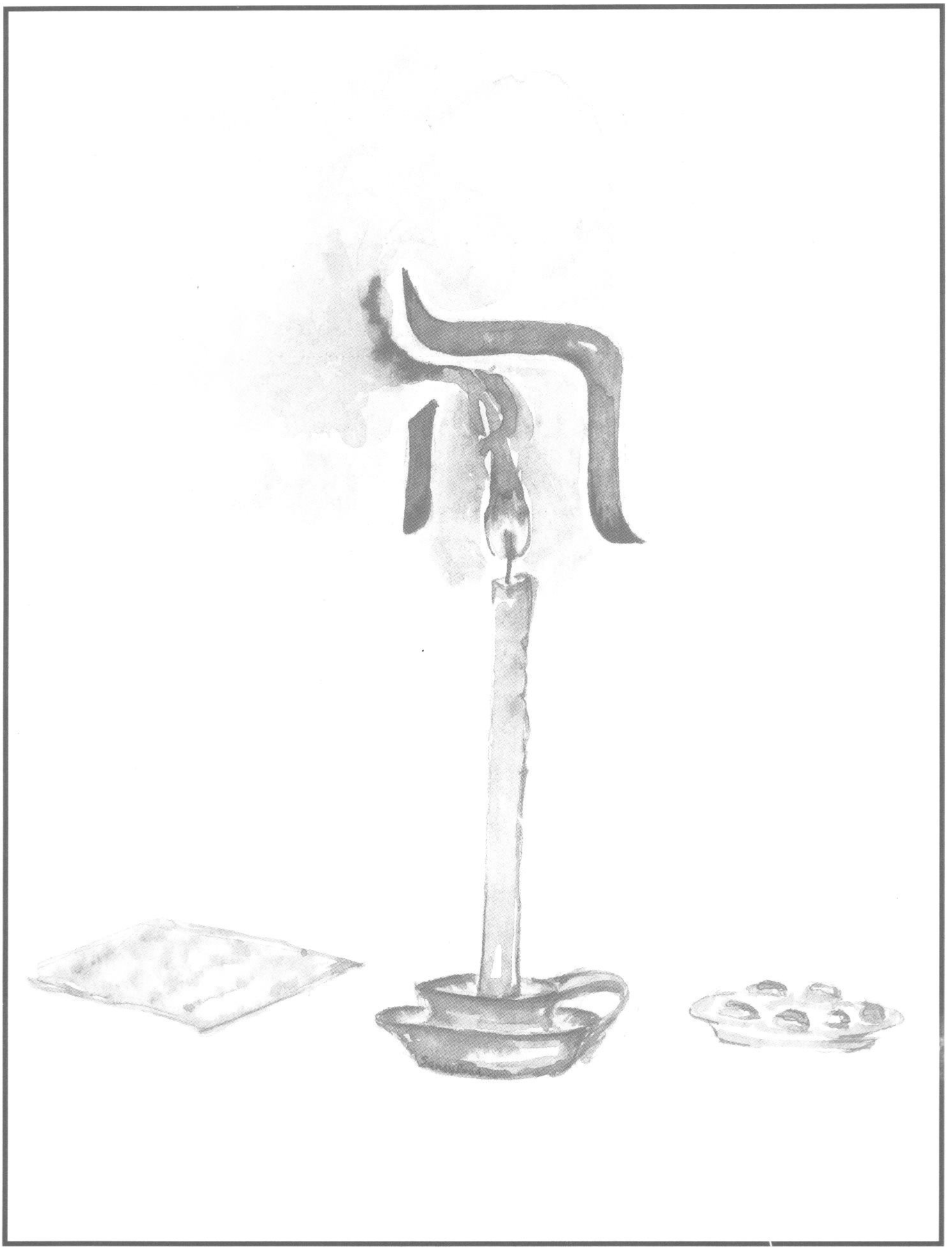

בדיקת חמץ

After dusk on the day before the Seder the search begins for any remaining ḥametz in any location owned by the household; this includes the residence, cars, office, etc. It is traditional that in order to make the search real, ten pieces of ḥametz (bread, cake, etc.) are carefully wrapped in aluminum foil or small plastic bags and distributed in each room at floor level. The children can do this "hiding" of the ḥametz but an adult should supervise in order that the hidden packets not get lost. The search is traditionally made using a candle in a darkened room, although a pinpoint flashlight will do. A feather or small brush is used to brush the found ḥametz into a bag. Effort should be made to search in corners and under furniture in a serious way. Care should be taken not to drip candle wax all over the floor and special care should be taken not to set the curtains alight. At the end of the search the candle and brush are added to the bag.

The blessing is made before the search starts. From that moment the searcher remains in silence until all the packets are found and then reads the Aramaic statement in a language that is comprehensible.

בָּרוּךְ אַתָּה יְיָ, אֱלֹהֵינוּ מֶלֶךְ הָעוֹלָם, אֲשֶׁר קִדְּשָׁנוּ בְּמִצְוֹתָיו, וְצִוָּנוּ עַל בִּעוּר חָמֵץ:

כָּל חֲמִירָא וַחֲמִיעָא דְּאִכָּא בִּרְשׁוּתִי דְּלָא חֲמִתֵּהּ וּדְלָא בִעַרְתֵּהּ וּדְלָא יְדַעְנָא לֵהּ, לִבָּטֵל וְלֶהֱוֵי הֶפְקֵר כְּעַפְרָא דְּאַרְעָא.

BEING

The search for ḥametz around the house takes place in the dark under the scrutinizing light of a single candle. Take time to look scrupulously within for parts of yourself that have fermented and gone sour, that have become "old stuff," out-dated. But be gentle; search with a candle but clean with a feather, not a pneumatic drill or chain saw. It is so easy to hurt ourselves more, to beat ourselves up, to be our own taskmasters. Flood yourself with the light of awareness and purification but let the accusing mind be still.

The ability to nullify any remaining ḥametz is an example of the way our intentions can affect the spiritual world. The ten pieces of hidden bread represent the parts of our own Tree of Life* that have become fermented and have become barriers to the Divine flow.

* In kabbalistic terminology these barriers are referred to as *klipot*, or shells, that block the full *shefah*, or Divine sustenance, from flowing through the Tree. For more on the Tree of Life see the final section on the Counting of the Omer.

❧ B'dikat Ḥametz – Searching for Ḥametz ☙

Searching for inner spoilage

After dusk on the day before the Seder the search begins for any remaining ḥametz in any location owned by the household; this includes the residence, cars, office, etc. It is traditional that in order to make the search real, ten pieces of ḥametz (bread, cake, etc.) are carefully wrapped in aluminum foil or small plastic bags and distributed in each room at floor level. The children can do this "hiding" of the ḥametz but an adult should supervise in order that the hidden packets not get lost. The search is traditionally made using a candle in a darkened room, although a pinpoint flashlight will do. A feather or small brush is used to brush the found ḥametz into a bag. Effort should be made to search in corners and under furniture in a serious way. Care should be taken not to drip candle wax all over the floor and special care should be taken not to set the curtains alight. At the end of the search the candle and brush are added to the bag.

The blessing is made before the search starts. From that moment the searcher remains in silence until all the packets are found and then reads the Aramaic statement in a language that is comprehensible.

[Before:]

Blessed are you, Lord our God, Majesty of the Universe, who has sanctified us through unification and commanded us to remove all the ḥametz.

[After:]

All ḥametz in my possession which I have not seen and have not removed shall be nullified and be ownerless as the dust of the earth.

DEEPENING

From the beginning of the month of Nisan start writing a list of what you are a slave to in the physical, emotional, psychological and spiritual planes of your life. Food, sex, money, time, car, house, family, wife, husband, work, alcohol, looking good, clothes, etc. Fear of loss, fear of success, fear of embarrassment, fear of being small, etc. Expectations of parents, teachers, friends, leaders, advertisers, society, etc. Suffering, being happy, being critical, being serious, worrying, etc. Self-improvement, workshops, books, finding meaning, self-discipline, being obedient, etc.

ביעור חמץ

In the morning, before about 10:30 a.m., the ḥametz collected from the night before plus any other ḥametz is burnt in a small, controlled fire.

כָּל חֲמִירָא וַחֲמִיעָא דְּאִכָּא בִרְשׁוּתִי דַּחֲזִיתֵהּ וּדְלָא חֲזִיתֵהּ, דַּחֲמִתֵּהּ וּדְלָא חֲמִתֵּהּ, דְּבִעַרְתֵּהּ וּדְלָא בִעַרְתֵּהּ, לִבָּטֵל וְלֶהֱוֵי הֶפְקֵר כְּעַפְרָא דְאַרְעָא.

Write. Be honest with yourself, for you know when you are lying. We could all easily fill several pages with our slaveries and that which we enslave (dependency and co-dependency). On the night of the fourteenth, when the search for ḥametz takes place, shred the list into little pieces and scatter them on the floor. If you find it difficult to tear up 'such a well thought out list' that has taken you so much time and effort to compose, then write that down as another slavery and then tear up the list. Go on you hands and knees and search for all the torn pieces and collect them in an envelope. In the morning burn it with the *Kavannah* (proper intention) that you are burning that which prevents you from being free, the gods of your ego-mind.

BEING

There is a custom of burning the ḥametz using the *lulav* (palm frond), kept from Succot half a year earlier, as kindling. What a beautiful example of Jewish recycling! The palm branch that was so tall, straight and proud is now withered and frayed. Its backbone has collapsed. It's time for change. It's time for a resurrection. Throw it into the flames. It's time to come out of Mitzraim. It's time to start another cycle in the spiral of life.

DEEPENING

Before Pesaḥ we search for ḥametz in the seams of our pockets. Any ḥametz found is collected and cast into the flames. During Rosh HaShannah there is a tradition to do *Tashliḥ* – casting off of sins – where the pockets are turned inside out over a body of water. What's the difference? At Pesaḥ we

❧ Biur Ḥametz – Burning the Ḥametz ❧

Willingness to let go of attachments

In the morning, before about 10:30 a.m., the ḥametz collected from the night before plus any other ḥametz is burnt in a small, controlled fire.

All ḥametz in my possession, whether I have seen it or not, whether I have removed it or not, shall be nullified and be ownerless as the dust of the earth.

were deep into our slavery, cut-off, desperate for air. We would do anything (or nothing) to get out. To be free from Mitzraim we must be radical. Whatever is enslaving us, trapping us, trapped by us, must be destroyed – and quickly. Our over-inflated, fear-filled egos that create the illusions of our reality, our reality of illusions, must be deflated and reduced to naught in fire. No mercy. Every crumb, every hint, cast into the flames. Dis-illusionment into the light of the fire of Truth. This is *bitul* – self-nullification.* At Rosh HaShannah we are dealing with our sins (misguided actions). Breadcrumbs now symbolize our iniquities (loss of balance) and transgressions (going out of bounds), whose roots originate in some form of ego inflation. These are cast into the waters and are thereby transformed into food for the fish. Sins are misguided events in the past and *Teshuvah* (turning back to God) transforms the past and karmic consequences of our actions. Ḥametz, on the other hand, represents a state of being now, in present time. It can only be transformed through fire.

Let go. Just let go. For God's sake, let go. For your sake, let go. You're still holding on to what doesn't work for you. Cast it into the flames.

What is the difference between matzah and ḥametz? Just this much.** It is the difference between a little bit less than 18 minutes and a little bit

* Reb Zalman Schachter-Shalomi understands self-nullification as becoming transparent to the will of God so that God shines through us without hindrance. In the case of Moses this led to his face literally glowing with beams of light (Exodus 34:29).

** The term, "Just this much" is from Stephan Levine's *Healing into Life and Death*. He uses the term to imply that when starting out on the path of healing one should take whatever size steps feel appropriate, that even the smallest step is actually a giant leap forward ("One small step for man..."). In the context of Pesaḥ we see that one small candle is all that is needed to cast away a lot of darkness. The shift between these opposites involves small subtle changes in attitude. It's like looking at the stars – a tiny shift in perspective by our eyes results in a sweep of millions of light years across the heavens.

Don't forget to start the Seder w/ music = worship.
incense! I worship you Almighty G-d, Holy Spirit Medley!
& El Shaddai tape
(See sheet)

✿ הדלקת נרות ✿

bo

A 24-hour candle is lit from which fire can be transferred during the festival.
Festival candles are lit as on Shabbat except that the blessing is recited after the match
is lit but before the candles are lit. If your preference is to say the blessing slowly then it
is recommended to first light a small kindling candle, say the blessing and then light the
main candles. The general rule is to first say a blessing and then do the action. However,
on Shabbat, since the saying of the blessing registers the onset of the Shabbat, which
would then prevent the lighting of the candles, the candles are lit first, the eyes covered,
the blessing recited and only then the hands removed to reveal the candles already lit!
Care should be taken not to purposely extinguish the match or kindling candle. Just leave
it in a safe place to burn itself out.

בָּרוּךְ אַתָּה יְיָ, אֱלֹהֵינוּ מֶלֶךְ
הָעוֹלָם, אֲשֶׁר קִדְּשָׁנוּ בְּמִצְוֹתָיו
וְצִוָּנוּ לְהַדְלִיק נֵר שֶׁל (בשבת: שַׁבָּת וְשֶׁל)
יוֹם טוֹב:

בָּרוּךְ אַתָּה יְיָ, אֱלֹהֵינוּ מֶלֶךְ הָעוֹלָם, שֶׁהֶחֱיָנוּ וְקִיְּמָנוּ
וְהִגִּיעָנוּ לַזְּמַן הַזֶּה:

◆

more than 18 minutes. Look at the Hebrew: "matzah" is comprised of the
letters מ (mem), צ (tzaddik) and ה (heh). "Ḥametz" consists of the letters ח
(ḥet), מ (mem) and צ (tzaddik). The difference between these two words is a
ה (heh) and a ח (ḥet). And what's the difference between these two letters?
The ה (heh) is the same as the ח (ḥet) except that it has a small opening on
its top left. That's it – just a small gap, no bigger than the eye of a needle. √
That's the difference between reality and illusion, between ignorance
and enlightenment, between darkness and light, between arrogance and
humility, between broken and fixed.* Just this much. √

use Aly Bet Wheel!

---

*   Reb Shlomo Carlebach z"l was wont to say that healing takes time whereas fixing
(tikkun) is immediate.

You might want to have a blanket available to cover yourself. Allow yourself to be wrapped in the loving arms of the *Shekhinah*.* *yes.*

A = The real Complete Passover Sedu
B = Ian Peerce
  A Passover Sedu.

❧ Lighting the Candles ❧
Bringing in the Light

1st Pg 35 order
Then B-1
Here

A 24-hour candle is lit from which fire can be transferred during the festival. Festival candles are lit as on Shabbat except that the blessing is recited after the match is lit but before the candles are lit. If your preference is to say the blessing slowly then it is recommended to first light a small kindling candle, say the blessing and then light the main candles. The general rule is to first say a blessing and then do the action. However, on Shabbat, since the saying of the blessing registers the onset of the Shabbat, which would then prevent the lighting of the candles, the candles are lit first, the eyes covered, the blessing recited and only then the hands removed to reveal the candles already lit! Care should be taken not to purposely extinguish the match or kindling candle. Just leave it in a safe place to burn itself out.

Blessed are you, Lord our God, Majesty of the Universe, who sanctified us through unification and commanded us to light the [Shabbat and] holiday candles.

Blessed are you, Lord our God, Majesty of the Universe, who has given us life and the opportunity to arrive here now at this moment.

BEING

No hurry
no worry

Welcome the light into your heart. Let your being become infused with warmth. Don't hurry. Now is a time to take time. So much rushing has taken place to reach *yes* this moment. Just relax. Know that all your efforts on behalf of yourself, your family and your guests will soon come to fruition. Do not say "soon it will be all over," but rather "soon it will all begin." If you have felt like a slave over the last few days (weeks), try to ensure that this evening you will be treated as a king or queen, that you will be served, that this night will be different for you, too.

DEEPENING

Why, specifically on Shabbat, are two principle candles lit? The two candles represent the duality of the world as we generally experience it. This is the letter ב (*bet*), the first letter of the Bible, which has a numerical value of two. This is the illusion of our existence: there is I and thou,

ברכת בנים

On this night, when the *mitzvah* is to relate the story of our past to the carriers of our future, it is traditional to give the children the blessing that is usually reserved for Friday nights. Mother and father, either together or separately, place their hands on the child's head.

לבנים: יְשִׂמְךָ אֱלֹהִים כְּאֶפְרַיִם וְכִמְנַשֶּׁה

לבנות: יְשִׂמֵךְ אֱלֹהִים כְּשָׂרָה רִבְקָה רָחֵל וְלֵאָה

יְבָרֶכְךָ יהוה וְיִשְׁמְרֶךָ׃
יָאֵר יהוה פָּנָיו אֵלֶיךָ וִיחֻנֶּךָּ׃
יִשָּׂא יהוה פָּנָיו אֵלֶיךָ וְיָשֵׂם לְךָ שָׁלוֹם׃

inside and outside, male and female; there is God and there is me. Where is the true reality? In the letter that comes before the *bet*. Where is it? It's in the silent, invisible א (*aleph*), which equals the number one. So for six days of the week we live our lives in continuous struggle or tension with this duality. On Shabbat we can become dis-illusioned (freed from illusions) and settle back into the One. And so the Shabbat is called the ONE. This is the offering of the Shabbat – to remember that we are ONE. And when Shabbat ends we light a *havdalah* candle, which is made from a number of wicks intertwined to form one flame. The two have become ONE. In a similar way the *ḥallah* bread of a regular Shabbat consists of many braids fusing into the ONE. And so it is for male and female to become ONE, especially on the Shabbat.

BEING

Bless your loved ones. Bless yourself. Bless your table. Bless your house. The Hebrew for blessing is *brakhah*, which is associated with the word *breikhah* (pool). We all need to receive blessings to fill our pool. We all need to give blessings to share from our reservoir. Open your heart and let yourself be a channel for the Divine blessings to flow through.

If there are no children around the table then bless each other. If there are

❧ Blessing the Children ❧

For they are our future

On this night, when the *mitzvah* is to relate the story of our past to the carriers of our future, it is traditional to give the children the blessing that is usually reserved for Friday nights. Mother and father, either together or separately, place their hands on the child's head.

[For a son:] ***May God make you like Ephraim and Menashe.***

[For a daughter:] ***May God make you like Sarah, Rivkah, Raḥel and Leah.***

[For both:] ***May God bless you and look after you.***

May the light of God's face shine upon you and may you be graced.

May the face of God be turned to you and give you peace.

children then bless them and then bless each other. Breathe in the blessings. And when you have finished, bless yourself and the child inside you.

DEEPENING

From the beginning of the month of Nisan (the First Month) there is the opportunity to say a blessing upon seeing blossoming fruit trees (*Birkhat HaIlanot*). Why now and not two months earlier around Tu B'Shvat when the almond trees are flowering? Why wait? Why specifically fruit trees? Because this is the month when we pass on our story to the next generation, when the tree gives its energy to its future.

When the *Kohen* (priest) raises his hands to give a blessing his fingers part – two and two; his hands are raised with the outstretched thumbs touching each other and the index fingers touching; his upper body and hands are covered by his *tallit* (prayer shawl). What is all this about? The *Kohen* is taking on the stance of the Holy Cherubim that were standing on the lid of the Holy Receptacle that was in the Holy of Holies. His fingers are parted like the tip feathers of wings; his arms are raised like

the Angels' wings, stretched out to touch each other. The *tallit* hides the energy hot spot like the *Parokhet* (curtain) hid the inner sanctum. And the Holy Spirit came down between the gap in the outstretched wings, down to the level of the breasts, and then projected outwards spreading its blessing amongst the people. The *Kohen* is not the source of the blessing. He is a channel for the blessing to come down from the Most High. The blessing comes down through his outstretched fingers, down to the level of his heart and then outwards. And so it is that if the heart of the priest is blocked through anger or grief then he is not to bless because his heart is blocked to the blessing of peace.

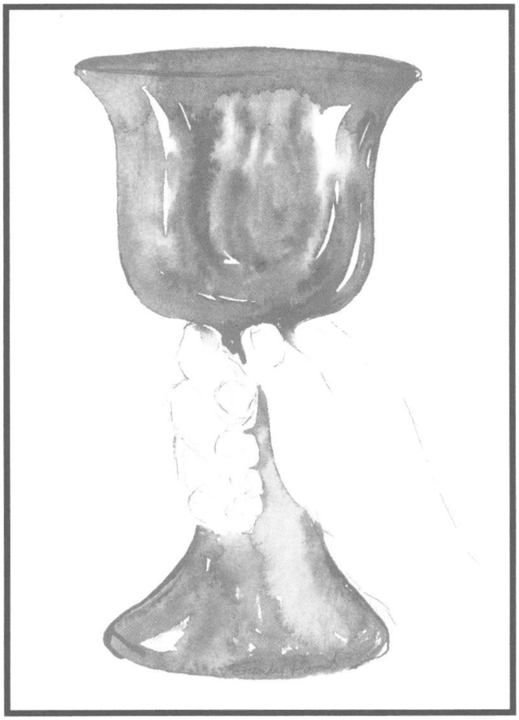

סדר ליל פסח

The Seder Night

Tonight, Jews all over the world are going to a magical place. The seder. A place filled with special foods, with family and friends and with exciting stories. And kiddush is the entrance into the seder.

When the person leading your seder stands up with a beautiful cup in his hand filled with wine and begins to say the kiddush, he is actually welcoming everyone to a very wonderful place. A place where you will hear stories from three thousand years ago. A place where frogs might jump on your table, where hail might fall from the ceiling and where you will get special treats, prizes and delicious foods.

סימני הסדר

The table is set for the evening's journey. If possible, all participants should have three matzot separated by napkins before them. The various special items on the table are pointed out to all. The ceremonial plate consists of a roasted egg, a burnt piece of boned meat (*z'roah*), bitter lettuce leaf or freshly grated horseradish (*maror*), sweet mixture (*ḥaroset*) and green vegetable (*karpas*). The three matzot lie hidden in their coverings. The goblet of wine and the stockpile of wine bottles wait to be opened. The mysterious Cup of Elijah. The innovative Cup of Miriam. The salt water for the dipping of the karpas. The cushions for leaning on.

The Order of the evening's ceremony is recited, usually in song.

קַדֵּשׁ וּרְחַץ

כַּרְפַּס יַחַץ

מַגִּיד רָחְצָה

מוֹצִיא מַצָּה

מָרוֹר כּוֹרֵךְ

שֻׁלְחָן עוֹרֵךְ

צָפוּן בָּרֵךְ

הַלֵּל נִרְצָה

Can use R. Simonson's Passover CD for Chanting the Order

The Fifteen Steps – *Order Out of Chaos*

B-1

The table is set for the evening's journey. If possible, all participants should have three matzot separated by napkins before them. The various special items on the table are pointed out to all. The ceremonial plate consists of a roasted egg, a burnt piece of boned meat (*z'roah*), bitter lettuce leaf or freshly grated horseradish (*maror*), sweet mixture (*ḥaroset*) and green vegetable (*karpas*). The three matzot lie hidden in their coverings. The goblet of wine and the stockpile of wine bottles wait to be opened. The mysterious Cup of Elijah The innovative Cup of Miriam. The salt water for the dipping of the karpas. The cushions for leaning on.

The Order of the evening's ceremony is recited, usually in song.

Kadesh – Kiddush and the First Cup of wine
UrḤatz – Washing the hands (without blessing)
Karpas – First dipping: green vegetable into salt water
Yaḥatz – Breaking the matzah
Maggid – Telling the story
Raḥtzah – Second washing of the hands (with blessing)
Motzi – First blessing over matzah
Matzah – Second blessing over matzah
Maror – Second dipping: bitter herb into ḥaroset (sweet mixture)
Koreḥ – The sandwich of Hillel
Shulḥan Oreḥ – The meal
Tzafun – The Afikoman
Barekh – Blessing the Source of the Meal
Hallel – Praising
Nirtzah – Conclusion

BEING

The Haggadah is a beautifully constructed book that has the power and mystery to take us on an experiential journey down into our inner Mitzraim and then out into freedom. It accomplishes this through various levels of sacred ritual: eating, drinking, story telling, meditating, learning, questioning, reciting, chanting,

singing, rejoicing, praying and playing. It is not just an intellectual exercise.

The Seder night is built around the dialectic of slavery and freedom. In every section these themes play themselves out. In the first half of the Seder the emphasis is more on the slavery, whereas in the second part it is on the freedom. And where is the turning point? Look out for it.

The Seder Plate has five (or six) elements on it: a roasted egg (*baitzah*), a burnt piece of boned meat (*z'roah*), a lettuce leaf (*maror*), sweet mixture (*ḥaroset*), and a green vegetable (*karpas*) – horseradish (*ḥazeret*) is the optional sixth. What can these symbolize? The ḥaroset – the sweet people; the maror – the bitter ones; karpas – the ones full of life; the burnt meat – our ancestors; and the roasted egg – those yet to be born.* They are all on one plate, for together we make up the experience of life. (This is also reminiscent of the festival of Succot when we tie and shake different vegetation together. Each can be seen as different personality types or different aspects of oneself.)

DEEPENING

Seder literally means "order." Pesaḥ follows after Purim.** Purim is the festival that celebrates the hidden hand of order in the chaos of our regular lives. The Book of Esther doesn't even contain a mention of God's name, hand or direct intervention in the unfolding of history. Everything seems to occur randomly, with no rhythm or reason. God's face is hidden. By reading the Megillah (lit.: "scroll," but also "to reveal") and focusing in on the space between the letters – the unwritten story – the Divine Order begins to become apparent. When we look at our lives through our regular eyes all we can see is a series of coincidences. Only when we rise up and look down can we see the connections between events and the Hand that assists. It is for this reason that Purim must occur before Pesaḥ for, if we have no appreciation of this reality, then we might as well stay in Mitzraim – why bother swapping one prison for another? God's Order is revealed right up front, right now.

* This insight was shared by Sariel Rabinovitz, age 9 (Pesaḥ 5758). The Ari *z"l* uses six elements and identifies the bone with the *sefirah* of *Ḥesed*, the egg with *Gevurah*, bitter herbs with *Tiferet*, ḥaroset with *Netzaḥ*, karpas with *Hod* and horseradish with *Yesod*. The three matzot are *Keter*, *Ḥokhmah* and *Binah* respectively (see *Counting of Omer*).

** See Introduction

The Cup of Eliyahu* (Elijah) the Prophet holds a mystical fascination over children's imaginations and is a central feature of the Seder table. What is it doing here? The source comes from a dispute in the Talmud regarding the levels of redemption that we are to celebrate with the drinking of wine. The levels appear as separate expressions in Exodus 6: 6–8, "*Therefore say to the Children of Israel, I am the Lord, and I will **bring** you from under the burdens of Mitzraim, and I will **rescue** you out of their bondage, and I will **redeem** you with an outstretched arm, and with great judgments; and I will **take** you to me for a people…And I will **bring** you into the land…*" Is the last verb part of the drama of the Exodus or not? The answer is left undecided until the arrival of Eliyahu, the herald of the Messiah, who will resolve all such disputes. Thus, in the meantime, we drink Four Cups and leave a fifth one undrunk on the table. Is that all? Listen, for here lies a great secret. The importance of Eliyahu at the Seder table is because of our deepest slavery – our slavery to our family dramas. This inter-generational gathering brings out all the worst – and best – memories of family interactions. The family drama – the most insidious of all slaveries – is ever present. The voices of our fathers; the voices of our mothers; the voices of our siblings; our own voice as a child; they are all present at the Seder table. Whether physically present or as memories, they are all there, still pulling us this way and that. And the Seder table, like everything else mentioned here, is only an encapsulation, a microcosm of our lives. The manner in which we then relate to our children and partners is influenced by these voices that conjure up such deep emotions. In the *Haftorah* (Reading from the Prophets) on the Shabbat immediately before Pesaḥ (called *Shabbat HaGadol* – the Great Shabbat) the last lines from the last canonized Prophet, Malakhi, are read, "*Behold, I will send you Eliyah, the Prophet, before the coming of the great and awesome day of the Lord; and he shall turn the heart of the fathers to the children, and the heart of the children to their fathers…*" (Malakhi 3:23–24). Here is the goal and here is the promise. The Messiah, the great healing, will come when we can open our hearts to our parents and when we can, as parents, open our hearts to our children. And hear them, and be heard. And love them, and be loved by them.

---

* This teaching is given here because it relates to the family dynamic that is about to begin around the table. It is repeated later in the section on Eliyahu's Cup.

קַדֵּשׁ

The first of the four glasses of wine are poured. It is customary that everyone pours for someone else, thus introducing the spirit of majesty and freedom to the table.

It is advisable that there be bottles of grape juice available for those who are overly sensitive to alcohol (apple juice and even milk is permissible).

If there is a Master of Ceremonies for the evening then he or she will raise the goblet and recite the sanctification over the wine and time on behalf of all the others. If not then everyone raises their own glasses and recites together.

After the blessings are recited, be seated. The majority of the liquid is drunk while leaning on one's left side.

הִנְנִי מוּכָן וּמְזֻמָּן לְקַיֵּם מִצְוַת כּוֹס רִאשׁוֹן מֵאַרְבַּע כּוֹסוֹת. לְשֵׁם יִחוּד קוּדְשָׁא בְּרִיךְ הוּא וּשְׁכִינְתֵּיהּ עַל יְדֵי הַהוּא טָמִיר וְנֶעְלָם בְּשֵׁם כָּל יִשְׂרָאֵל:

On the Eve of Shabbat begin here:

בלחש: וַיְהִי עֶרֶב וַיְהִי בֹקֶר

יוֹם הַשִּׁשִּׁי, וַיְכֻלּוּ הַשָּׁמַיִם וְהָאָרֶץ וְכָל־צְבָאָם: וַיְכַל אֱלֹהִים בַּיּוֹם הַשְּׁבִיעִי מְלַאכְתּוֹ אֲשֶׁר עָשָׂה, וַיִּשְׁבֹּת בַּיּוֹם הַשְּׁבִיעִי מִכָּל־מְלַאכְתּוֹ אֲשֶׁר עָשָׂה: וַיְבָרֶךְ אֱלֹהִים אֶת־יוֹם הַשְּׁבִיעִי, וַיְקַדֵּשׁ אֹתוֹ, כִּי בוֹ שָׁבַת מִכָּל־מְלַאכְתּוֹ אֲשֶׁר בָּרָא אֱלֹהִים לַעֲשׂוֹת:

When the festival begins on a weekday, begin here:

סַבְרִי מָרָנָן וְרַבָּנָן וְרַבּוֹתַי

בָּרוּךְ אַתָּה יְיָ, אֱלֹהֵינוּ מֶלֶךְ הָעוֹלָם, בּוֹרֵא פְּרִי הַגָּפֶן:

בָּרוּךְ אַתָּה יְיָ, אֱלֹהֵינוּ מֶלֶךְ הָעוֹלָם, אֲשֶׁר בָּחַר בָּנוּ מִכָּל־עָם, וְרוֹמְמָנוּ מִכָּל־לָשׁוֹן, וְקִדְּשָׁנוּ בְּמִצְוֹתָיו, וַתִּתֶּן־לָנוּ

(A) Reel Complete Passover Seder
(B) Jan Peerce Passover Seder

Kadesh – *Making Holy*

The first of the four glasses of wine are poured. It is customary that everyone pours for someone else, thus introducing the spirit of majesty and freedom to the table.
It is advisable that there be bottles of grape juice available for those who are overly sensitive to alcohol (apple juice and even milk is permissible).
If there is a Master of Ceremonies for the evening then he or she will raise the goblet and recite the sanctification over the wine and time on behalf of all the others. If not then everyone raises their own glasses and recites together.
After the blessings are recited, be seated. The majority of the liquid is drunk while leaning on one's left side.

(A) 1 *Here I am right now, ready and mindful to participate in the unification of the Transcendent Holy One with the Immanent Shekhinah through the* ***first*** *of the Four Cups.*

On the Eve of Shabbat begin here:

And it was evening and it was morning -
The completion of the sixth phase.
Heaven and Earth were brided
Together with all their hosts.
And God brought to contain on the Seventh Day
All the works that God had made.
And God blessed the Seventh day
And wedded it to become sacred.
In this, God found repose
From all the action that God had created
So that we have something significant to do.

When the festival begins on a weekday, begin here:

A (2) *Blessed are You, Lord our God, Majesty of the Universe, who brings into being the fruit of the vine!* Partak[e]

Blessed are You, Lord our God, Majesty of the Universe, who has chosen us from all the other peoples and has distinguished us from all other tongues, by sanctifying us with your commandments. You have given us,

Remem to announce each step of the seder

Kadesh
Urḥatz
Karpas
Yaḥatz
Maggid
Raḥtzah
Motzi
Matzah
Maror
Korekh
Shulḥan Orekh
Tzafun
Barekh
Hallel
Nirtzah

יְיָ אֱלֹהֵינוּ בְּאַהֲבָה (לשבת: שַׁבָּתוֹת לִמְנוּחָה וּ) מוֹעֲדִים
לְשִׂמְחָה, חַגִּים וּזְמַנִּים לְשָׂשׂוֹן אֶת־יוֹם (לשבת: הַשַּׁבָּת הַזֶּה
וְאֶת יוֹם) חַג הַמַּצּוֹת הַזֶּה. זְמַן חֵרוּתֵנוּ, (לשבת: בְּאַהֲבָה,)
מִקְרָא קֹדֶשׁ, זֵכֶר לִיצִיאַת מִצְרָיִם. כִּי בָנוּ בָחַרְתָּ וְאוֹתָנוּ
קִדַּשְׁתָּ מִכָּל הָעַמִּים. (לשבת: וְשַׁבָּת) וּמוֹעֲדֵי קָדְשֶׁךָ (לשבת:
בְּאַהֲבָה וּבְרָצוֹן) בְּשִׂמְחָה וּבְשָׂשׂוֹן הִנְחַלְתָּנוּ: בָּרוּךְ אַתָּה יְיָ,
מְקַדֵּשׁ (לשבת: הַשַּׁבָּת וְ) יִשְׂרָאֵל וְהַזְּמַנִּים:

[If the Seder night falls out on Saturday evening then add:]

בָּרוּךְ אַתָּה יְיָ, אֱלֹהֵינוּ מֶלֶךְ הָעוֹלָם, בּוֹרֵא מְאוֹרֵי הָאֵשׁ:

בָּרוּךְ אַתָּה יְיָ, אֱלֹהֵינוּ מֶלֶךְ הָעוֹלָם, הַמַּבְדִּיל בֵּין קֹדֶשׁ לְחֹל בֵּין אוֹר לְחֹשֶׁךְ, בֵּין יִשְׂרָאֵל לָעַמִּים, בֵּין יוֹם הַשְּׁבִיעִי לְשֵׁשֶׁת יְמֵי הַמַּעֲשֶׂה. בֵּין קְדֻשַּׁת שַׁבָּת לִקְדֻשַּׁת יוֹם טוֹב הִבְדַּלְתָּ, וְאֶת־יוֹם הַשְּׁבִיעִי מִשֵּׁשֶׁת יְמֵי הַמַּעֲשֶׂה קִדַּשְׁתָּ. הִבְדַּלְתָּ וְקִדַּשְׁתָּ אֶת־עַמְּךָ יִשְׂרָאֵל בִּקְדֻשָּׁתֶךָ. בָּרוּךְ אַתָּה יְיָ, הַמַּבְדִּיל בֵּין קֹדֶשׁ לְקֹדֶשׁ:

[On all nights continue here:]

בָּרוּךְ אַתָּה יְיָ, אֱלֹהֵינוּ מֶלֶךְ הָעוֹלָם, שֶׁהֶחֱיָנוּ וְקִיְּמָנוּ
וְהִגִּיעָנוּ לַזְּמַן הַזֶּה:

קדש
ורחץ
כרפס
יחץ
מגיד
רחצה
מוציא
מצה
מרור
כורך
שלחן עורך
צפון
ברך
הלל
נרצה

BEING

In Mitzraim we had descended to the lowest rung on the ladder of the Profane. We were the living dead. Physically, our Life Energies were literally being stolen as slaves. Spiritually, metaphorical Mitzraim is the place of narrowing Life's potential, the place of becoming the Living Dead. We must be free to be alive. Let us ascend the ladder to the Holy Mountain of God. The Journey starts right NOW!

Why lean on the left side? Why not the right side? In the kabbalistic understanding of the Tree of Life (see "Counting the Omer" for a more detailed explanation), the left side is associated with constriction while the right side is associated with expansion; the left side with judgment while the right side with

Lord our God, in love [the Sabbaths to rest in and] the appointed times to be joyous in, including today [this Sabbath and today] this festival of Matzot, the season of our liberation [in love] that is proclaimed Holy. Remember the Exodus from Mitzraim for through it you have chosen us and separated us from all the other peoples. You have granted us [the Sabbath] and the Holy Moments [in love and intention] in joy and in bliss. Blessed are You who has sanctified [the Sabbath,] Israel and the festivals.

[If the Seder night falls out on Saturday evening then add:]

Blessed are You, Lord our God, Majesty of the Universe, who brings into being the lights of the fire.

Blessed are You, Lord our God, Majesty of the Universe, who differentiates between Holy and Profane, between light and dark, between Israel and the other peoples, between the seventh day of being and the six days of doing. Furthermore you have created a differentiation between the level of Holiness of the Shabbat and the level of Holiness of the Festival as you have raised in Holiness the seventh day of Being from the six days of doing. You differentiated and raised up in Holiness your people Israel within your Holiness. Blessed are You, Lord, who differentiates between Holy (Shabbat) and Holy (Festival).]

[On all nights continue here:]

Kadesh
Karpas
Yahatz
Maggid
Rahtzah
Motzi
Matzah
Maror
Korekh
Shulhan Orekh
Tzafun
Barekh
Hallel
Nirtzah

Blessed are You, Lord our God, Majesty of the Universe, who has lived us, has sustained us and has entered us into this moment right now.

grace; the left side with tension while the right side with ease. Mitzraim means "The Place of Constriction." God leaned on the Mitzrim and had to put the squeeze on them to release the Children of Israel. On the other hand, the Children of Israel were eased out of Mitzraim by the gentle, loving hand of God. To what can this be compared? To a woman giving birth* with a midwife in attendance.

The wine is drunk to help lower your resistance; to help you let go; to break habits. For instance, leaning while eating (weren't you always told to "Take your elbows off the table!"?).

---

* The Hebrew term for labor contractions is *tzirim*, connected to the word Mi*tzraim*.

DEEPENING

What is it to make Holy? To be Holy? For it says, "Be Holy! For I, the Lord your God, am Holy."* Holiness is a velocity vector, meaning it has both direction and movement. Imagine a ladder that reaches up, higher and higher, but also reaches down, lower and lower. Ascending the ladder is Holy (*Kodesh*), descending it is called Profane (*Ḥol*), the antithesis of Holy. The Temple that once stood in Jerusalem, Israel, the Middle East, Earth, had several segregated areas. At the very center stood the Holy of Holies. This could only be entered once a year – on Yom Kippur – by one person – the High Priest. The surrounding areas could only be entered by certain people under certain conditions. The High Priest had to be on the highest level of purity (*Taharah*) otherwise he would not survive the experience. This can be compared to an electrician fixing an electric generator that is putting out millions of volts of electricity. If he isn't properly grounded, if he isn't totally focused, if he doesn't have the correct tools, if he makes one slip, then he will not survive. So it was with the High Priest when he entered the Holy of Holies, for this was the place where God's energy flowed the highest that a human could withstand. What is this energy? It is the energy of LIFE (*Hayut–Ki–Chi–Prana***) in its most intensive form. If the High Priest was not a perfect conductor, if he was not as fully alive as a human being could be – physically, emotionally, mentally and spiritually – then he would not be able to dwell in the Presence of the full Energy of Life. Anything less than being fully, 100% alive is called impure (*Tamei*). This is Death – the antithesis of Life.*** It's not that dying is bad. It's that not being fully alive, while you're alive, is deadly. From the Holy of Holies the level of Life Energy spread out in decreasing intensity. The inner court, then the outer court, then the City, then the Land and finally the whole Earth. The closer a person wanted to come, the purer she had to be. How do we become pure? By removing ourselves from all contact with death – physically, emotionally, mentally and spiritually. An essential stage in such a process involves entering the Waters of Life (*Mikvah*); that is, returning to the womb state of total purity or, in

קדש
ורחץ
כרפס
יחץ
מגיד
רחצה
מוציא
מצה
מרור
כורך
שלחן עורך
צפון
ברך
הלל
נרצה

* Leviticus 19:2

** *Ki* – Japanese; *Chi* – Chinese; *Prana* - Sanskrit

*** "If the opposite of birth is death then what is the opposite of life?" From *The Seventh Telling* by Mitch Chefitz (St. Martin's Press, 2001).

spiritual terms, returning to the Garden of Eden and then rebirthing anew, alive. How do we become impure? By stealing life, by diminishing life from others, from yourself, from the planet, from the Universe. We steal life because we don't believe that there is enough to go around. If we open ourselves up to the Source of All Life then we would interrupt the illusion of scarcity and our fear of death would dissipate. The more we steal, the more we descend the ladder of the Profane. The more we channel Life Energy (*Ḥayut*), the higher we ascend the ladder of Holiness. Give, share – stop taking.

The First Cup represents the letter י (*yud*) of the Divine name.* This is the cup of Holiness that opens the channel for the energy to come down from the High Place of *Atzilut* – the World of Emanation, the World before Conception, our Being before we have even started the journey of this Telling. As the night progresses, we draw the Divine Presence down and as we do so, we ourselves ascend. This is the Ladder of Jacob. This is the triangle with its apex facing downwards, descending from the Heavens, while simultaneously the triangle with its base on the Earth is ascending. In the space in between the tips touch, kiss and proceed to interlock in an Eternal hug. This is the *Magen David*, the Star of David. This is Israel – the Ladder between Heaven and Earth.

At this point in the evening each participant is encouraged to introduce her/himself and briefly relate where they were at the previous year's Seder. Reflect not only on where you were physically but also where you were on your own life path.

Kadesh
Urḥatz
Karpas
Yaḥatz
Maggid
Raḥtzah
Motzi
Matzah
Maror
Korekh
Shulḥan Orekh
Tzafun
Barekh
Hallel
Nirtzah

* This teaching was given over to me by Reb Zalman Schachter-Shalomi on ב Nisan, 5762 (March 14th, 2002).

⊰ וּרְחַץ ⊱

Each person at the table washes his or her hands and dries them without reciting a blessing. The water should not be recycled back into the pitcher. If it is convenient, the heads of the household wash everyone's hands using a pitcher and bowl.* This act of kindness is a reminder of the necessity of humility in the journey to true freedom.

BEING

Why the washing of hands without a blessing? What other times is there a ritual washing of hands with no blessing? Upon rising in the morning (the blessing is actually delayed until morning prayers commence) and upon leaving a cemetery. The reason given for the former is that sleep is like a sixtieth part of death and that the taint of death remains on the fingertips. Likewise when leaving a cemetery. The Talmud (*Kiddushin* 49b) states that 10 measures of sleep were given to the world – nine went to slaves. Being confined in Mitzraim is like being buried alive – it's the living death. The opening volley in the road to freedom is to wash your hands of the antithesis of life.

⊰ כַּרְפַּס ⊱

Celery sticks or parsley leaves are distributed and dipped into bowls of salt water. The blessing is said and the greenery is chewed contemplatively. Taste the saltiness of the vegetable with the added saltiness of the water.

There is an accepted, historical practice to expand this "hors d'oeuvres" section in order to ease the hunger pangs that might develop, as the meal is still a long way off. Suggested dips: chips (crisps), carrots and more celery dipped in salsa or ketchup; artichoke and boiled potatoes dipped in salt water.

בָּרוּךְ אַתָּה יְיָ, אֱלֹהֵינוּ מֶלֶךְ הָעוֹלָם, בּוֹרֵא פְּרִי הָאֲדָמָה:

BEING

Karpas: what is it? Karpas is usually a green, leafy, salty vegetable like parsley, celery or watercress dipped into salt water. These are your tears; those that you have shed and those that you haven't allowed yourself to shed. Remember how

---

* This touching act of serving others was learnt from Rabbi Meir and Anne Sendor.

קדש
ורחץ
כרפס
יחץ
מגיד
רחצה
מוציא
מצה
מרור
כורך
שלחן עורך
צפון
ברך
הלל
נרצה

44

Urḥatz – *Purifying*

Each person at the table washes his or her hands and dries them without reciting a blessing. The water should not be recycled back into the pitcher. If it is convenient, the heads of the household wash everyone's hands using a pitcher and bowl.* This act of kindness is a reminder of the necessity of humility in the journey to true freedom.

Nothing is said. Silence is preferred.

DEEPENING

Another occasion when the hands are ritually washed with no blessing is when the *Kohanim* (Priests) prepare to give the Priestly blessing. Tonight, be priestly! Have your hands washed and prepare yourself to be a channel for the Divine blessing of freedom.

Karpas - *Connecting Inside*

Celery sticks or parsley leaves are distributed and dipped into bowls of salt water. The blessing is said and the greenery is chewed contemplatively. Taste the saltiness of the vegetable with the added saltiness of the water.

There is an accepted, historical practice to expand this "hors d'oeuvres" section in order to ease the hunger pangs that might develop, as the meal is still a long way off. Suggested dips: chips (crisps), carrots and more celery dipped in salsa or ketchup; artichoke and boiled potatoes dipped in salt water.

Blessed are You, Lord our God, Majesty of the Universe, who creates the fruit of the ground.

they tasted as they ran down your cheeks? Breathe. The Haggadah is bringing you into contact with your inner Mitzraim. All those times that you have felt trapped, lost, out of touch with yourself and the Source of Life – unfulfilled. Feel the constriction in your chest, the knots in your stomach. The Journey has begun.

Kadesh
Urḥatz
Karpas
Yaḥatz
Maggid
Raḥtzah
Motzi
Matzah
Maror
Korekh
Shulḥan Orekh
Tzafun
Barekh
Hallel
Nirtzah

יחץ

Each participant removes the middle matzah and holds it up to view. It is important that the piece is whole, without blemish. If an edge is chipped then it should either be replaced or, provided it is not Shabbat, the corner can be browned in the flame of the candle. Spend some time meditating on the matzah. Note its texture, its lightness of being, its simplicity.

With quiet determination break the matzah into two parts, approximately one-third to two-thirds. The larger piece is wrapped up in a cloth or napkin and put aside becoming the *Afikoman,* while the smaller piece is held as the next section is chanted together. The children should be made aware that the Afikoman of the leader is for capturing and hiding, and will have to be ransomed for the Seder to end. The capturing of the Afikoman should take place during the confusion of the meal.

Silent mindfulness

BEING

WAIT!! Bring *Kavannah* ("proper intent") to one of the most poignant rituals of the evening. Hold the unbroken matzah in your hands. This represents your true self; that is why it is so important that the slice of matzah is totally whole. Whole without any ego-inflation, without the swelling of pride, without being stuck in the head, without any fermentation spoilage, without any masks. Just you, as you were as a child. *Tam* – innocent – before the questioning began, before the answers were provided, before you had to pass exams. And this is how you wish to be again. And this is how you actually are if only you believed it. Break it.... This is you now: lost innocence, lost faith, broken spirit, distance from God, *Galut* – Exile – from Self. The smaller piece is held up and the declaration made, "This is the bread of my poverty...." The larger piece is wrapped up and hidden. It becomes transformed into the Afikoman – the last taste of the evening, the bread of freedom, the bread of healing, the bread of wholeness, the bread of the Messiah. It originates from the same material and yet it is so different. This is the miracle of redemption.

Yaḥatz – *The Broken Self*

Each participant removes the middle matzah and holds it up to view. It is important that the piece is whole, without blemish. If an edge is chipped then it should either be replaced or, provided it is not Shabbat, the corner can be browned in the flame of the candle. Spend some time meditating on the matzah. Note its texture, its lightness of being, its simplicity.

With quiet determination break the matzah into two parts, approximately one-third to two-thirds. The larger piece is wrapped up in a cloth or napkin and put aside becoming the *Afikoman,* while the smaller piece is held as the next section is chanted together. The children should be made aware that the Afikoman of the leader is for capturing and hiding, and will have to be ransomed for the Seder to end. The capturing of the Afikoman should take place during the confusion of the meal.

Silent mindfulness

DEEPENING

This theme of whole–broken–healing–whole can also be identified in the sounds of the shofar blown on Rosh HaShannah. There are three notes: *Tekiah* – one long blast (matzah); *Shvarim* – three broken notes (maror); and *Teruah* – nine staccato notes (ḥaroset). Why these notes and why in this order – one:three:nine:one? The Tekiah is the ONE that we all emerged from, that we all knew before our lives lost their innocence and we became broken, removed (Galut – Exile) from the Source. This state of Galut is heard in the *Shvarim*. The *Teruah* is our recognizing this loss, entering the pain and crying out (Teshuvah – Return). We then return to the ONE but as conscious, mature HUmans ("Man" with heh and vav – God's name) – this is Geulah (Redemption). The length of the Tekiah must be as long as the Shvarim-Teruah. Three notes of the Teruah must equal one of the Shvarim. This sandwich must be constructed so that the salami and pickle do not stick out over the sides. In other words, the spiritual reality is that everything is contained within the ONE all the time even though it may not feel like it. And it is this sandwich as Hillel's Sandwich (Korekh) that we will be eating, not hearing, later this evening.

Kadesh
Urḥatz
Karpas
Yaḥatz
Maggid
Raḥtzah
Motzi
Matzah
Maror
Korekh
Shulḥan Orekh
Tzafun
Barekh
Hallel
Nirtzah

מגיד

The smaller part of the broken matzah is held in the hand. After the following recitation it is placed back in its middle position. The top matzah is left uncovered.

הָא לַחְמָא עַנְיָא דִּי אֲכָלוּ אַבְהָתָנָא
בְּאַרְעָא דְמִצְרָיִם. כָּל דִּכְפִין יֵיתֵי וְיֵכוֹל כָּל
דִּצְרִיךְ יֵיתֵי וְיִפְסַח. הָשַׁתָּא הָכָא, לְשָׁנָה
הַבָּאָה בְּאַרְעָא דְיִשְׂרָאֵל. הָשַׁתָּא עַבְדֵי,
לְשָׁנָה הַבָּאָה בְּנֵי חוֹרִין:

BEING

To fully appreciate the Haggadah it is necessary to bring your full awareness to everything that is done and said. Learn to think in metaphors. Do not let explanations such as: "So that the children will ask…" satisfy you. Go deeper. This is your story. Use your imagination and understand it your way.

DEEPENING

Who is hungry? It is we who are hungry, hungry for spiritual sustenance. The Prophet Amos said, "Days are coming when the people will hunger not for bread but to hear the word of the Lord."* We are all so hungry. Mitzraim oppresses us. It separates us from ourSelves. The irony is, though, that this same hunger caused us to descend into Mitzraim in the first place.** We were hungry for love, for answers, for peace, for soul-connectivity. Where else could we have turned? But now comes the time to realize where the Truth lies. And it isn't in Mitzraim!

* Amos 8:11. Reb Shlomo Carlebach *z"l* spoke and sang at length about this hunger.

** There was a famine in the Land of Canaan (Genesis 42:1).

Maggid – *Telling my story*

The smaller part of the broken matzah is held in the hand. After the following recitation it is placed back in its middle position. The top matzah is left uncovered.

This is the bread of my poverty that was eaten by my ancestors in Mitzraim. All who are hungry come and eat. All who are in need come and join in the Pesaḥ celebration. This year we are here; next year in the Land of Israel. This year we are still slaves; next year may we be children of freedom.

What is true freedom? Here there is an apparent paradox: to be truly free is to let go of being a slave of Pharaoh, the god of Mitzraim, and to choose instead to become a servant of God, thereby shifting the axis of devotion from the horizontal to the vertical. But isn't this just another form of slavery? Freedom is to be totally free to choose to live fully the life that God has destined for us. And what prevents this? The fear that arises from the mind (ego), that without holding on to something we are a nothing. So we become enslaved by the illusion that by holding on to something in the temporal plane of existence we will find an anchor in the sea of chaos and this anchor creates the illusion of security and this "security" creates the illusion of freedom. "The closer to living one's destiny the freer one is."* Thus it says of Moses that he was the meekest of men for he totally let go of the needs of his ego and aligned his life fully with the will of God.

Kadesh
Urḥatz
Karpas
Yaḥatz
Maggid
Raḥtzah
Motzi
Matzah
Maror
Korekh
Shulḥan Orekh
Tzafun
Barekh
Hallel
Nirtzah

* Martin Buber: *I and Thou.* (Free Press 1971)

מה נשתנה

The Second Cup is poured for everyone. Again, pour the wine or grape juice for someone else. Get used to serving, for God said: "Let my people go that they may serve me!"

מַה נִּשְׁתַּנָּה הַלַּיְלָה הַזֶּה מִכָּל הַלֵּילוֹת?
שֶׁבְּכָל הַלֵּילוֹת אָנוּ אוֹכְלִין חָמֵץ וּמַצָּה.
הַלַּיְלָה הַזֶּה כֻּלּוֹ מַצָּה:
שֶׁבְּכָל הַלֵּילוֹת אָנוּ אוֹכְלִין שְׁאָר יְרָקוֹת.
הַלַּיְלָה הַזֶּה מָרוֹר:
שֶׁבְּכָל הַלֵּילוֹת אֵין אָנוּ מַטְבִּילִין אֲפִילוּ פַּעַם אֶחָת.
הַלַּיְלָה הַזֶּה שְׁתֵּי פְעָמִים:
שֶׁבְּכָל הַלֵּילוֹת אָנוּ אוֹכְלִין בֵּין יוֹשְׁבִין וּבֵין מְסֻבִּין.
הַלַּיְלָה הַזֶּה כֻּלָּנוּ מְסֻבִּין:

BEING

Give your inner child a voice. Let it ask the questions. This is her/his night too.

On Tisha B'Av the question is "*Eikha*" – How am I living my life? On Rosh HaShannah the question is "*Ayekah*" – Where am I on my life's path? On Pesah the question is "*Mah*" – What am I? A slave to Pharaoh or a servant to God? Don't ever stop asking – never be too frightened to ask.

So, what is different about you this night from all other nights? In what way are you prepared to be different after this night? The Exodus from Mitzraim is about the willingness to let go and be different. If, by the end of this experiential evening, you come away unmoved, unwilling to shift, uncompromising in your self-righteousness, then it will be as if you were never there. Remember, more than half of the Children of Israel opted to stay behind rather than take the risk of letting go!

קדש
ורחץ
כרפס
יחץ
מגיד
רחצה
מוציא
מצה
מרור
כורך
שלחן עורך
צפון
ברך
הלל
נרצה

AG

❧ The Four Questions* ❧

The Second Cup is poured for everyone. Again, pour the wine or grape juice for someone else. Get used to serving, for God said: "Let my people go that they may serve me!"

What has changed this night from all other nights:
That on all other nights we can eat both ḥametz and matzah, but on this night everything is matzah?
That on all other nights we eat other vegetables, but on this night maror [bitter ones]?
That on all other nights we don't dip our food even once, but on this night we dip twice?
That on all other nights we eat either sitting or reclining, but on this night we are all reclining?

DEEPENING

The order of these questions is significant and can be seen as an abbreviated process of healing into God like a four step program:**

Kadesh
Urḥatz
Karpas
Yaḥatz
Maggid
Raḥtzah
Motzi
Matzah
Maror
Korekh
Shulḥan Orekh
Tzafun
Barekh
Hallel
Nirtzah

Step 1. Recognize that you are trapped and living the life of a slave. Be willing to deflate your ego (*matzah*). Begin practicing humility. Admit that you cannot do this on your own and allow yourself to turn back to God. *I did when I let it go away*

Step 2. Be willing to face the bitter truth (*maror*) of who you are and how you are living your lies. Practice telling the Truth. *Just don't I would know*

Step 3. Do not be afraid to step into the layers of pain that surround the heart. Grieve all the losses and be willing to let the tears (*karpas*) flow. Renew the contact with your heart energy. Let the inner bitterness be miraculously transformed by love into love (*maror* dipped into the ḥaroset). *& into Perhaps in time to forgiveness! It will happen · 2017 / 2018!*

---

* The Hebrew text does not use the word "*she'elot*" – questions – but rather the word "*kushiot*" – apparent contradictions. Questions can be answered whereas contradictions need to be resolved.

** This will become clearer as matzah, maror and ḥaroset are explained below.

עבדים היינו

The top matzah is uncovered.

עֲבָדִים הָיִינוּ לְפַרְעֹה בְּמִצְרָיִם. וַיּוֹצִיאֵנוּ יְיָ אֱלֹהֵינוּ מִשָּׁם, בְּיָד חֲזָקָה וּבִזְרֹעַ נְטוּיָה.

Step 4. Let your over-judgmental self* rest by practicing acts of loving-kindness.** Let yourself be filled with compassion. Hand over to God the heaviness of your burden and let yourself rest in God's hands, for *HaShem Tzva'ot* (God of the Battle) has promised to deliver if you are willing to be delivered.

◆

BEING

"A determined hand." This refers to God's attributes of *Gevurah* and *Din* – Strength and Judgment – against the Mitzrim. While "an outstretched arm" refers to God's attribute of *Ḥesed* – Loving-kindness – towards the Children of Israel.

This is the account of our past according to the Talmudic Rabbi Shmuel. The emphasis is on the immediate experience of physical slavery and the power and grace of God that delivered us. Further on, another "starting point" is introduced – that of Rav. He paints a wider canvas by framing the descent and deliverance within the broader context of God's plan for returning those "made in His image" to full consciousness and thus to True worship.

DEEPENING

What is the purpose of retelling the story? So that we will remember.*** Remember what? Remember that life was once different, that once we used to be free, that our relationship with our Creator was more intimate

---

* This is the left side of the Tree of Life, the *sefirah* of *Din* – Judgment.

** This is the right side of the Tree of Life, the *sefirah* of *Ḥesed* – Loving-kindness. By leaning into the left (contraction) we make more room for the right (expansion).

*** Maimonides, in his Laws of Pesaḥ, stresses this aspect of the night more than any other.

We Were Slaves

The top matzah is uncovered.

*We were slaves to Pharaoh in Mitzraim. And the Lord our God brought us out from there, with a determined hand and an outstretched arm."**

and intuitive, that once upon a time everything in the world was beautiful and filled with mystery [my-story (*sic*)], that once we were one with our Source. What does "remember" mean? Re-member: to bring the separated parts back to wholeness. Becoming whole is not an illusion. Slavery is a consequence of the duality created by the mind. The apparent reality that there is God and there is I; that there is It and there is I; that there is You and there is I. Remembering leads to dis-illusionment (freedom from illusions).**

---

* This verse is part of a longer passage that appears in Deut. 6:20–23: "When in the future your child will ask you saying: 'What is the meaning of all these testimonies, laws and rules that the Lord, our God has commanded you?' Then you will say to your child: 'we were slaves to Pharaoh in Mitzraim. And the Lord brought us out from Mitzraim with a determined hand. And before our very eyes the Lord brought down signs and wonders, both great and terrible, upon Mitzraim and upon Pharaoh and his court. And He took us out from there in order to bring us to fulfill the promise He had made with our forbearers to give us the Land.'"

** Here is a section from the *Tale of the Seven Beggars* by Rebbe Naḥman of Bratzlav that illustrates the power of remembering.

> The people began to converse and they decided that each one should tell an ancient story involving his earliest memory. Each one would tell what he remembered from the time that his memory began.
>
> There were both old and young people present. They honored the oldest man among them to tell his story first. "What shall I tell you?" he said. "I can even remember when they cut the apple from off the branch" No one understood what he meant. However, there were wise men there, and they said, "This is obviously a very ancient story." The second one, who was not as old as the first, said, "Is that then an old story? That story even I remember! But I can also remember when the lamp was lit!" "This story is even older than the first!" said the listeners. But they were quite surprised, since the second one was not quite as old as the first, but still he remembered an older event. The third one, who was even younger, said, "I remember when the fruit began to have structure – that is, when the fruit began to be put together." "That story is even older," they responded. The fourth one, who was still younger, spoke up, "I can even remember when the seed was brought to plant the fruit." The fifth one, who was younger yet, said, "I even remember when the wise men invented the seed." The sixth one, who was younger still, said, "I remember the taste of the fruit before it

Kadesh
Urḥatz
Karpas
Yaḥatz
Maggid
Raḥtzah
Motzi
Matzah
Maror
Korekh
Shulḥan Orekh
Tzafun
Barekh
Hallel
Nirtzah

וְאִלּוּ לֹא הוֹצִיא הַקָּדוֹשׁ בָּרוּךְ הוּא אֶת־אֲבוֹתֵינוּ מִמִּצְרַיִם, הֲרֵי אָנוּ וּבָנֵינוּ וּבְנֵי בָנֵינוּ, מְשֻׁעְבָּדִים הָיִינוּ לְפַרְעֹה בְּמִצְרַיִם. וַאֲפִילוּ כֻּלָּנוּ חֲכָמִים, כֻּלָּנוּ נְבוֹנִים, כֻּלָּנוּ זְקֵנִים, כֻּלָּנוּ יוֹדְעִים אֶת־הַתּוֹרָה, מִצְוָה עָלֵינוּ לְסַפֵּר בִּיצִיאַת מִצְרַיִם. וְכָל הַמַּרְבֶּה לְסַפֵּר בִּיצִיאַת מִצְרַיִם, הֲרֵי זֶה מְשֻׁבָּח:

BEING

Knowledge is not a substitute for experience; therefore don't stick to this story line, follow your own.

מַעֲשֶׂה בְּרַבִּי אֱלִיעֶזֶר, וְרַבִּי יְהוֹשֻׁעַ, וְרַבִּי אֶלְעָזָר בֶּן־עֲזַרְיָה, וְרַבִּי עֲקִיבָא, וְרַבִּי טַרְפוֹן, שֶׁהָיוּ מְסֻבִּין בִּבְנֵי־ בְרַק, וְהָיוּ מְסַפְּרִים בִּיצִיאַת מִצְרַיִם, כָּל־אוֹתוֹ הַלַּיְלָה, עַד שֶׁבָּאוּ תַלְמִידֵיהֶם וְאָמְרוּ לָהֶם: רַבּוֹתֵינוּ, הִגִּיעַ זְמַן קְרִיאַת שְׁמַע, שֶׁל שַׁחֲרִית:

BEING

Bless G-d *Please* *always to shout!*

The night will end. The dawn will occur. The Light will shine. And God's name will be ONE again. This is the declaration of the Shemah Yisrael prayer. And

G-d 71 6ל

entered the fruit." The seventh one spoke up, "I remember the fragrance of the fruit before it entered the fruit." The eighth one said, "I remember the appearance of the fruit before it was drawn onto the fruit." I was also there at the time, and I was still an infant. I spoke up and said to them, "I remember all these events and I remember absolutely nothing." "This is a very ancient story," said the wise men, "more so than all the others." They were very surprised that a child remembered more than any of them. The Great Eagle (or Vulture) then said, "I will explain the stories that each one told. "The first one remembers when they cut the umbilical cord. The second

If the Holy One blessed be He, would not have brought our ancestors out from Mitzraim, then we and our children and our children's children would still be enslaved in Mitzraim.
And even if all of us were wise, discerning, venerated and completely knowledgeable in Torah, it is still necessary to unify ourselves by telling the story of the deliverance from Mitzraim.
And the more one extrapolates and embellishes the telling of the deliverance from Mitzraim, the more it is praise worthy.

The incident concerning Rabbi Eliezer, and Rabbi Yehoshua, and Rabbi Elazar son of Azarya, and Rabbi Akiva, and Rabbi Tarfon when they were reclining in Bnai B'rak: they were telling about the Exodus from Mitzraim all that night, until their disciples came to them and said: "Our Teachers, the time has come to recite the Shemah of the morning."

even if we ever forget this Truth our disciples (children) are there to remind us.

And this is part of what they said....

---

one remembers when he was in the womb. The third remembers when his body began to knit together as the fetus took form. The fourth remembers how the drop was emitted at the time of conception. The fifth remembers when the semen formed. The sixth remembers the soul (*nefesh*). The seventh remembers the spirit (*ruaḥ*). The eighth remembers the essence (*neshamah*). Finally, there is the child who said that he remembers absolutely nothing. He is even higher than all the rest since he remembers even what was before and that is Nothingness (*Ayn Sof*). (*Rabbi Nachman Stories*, Trans. by Rabbi A. Kaplan, Breslov Research Institute, 1983)

אָמַר רַבִּי אֶלְעָזָר בֶּן־עֲזַרְיָה. הֲרֵי אֲנִי כְּבֶן שִׁבְעִים שָׁנָה, וְלֹא זָכִיתִי שֶׁתֵּאָמֵר יְצִיאַת מִצְרַיִם בַּלֵּילוֹת. עַד שֶׁדְּרָשָׁהּ בֶּן זוֹמָא. שֶׁנֶּאֱמַר לְמַעַן תִּזְכֹּר, אֶת יוֹם צֵאתְךָ מֵאֶרֶץ מִצְרַיִם, כֹּל יְמֵי חַיֶּיךָ. יְמֵי חַיֶּיךָ הַיָּמִים. כֹּל יְמֵי חַיֶּיךָ הַלֵּילוֹת. וַחֲכָמִים אוֹמְרִים: יְמֵי חַיֶּיךָ הָעוֹלָם הַזֶּה. כֹּל יְמֵי חַיֶּיךָ לְהָבִיא לִימוֹת הַמָּשִׁיחַ:

BEING

Why does Rabbi Elazar say: "I am like a seventy year old?" The Talmud relates* that he was in fact much younger when he was appointed as president of the Sanhedrin. He was afraid that his youthful appearance would cause a loss of respect to the esteemed position. In response to his prayers his hair turned white and he appeared as if he were a seventy-year-old sage. There is a general understanding in wisdom-based traditions that in order to teach the tradition you must have life experience and that a sign of such a quality is that your hair is white. The idea is that wisdom comes from the application of knowledge over time. And time can be counted by the number of one's white hairs.** Rabbi Elazar had attained this level of wisdom in spite of his few years, but the white hairs were necessary for public consumption.

DEEPENING

All spiritual paths demand the same thing: to break through the illusions created by the ego-mind and thereby become healed, to come back home, to end the exile, to awaken Messianic consciousness. The *Shemah* prayer ends with a reminder of this by mentioning the redemption from Mitzraim.

* Talmud Bavli, *Brakhot* 28a

** This truism is beautifully told over in Carl Hammerschlag's book *The Dancing Healers* (Harper SanFrancisco 1983).

Rabbi Elazar son of Azarya said: "Even though I am like a seventy-year-old, I have not been privileged to understand that the coming out of Mitzraim should be recited at night until Ben Zoma expounded upon the verse: 'So that you will remember the day that you came out of Mitzraim, all the days of your life.** If it would only say, 'The days of your life' then it would mean just during the daytime but it says, '**All** the days of your life,' thereby implying nighttime as well." However the Wise Ones add by saying: "'The days of your life' refers to life in this world, whereas '**All** the days of your life' means to include the coming days of the Messiah."*

Ben Zoma's comment about "...all the days of your life" suggests that the redemption from Mitzraim should not only be referred to in the light (day) during the good times, but must also be prayed for in the dark (night) that we are in now. The Sages go one step further and declare that the seemingly endless cycle of going down into Mitzraim (dusk), suffering in bondage (night) and being redeemed (dawn) does have an end – it is in the promise, by the grace of God, of the coming of the Messiah. The Messiah is the potential for total healing on the personal, national, global and cosmic levels. And, furthermore, the promise that this process will start this very night...

---

* This is a reference to the recitation of the third paragraph of the *Shemah,* which ends with the statement: "So that you will remember and do all the commandments and you will be holy to your God. I, the ineffable Lord, is your God which brought you out from the Land of Mitzraim to be your God: I, the ineffable Lord, am your God" (Numbers 15: 40–41).

** Deuteronomy 16:3

ארבעה בנים

בָּרוּךְ הַמָּקוֹם.
בָּרוּךְ הוּא.
בָּרוּךְ שֶׁנָּתַן תּוֹרָה לְעַמּוֹ יִשְׂרָאֵל.
בָּרוּךְ הוּא.

כְּנֶגֶד אַרְבָּעָה בָּנִים דִּבְּרָה תוֹרָה.
אֶחָד חָכָם,
וְאֶחָד רָשָׁע,
וְאֶחָד תָּם,
וְאֶחָד שֶׁאֵינוֹ יוֹדֵעַ לִשְׁאוֹל:

חָכָם מַה הוּא אוֹמֵר? מָה הָעֵדֹת וְהַחֻקִּים וְהַמִּשְׁפָּטִים, אֲשֶׁר צִוָּה יְיָ אֱלֹהֵינוּ אֶתְכֶם? וְאַף אַתָּה אֱמָר־לוֹ כְּהִלְכוֹת הַפֶּסַח: אֵין מַפְטִירִין אַחַר הַפֶּסַח אֲפִיקוֹמָן:

קדש
ורחץ
כרפס
יחץ
מגיד
רחצה
מוציא
מצה
מרור
כורך
שלחן עורך
צפון
ברך
הלל
נרצה

* The original text talks about four male children. I thought that it would make a nice change to have four female children. The first letter of each child spells the word חרות (*ḥerut*) – freedom (an insight by Dr. Jonathan Zuess).

** In the Septuagint (the Greek translation of the Bible) this reads: "...has commanded **us** to do?"

*** Deuteronomy 6:20–25, source: "...And the time will come when your child will **ask**

The Four Children

Blessed is the Present One
Blessed is He
Blessed is the One who gave the Torah
to Her people Israel
Blessed is He.

About four children did the Torah speak:
One wise, and one alienated, and one naïve,
and one who doesn't know how to ask.

The ***Wise*** *one: what does she* say?*
*"What are these testimonies, rules and legalities which the Lord our God has commanded you** to do?"****
In spite of this, you will tell her about the laws of the Pesaḥ sacrifice:
"Nothing follows after the Pascal lamb
Afikoman [dessert]."

Kadesh
Urḥatz
Karpas
Yaḥatz
Maggid
Raḥtzah
Motzi
Matzah
Maror
Korekh
Shulḥan Orekh
Tzafun
Barekh
Hallel
Nirtzah

---

you saying, 'What are these testimonies, rules and legalities which the Lord our God has commanded you to do?' And you will explain to your child that we were slaves to Pharaoh in Mitzraim. And God brought us out from Mitzraim with a determined hand. And God bestowed signs and wonders, great and evil, upon Mitzraim, upon Pharaoh and upon his entire dynasty right before our eyes. And He brought us out from there so that He may bring us to the Land which He promised to our ancestors. And God enjoined us to perform all these laws, to be in awe of the Lord our God, for our own good for all time to give us life as has been done to this day."

רָשָׁע מַה הוּא אוֹמֵר? מָה הָעֲבוֹדָה הַזֹּאת לָכֶם?
לָכֶם, וְלֹא לוֹ. וּלְפִי שֶׁהוֹצִיא אֶת־עַצְמוֹ מִן הַכְּלָל,
כָּפַר בָּעִקָּר. וְאַף אַתָּה הַקְהֵה אֶת־שִׁנָּיו, וֶאֱמָר־
לוֹ: בַּעֲבוּר זֶה, עָשָׂה יְיָ לִי, בְּצֵאתִי מִמִּצְרָיִם. לִי
וְלֹא־לוֹ. אִלּוּ הָיָה שָׁם, לֹא הָיָה נִגְאָל:

תָּם מַה הוּא אוֹמֵר? מַה זֹּאת? וְאָמַרְתָּ אֵלָיו:
בְּחֹזֶק יָד הוֹצִיאָנוּ יְיָ מִמִּצְרַיִם מִבֵּית עֲבָדִים:

וְשֶׁאֵינוֹ יוֹדֵעַ לִשְׁאוֹל, אַתְּ פְּתַח לוֹ. שֶׁנֶּאֱמַר
וְהִגַּדְתָּ לְבִנְךָ, בַּיּוֹם הַהוּא לֵאמֹר: בַּעֲבוּר זֶה
עָשָׂה יְיָ לִי, בְּצֵאתִי מִמִּצְרָיִם:

* Exodus 12:24–27, source: "...And you will preserve this thing as a rule for yourselves and for your descendents forever. And the time will come when you will have come into the Land, which the Lord has given you as He said He would, that you will practice this Service. And it will happen that your children will **say** to you, 'What does all this Service mean to you?' Then you will tell them that this is the Pesaḥ sacrifice to the Lord because He passed over the Children of Israel in Mitzraim when he slaughtered

*The **Alienated** one: what does she say?*
*"What does all this Service mean to you?"****
"To you" rather than herself. And thus she excludes herself from the community and rejects a fundamental tenet [alt: And thus, by excluding herself from the community, she thereby rejects a fundamental tenet]; then you need to soften the sharpness of her bite and say to her: "[This Service is done] *because of what the Lord did for me in bringing me out from Mitzraim."***
"Me" rather than her, as if to say that had she been there [with an attitude like that] *she would not have been redeemed.*

*The **Naïve** one: what does she say?*
*"What is this?"****
And you will say to her, "With a determined hand the Lord brought us out of Mitzraim from the crucible of slavery."

*And the **One that doesn't know how to ask**?*
*Prompt her, like it says: "And on that day you will tell your child saying: 'We are doing this because of what God did for me when I came out of Mitzraim.'"*****

Kadesh
Urḥatz
Karpas
Yaḥatz
Maggid
Raḥtzah
Motzi
Matzah
Maror
Korekh
Shulḥan Orekh
Tzafun
Barekh
Hallel
Nirtzah

---

the Mitzrim but spared our households. And when they heard this, the people bowed their heads and knelt in worship."

** Exodus 13:8

*** Exodus 13:14, source: "...And all the first-born of humans among yours sons you shall redeem. And when your child will one day **ask** you, 'What's all this about?' You will say to him, 'With a determined hand God brought us out from Mitzraim from the house of slavery. And it was when Pharaoh stubbornly refused to send us out that God killed all the first-born in the land of Mitzraim, from the first-born of humans to the first-born of animals. So therefore, I sacrifice to the Lord all the males that first breech the womb, except for my children – them I redeem.'"

**** Exodus 13:8

BEING

The Wise one: What kind of a question is she asking? Is this really the question one would expect from a "wise" child? And what kind of an answer is being given? Why does it say "*...haPesaḥ Afikoman* (*The Pascal Lamb dessert*)"? Surely it should say "*ein matirin Afikoman aḥar haPesaḥ* (*no dessert follows after the eating of the Pesaḥ sacrifice*)." And what does "Afikoman" actually mean? One way of understanding this is as follows: The child is actually asking: what are we to do with all these Divine instructions concerning the particulars of the observance of the Pascal sacrifice if we no longer have a Temple or sacrifices? How are we supposed to remember now? The answer comes: In the past we used to finish the meal by eating a piece of the Pesaḥ sacrifice after which no dessert was to be consumed. But now, having re-entered the darkness of exile and loss of freedom, everything has changed. Now the Pesaḥ sacrifice is replaced by a piece of matzah that is called Afikoman, after which no dessert may be eaten. The child is concerned with the question of continuity. The parent answers "*k'hilkhot*" (i.e., approximating the practice of the Pesaḥ); it is time for a paradigm shift,* the times have changed and so must our practice – this is the sign of true wisdom; from now on, instead of concluding with the sacrifice that was, we taste the Messiah that will be, for the Afikoman now becomes a symbolic reference to the coming of the Messiah!**

The Alienated One: she is not overly concerned with the future of the community, thereby becoming even more alienated from it. She is angry. She actually doesn't even ask a question but rather makes a rhetorical statement (see the Biblical quote in the footnote***). She demands to know what the point of all this Service is if God has allowed the destruction of the Temple to happen (again). With compassion and understanding must come the answer. Help her soften. Explain that a rejection of the Divine is a rejection of Self; that giving up leads to self-condemnation in the crucible of enslavement; that the Divine Love penetrates through the thickest darkness; that there are many questions but not

קדש
ורחץ
כרפס
יחץ
מגיד
רחצה
מוציא
מצה
מרור
כורך
שלחן עורך
צפון
ברך
הלל
נרצה

* See *Paradigm Shift* (Aronson, 1993), by Reb Zalman Schachter-Shalomi.

** According to Prof. David Daube *z"l*, the Biblical law scholar, it derives from the Greek word aphikomenos, "after he will come," referring to the Messiaḥ. This alternative reading suggests that it might be part of a Jewish-Christian polemic: "After the Messiah comes there will be no other coming."

*** See Dr Russell Jay Hendel's comments at www.rashiyomi.com/h1n8.htm.

necessarily corresponding answers. The entire evening, in fact, can be seen as being dedicated to this rejected and rejecting child.*

DEEPENING

The Four Children: the Wise one, the Alienated one, the Naive one, and the one who doesn't know how to ask. Taken in the opposite order they aptly describe the natural development of the human individual:** the stage at which we are too young to even formulate the questions; the stage at which we can only ask the innocent questions; the rebellious stage, when it's all "Your stuff, not mine!"; to the understanding stage of intellectual maturity. But that's not the end of the journey. After the natural developmental program comes the spiritual developmental opportunities. The "stuck-in-the-head" self needs to go through a rebellion against rationalism as a total means of understanding, maybe even a suspension of dogmatic religious practice in order to discover what's behind it. The innocent stage is when the true questions are rediscovered, simple questions that go straight to the heart of the matter. Finally, the point is reached when no more questions are necessary, when comfort and wisdom are found in silence, when the answer is simply, "Because."

The Four Parents:*** The types of questions that our children ask are a direct reflection of the kind of relationships that we have built with them. A parent who relates to a child on a singularly intellectual level will spawn a child who can only relate to the world, to the emotional world, to the experiential world, through the mind. Some would call this "wise," others might call it limited. Then there are parents who themselves feel alienated from the events of their ancestors and are not attempting to form a meaningful relationship with "The Present One, Blessed be She." What do they expect when their child turns around with anger and disdain? And how many of us don't take our children seriously? Not really listening

* I once led a Seder at which a guest confided that her brother had joined a cult and had totally rejected his Jewish path. I responded in the way that this passage is traditionally translated: "Smash his teeth in – he's so ungrateful that he doesn't deserve to be liberated!" Afterwards, I deeply regretted this attitude as I came to realize that the rest of the entire evening is actually dedicated to this rejected and rejecting child.

** The connection between developmental psychology and the four children was told to me by Prof. Julius Carlebach (cousin of Reb Shlomo) in 1975.

*** This indictment against the parent comes from Rabbi Danny Wise – a truly wise friend.

Kadesh
Urḥatz
Karpas
Yaḥatz
Maggid
Raḥtzah
Motzi
Matzah
Maror
Korekh
Shulḥan Orekh
Tzafun
Barekh
Hallel
Nirtzah

יָכוֹל מֵרֹאשׁ חֹדֶשׁ, תַּלְמוּד לוֹמַר בַּיּוֹם הַהוּא. אִי בַּיּוֹם הַהוּא. יָכוֹל מִבְּעוֹד יוֹם. תַּלְמוּד לוֹמַר. בַּעֲבוּר זֶה. בַּעֲבוּר זֶה לֹא אָמַרְתִּי, אֶלָּא בְּשָׁעָה שֶׁיֵּשׁ מַצָּה וּמָרוֹר מֻנָּחִים לְפָנֶיךָ:

to their questions, constantly dismissing them as silly? Maybe your child is not so much naïve as pure? Maybe you need to start listening more? Finally, there is the parent who is never around long enough for the child to even ask, the absentee parent. How about slowing down a bit and spending some time tending the garden? Or maybe the child is just being obedient – "little children should be seen but not heard!"*

By listening to your children, maybe you can learn something about yourself. By listening to your inner child, maybe you can learn to heal yourself. Open the child's mouth; help her give expression to the suppressed voices.

BEING

Having the experience is not sufficient; you must also share it with others and help them touch and be touched by it. Help them find the same archetypal experience in their own lives. On this night all the props are made available to create a multi-dimensional remembering experience.

And when you tell your story, tell the good with the bad; the sorrow with the joy; the desperation with the relief; the dark with the light. You don't have to pull punches in front of the children – they will see through a whitewash. Therefore the telling must be with the signs of slavery, hardship and freedom in front of you.

* The Baal Shem Tov sent his disciple Rabbi Yaakov Yosef of Polnoy to test the learning of Reb Yeḥiel, a prospective husband for his daughter Odel. Reb Yeḥiel came from a simple German Jewish family. When Rabbi Yaakov Yosef returned from his mission, he told the Baal Shem Tov, "To everything I asked him Reb Yeḥiel answered, 'I don't know.' I wonder about him." "Gevalt!" exclaimed the Baal Shem Tov. "I'd love to have him as a son-in-law."

The Full Experience

*Should the telling start from the beginning of this month?**
*It explicitly states, "...on **this** day..."* [the anniversary of the Exodus].
In that case should the telling start during the daytime?
*It explicitly states, "...because of **this**..." namely, only at such time that there is matzah and maror* [bitter herbs] *present before you.*

Kadesh
Urḥatz
Karpas
Yaḥatz
Maggid
Raḥtzah
Motzi
Matzah
Maror
Korekh
Shulḥan Orekh
Tzafun
Barekh
Hallel
Nirtzah

* The discussion that follows is based on the following verse which emphasizes the particular time the "telling should occur. "And you shall tell your children on **this** day saying, 'It is because of this which the Lord did for me when I came out of Mitzraim'" (exodus 13:8).

wanted to – they would not even hear it.

A physical transition can now be made away from the table to the area of lounging, thus allowing the participants to lean comfortably on sofas and cushions. One set of matzot and a cup of wine are placed in the center of the gathering.

מִתְּחִלָּה עוֹבְדֵי עֲבוֹדָה זָרָה הָיוּ אֲבוֹתֵינוּ. וְעַכְשָׁו קֵרְבָנוּ
הַמָּקוֹם לַעֲבוֹדָתוֹ. שֶׁנֶּאֱמַר וַיֹּאמֶר יְהוֹשֻׁעַ אֶל־כָּל־הָעָם.
כֹּה אָמַר יְיָ אֱלֹהֵי יִשְׂרָאֵל, בְּעֵבֶר הַנָּהָר יָשְׁבוּ אֲבוֹתֵיכֶם
מֵעוֹלָם, תֶּרַח אֲבִי אַבְרָהָם וַאֲבִי נָחוֹר. וַיַּעַבְדוּ אֱלֹהִים
אֲחֵרִים: וָאֶקַּח אֶת־אֲבִיכֶם אֶת־אַבְרָהָם מֵעֵבֶר הַנָּהָר,
וָאוֹלֵךְ אוֹתוֹ בְּכָל־אֶרֶץ כְּנָעַן. וָאַרְבֶּה אֶת־זַרְעוֹ וָאֶתֶּן לוֹ
אֶת־יִצְחָק: וָאֶתֵּן לְיִצְחָק אֶת־יַעֲקֹב וְאֶת־עֵשָׂו. וָאֶתֵּן לְעֵשָׂו
אֶת הַר־שֵׂעִיר, לָרֶשֶׁת אוֹתוֹ. וְיַעֲקֹב וּבָנָיו יָרְדוּ מִצְרָיִם:

BEING

Do you remember the film based on Arthur Hailey's book *Roots*?* While still in Africa, the father holds up his newborn son, Kunta Kinte, towards the heavens and retells the story of their ancestors, where they came from and how they lived their lives. Later, after his son had become enslaved and shipped over to Mitzraim (The Plantation States), he holds his newborn child to the sky and retells the story of their ancestors, where they came from and how they lived their lives. Except this time he adds his own story of how he was enslaved and his hope for future freedom. So too, we retell our story.

Esau was given the land of Seir (lit.: "hair"). He never "went down"; he never faced the internal demons of Mitzraim; he never got lost in order to be found – he just stayed the same way, living in the land that was so familiar to him.

* *Roots*, Alex Hailey (Dell 1980)

B-7 ❧ **Our Story** ☙

A physical transition can now be made away from the table to the area of lounging, thus allowing the participants to lean comfortably on sofas and cushions. One set of matzot and a cup of wine are placed in the center of the gathering.

From the very beginning our ancestors were worshippers of strange practices [idol worship]. But now the Present One has brought us close to true worship, as it says:*

"And Joshua said to all the people:
'Thus says the Lord God of Israel:
Your ancestors, including Teraḥ the father of Abraham and Naḥor, always lived on the other side of the river; and there they worshipped other gods. And I took your father Abraham from the other side of the river and led him throughout the Land of Canaan. And I multiplied his offspring by giving him Isaac, and by giving to Isaac, Jacob and Esau. And to Esau I gave the area of Mount Seir as an inheritance, while Jacob and his sons went down to Mitzraim.'"**

DEEPENING

This is the "starting point" according to Rav. He places the physical slavery in Mitzraim within the much larger context of the spiritual slavery that has been going on for almost always. Spiritual slavery is induced through forgetting: forgetting the True Source of all Creation; forgetting

Kadesh
Urḥatz
Karpas
Yaḥatz
Maggid
Raḥtzah
Motzi
Matzah
Maror
Korekh
Shulḥan Orekh
Tzafun
Barekh
Hallel
Nirtzah

---

* Joshua 24:3–4. This speech by Joshua is given after the Children of Israel have crossed over the river (Jordan), finally arriving back into the land promised to them by God. Thus it can be seen as closing the circle.

** The continuation of this quote is also significant and relevant: "And in reply the people declared: 'Far be it for us to forsake the Lord and serve other gods. For it was the Lord our God who brought us and our ancestors up from the Land of Mitzraim, the house of slavery, and who performed those wondrous signs before our very eyes... Now we too will serve the Lord, for the Lord is our God.'"

בָּרוּךְ שׁוֹמֵר הַבְטָחָתוֹ לְיִשְׂרָאֵל. בָּרוּךְ הוּא. שֶׁהַקָּדוֹשׁ בָּרוּךְ הוּא חִשַּׁב אֶת־הַקֵּץ, לַעֲשׂוֹת כְּמָה שֶּׁאָמַר לְאַבְרָהָם אָבִינוּ בִּבְרִית בֵּין הַבְּתָרִים, שֶׁנֶּאֱמַר וַיֹּאמֶר לְאַבְרָם יָדֹעַ תֵּדַע כִּי־גֵר יִהְיֶה זַרְעֲךָ בְּאֶרֶץ לֹא לָהֶם וַעֲבָדוּם וְעִנּוּ אֹתָם אַרְבַּע מֵאוֹת שָׁנָה: וְגַם אֶת־הַגּוֹי אֲשֶׁר יַעֲבֹדוּ דָּן אָנֹכִי. וְאַחֲרֵי כֵן יֵצְאוּ, בִּרְכֻשׁ גָּדוֹל:

that this world and everything in it is not owned by Humankind; that, in fact, we cannot "create" anything *ex-nihilo* but, at best, we can only transform. This forgetting leads us to worship foreign things like money, body, power, nature, people, the pursuit of happiness, etc. This forgetting leads us to confuse the product from the Source. This forgetting leads us to love the product rather than Love the Source. Thus money is not the root of all evil but rather, "The *love* of money is the root of all evil."* Money is just a means for transaction, energy to be used or misused.

The "over the other side of the river" refers to those who are still in a state of forgetting, who are wandering around as lost souls.** God took Abraham from over the other side of the river. He thus became a Hebrew (lit.: "the one who crossed over"). Abraham woke up to the Truth and turned his back on the ways of his and his ancestor's past.

Before the exit from the Garden of Eden, humankind lived with an innate knowledge (Torah) of how to live on this planet and the symbiotic relationship between all things. This knowledge (Torah) was not written down – it was known. After the exit, humankind forgot this knowing and lost its close relationship with God and Nature. The war against Creation was declared; humans began conquering the Earth rather than nurturing it; suppressing the female; the *Shekhinah* went into exile. These are the twenty generations recorded in Genesis until the time of Abraham. With the Awakened One the story starts to turn, albeit slowly and painfully. The innate Torah was too difficult to hold onto so a written version was

קדש
ורחץ
כרפס
יחץ
מגיד
רחצה
מוציא
מצה
מרור
כורך
שלחן עורך
צפון
ברך
הלל
נרצה

* Christian Bible: Timothy 6:10

** Genesis 12:5 "And Abram took his wife Sarai... and the souls that they had made [read: re-membered]."

*Blessed is the One that keeps His promises to Israel. Blessed be He. That the Holy One, Blessed be He, thought out the ending and did what He said to Abraham our Father at the time of the Covenant-between-the-Pieces; as it is said: "And He said to Abram: 'You should know what is known, that your descendents will be strangers in a land that is not theirs. And they will be enslaved and made to suffer for four hundred years. And I will also judge the enslaving nation. And afterwards they will leave with great wealth'"**

passed down. It contains remnants of life in Eden modified for life outside of Eden. We are messengers carrying this knowledge throughout history, waiting for the time that it is needed. Now is that time.

DEEPENING

The wealth that we took out of Mitzraim. Out of the darkness of your own imprisonment there is also a treasure to take out with you. It is never totally black or worthless. "And the Children of Israel left with the gold and silver of Mitzraim." The question then arises, what do you do with such a treasure? It can either be dedicated upwards to God (through the dedication of the Tabernacle) or corrupted into idolatry (the Golden Calf). So the questions for you are what did you learn from the time you spent in your inner Mitzraim and how can that be used for good in the world? And what is true for the individual is true for our people. After two-thousand years of exile, what have we learnt that can be used for the good of the world?

Kadesh
Urḥatz
Karpas
Yaḥatz
Maggid
Raḥtzah
Motzi
Matzah
Maror
Korekh
Shulḥan Orekh
Tzafun
Barekh
Hallel
Nirtzah

* Genesis 15:13–14

The matzot are covered and the wine glasses raised.

וְהִיא שֶׁעָמְדָה לַאֲבוֹתֵינוּ וְלָנוּ. שֶׁלֹּא אֶחָד בִּלְבָד, עָמַד עָלֵינוּ לְכַלּוֹתֵנוּ אֶלָּא שֶׁבְּכָל דּוֹר וָדוֹר, עוֹמְדִים עָלֵינוּ לְכַלּוֹתֵנוּ. וְהַקָּדוֹשׁ בָּרוּךְ הוּא מַצִּילֵנוּ מִיָּדָם:

Place the cup down and uncover the matzot again.

צֵא וּלְמַד, מַה בִּקֵּשׁ לָבָן הָאֲרַמִּי לַעֲשׂוֹת לְיַעֲקֹב אָבִינוּ. שֶׁפַּרְעֹה לֹא גָזַר אֶלָּא עַל הַזְּכָרִים, וְלָבָן בִּקֵּשׁ לַעֲקֹר אֶת־הַכֹּל:

אֲרַמִּי אֹבֵד אָבִי וַיֵּרֶד מִצְרַיְמָה וַיָּגָר שָׁם בִּמְתֵי מְעָט
וַיְהִי שָׁם לְגוֹי גָּדוֹל עָצוּם וָרָב:
וַיָּרֵעוּ אֹתָנוּ הַמִּצְרִים וַיְעַנּוּנוּ וַיִּתְּנוּ עָלֵינוּ עֲבֹדָה קָשָׁה:
וַנִּצְעַק אֶל יְיָ אֱלֹהֵי אֲבֹתֵינוּ וַיִּשְׁמַע יְיָ אֶת קֹלֵנוּ
וַיַּרְא אֶת עָנְיֵנוּ וְאֶת עֲמָלֵנוּ וְאֶת לַחֲצֵנוּ:
וַיּוֹצִאֵנוּ יְיָ מִמִּצְרַיִם בְּיָד חֲזָקָה וּבִזְרֹעַ נְטוּיָה וּבְמֹרָא גָּדֹל וּבְאֹתוֹת וּבְמֹפְתִים:
וַיְבִאֵנוּ אֶל הַמָּקוֹם הַזֶּה וַיִּתֶּן לָנוּ אֶת הָאָרֶץ הַזֹּאת אֶרֶץ זָבַת חָלָב וּדְבָשׁ:

BEING

The Haggadah now proceeds to expand upon each phrase of this passage. This is a classic form of exegesis in which every word and phrase has many layers of meaning: some literal, some imaginative, some intellectual, some esoteric.

This passage forms the central part of the storytelling and follows the dictate mentioned above that "*the more one extrapolates and embellishes the telling of the deliverance from Mitzraim, the more it is praise worthy.*"

The matzot are covered and the wine glasses raised.

And it is this [promise] *that has supported our ancestors and ourselves, for it has not only been this one that has stood against us to destroy us. In fact, in every generation there have been those who have stood against us to destroy us. And the Holy One, Blessed be He, has delivered us from their hands.*

Place the cup down and uncover the matzot again.

*Go out and learn what Lavan the Aramite wished to do to Jacob our ancestor. For Pharaoh only decreed against the newborn males whereas Lavan tried to uproot everything.**

An Aramean attempted to destroy my father. After that he went down to Mitzraim and lived there as a small tribe. And soon it grew into a great, powerful and populous nation. And the Mitzrim did evil to us and made us suffer and they burdened us with hard labor.

And we cried out to the Lord the God of our ancestors, and the Lord heard our voice and witnessed our suffering, our toil and our oppression.

And the Lord brought us out of Mitzraim, with a determined hand and an outstretched arm and with great awe and many signs and wonders.

*And He brought us to this Place and gave us this Land, a Land flowing with milk and honey.***

Kadesh
Urḥatz
Karpas
Yaḥatz
Maggid
Raḥtzah
Motzi
Matzah
Maror
Korekh
Shulḥan Orekh
Tzafun
Barekh
Hallel
Nirtzah

* I have shifted this passage down so that it forms an explanation of the verse above rather than an introduction to the whole passage. In this way it remains consistent with the flow of a quote followed by exegesis.

** Deuteronomy 26: 1–9, context: These verses describe how the farmer would bring up his first fruits in baskets to the Temple and make this declaration to the priest. By doing (the festival of Shavuot) so the people are continuously rooted into historical contexture.

שֶׁנֶּאֱמַר אֲרַמִּי אֹבֵד אָבִי, וַיֵּרֶד מִצְרַיְמָה, וַיָּגָר שָׁם בִּמְתֵי מְעָט. וַיְהִי שָׁם לְגוֹי גָּדוֹל, עָצוּם וָרָב:

DEEPENING

Lavan in Hebrew means "the White One." This is a code name that appears in many mythological stories for the Dark One. He appears to us as white and innocent whereas in fact he is a forked-tongued, evil spirit. He is insidious. He will twist reality and our perception of reality until we no longer know right from wrong, truth from lies. He will try to destroy us as soon as we attempt to begin the journey out of ignorance towards the Light of Truth. Either he will work through others or worse, will work within us, exploiting our weaknesses. To survive we must recognize it for what it is and separate ourselves from it. And when, with God's help, he is defeated, we will be able to look back and see that this "enemy" was in fact our greatest teacher. And so it was with Jacob. Just as he was embarking upon his journey of uplifting the Abrahamic torch, along came Lavan and tried to snuff it out. Eventually, twenty-two years later, Jacob manages to separate himself from Lavan's grip and returns home. He has survived. But more than just survive, he has learnt from Lavan the meaning of Truth. And as he embraces Truth he becomes Israel.

Lavan is like the snake in the Garden of Eden. Of the snake it says: "And the two of them were naked (*arumim*), the man and his wife, and were not ashamed. And the snake was more deceptive (*arum*) than all the other animals of the field which the Lord God had made...."* The Hebrew word for naked and deceptive are the same. In other words, the snake presented itself as naked and as innocent as the two humans, but was far from it.

---

* Genesis 2:25–3:1

As it says: An Aramean attempted to destroy my father. After that he went down to Mitzraim and lived there as a small tribe. And soon it grew into a great, powerful and populous nation.

וַיֵּרֶד מִצְרַיְמָה, אָנוּס עַל פִּי הַדִּבּוּר:

BEING

"Going down" implies "going inside" to face our worst demons. Joseph went down into the pit, then down to Mitzraim and then down into the pit of the pits. He had to face his arrogance, his manipulative self and his lack of trust in God. Judah went down away from his father and brothers and had to face the death of his wife and sons, and his actions towards Tamar. He had to face his inability to take responsibility for his actions. By working through these weaknesses, they both rose up, transformed,* becoming anointed ones.** Joseph learnt how to let go and let God in; Judah learnt how to take responsibility for his actions. The Children of Israel's descent into Mitzraim brought them (and us) face to face with the demon of attachment to the world of things. This attachment is the basis of idol worship, i.e., the worshipping of that which is idle – not giving of Life. By surviving this ordeal they were able to become God's servants rather than Pharaoh's slaves.

וַיָּגָר שָׁם. מְלַמֵּד שֶׁלֹּא יָרַד יַעֲקֹב אָבִינוּ לְהִשְׁתַּקֵּעַ בְּמִצְרַיִם, אֶלָּא לָגוּר שָׁם, שֶׁנֶּאֱמַר וַיֹּאמְרוּ אֶל־פַּרְעֹה, לָגוּר בָּאָרֶץ בָּאנוּ, כִּי אֵין מִרְעֶה לַצֹּאן אֲשֶׁר לַעֲבָדֶיךָ, כִּי כָבֵד הָרָעָב בְּאֶרֶץ כְּנָעַן. וְעַתָּה, יֵשְׁבוּ־נָא עֲבָדֶיךָ בְּאֶרֶץ גֹּשֶׁן:

* The idea that both Judah and Joseph underwent *Teshuvah* – repentance – was taught to me by Rabbi Neḥemia Polin.

** This is a reference to the Messiah that will come through Joseph (*Mashiaḥ Ben Yosef*) and the Messiah that will come through Judah (*Mashiaḥ Ben David*).

"...after that he went down to Mitzraim..." – *impelled by the word.*

DEEPENING

What does it mean, "impelled by the word"? This refers to the word of God when he revealed to Abraham the destiny of his descendents.* So what happened to free will? That we would go down to a strange land, be enslaved and finally be redeemed was already determined. Free choice comes into how we go down and how we come out and how long we are there for. The same is true in our own lives: it's how we face the events in our lives that counts, not necessarily the events themselves.

"...and resided there...." *We learn from this that Jacob our father did not go down in order to get stuck in Mitzraim but just to reside there temporarily, as it says: "And they said to Pharaoh: 'We have come to reside in this land because of the lack of pastures for the sheep of your servants due to the severity of the famine in the Land of Canaan, and therefore, with your permission, your servants would like to take up residency in the Land of Goshen'"* (Genesis 47:4).

BEING

See how almost permanent our most temporary plans can become!
As someone once said: "We plan, God laughs."

Kadesh
Urḥatz
Karpas
Yaḥatz
Maggid
Raḥtzah
Motzi
Matzah
Maror
Korekh
Shulḥan Orekh
Tzafun
Barekh
Hallel
Nirtzah

* "Your descendents will be strangers in a land not their own, where they will be enslaved and persecuted..." (Genesis 14:13).

בִּמְתֵי מְעָט. כְּמָה שֶׁנֶּאֱמַר בְּשִׁבְעִים נֶפֶשׁ יָרְדוּ אֲבוֹתֶיךָ מִצְרָיְמָה. וְעַתָּה שָׂמְךָ יְיָ אֱלֹהֶיךָ כְּכוֹכְבֵי הַשָּׁמַיִם לָרֹב.

DEEPENING

The Torah commands us to treat others in a compassionate manner: "And you shall not wrong the stranger, neither shall you oppress him because you were strangers in the Land of Mitzraim."* What does this refer to? When Jacob and his tribe first entered Mitzraim they were welcomed by Pharaoh and allotted the finest lands (Goshen). And even though they were looked down upon professionally, they were honored by the local population and allowed to settle in peace. We were strangers in a strange land and they treated us well. It is that relationship between the insiders and the outsiders that we must remember to practice.

We are all Broken people 2019

new/new knowledge! 2015

ESK JS

וַיְהִי שָׁם לְגוֹי. מְלַמֵּד שֶׁהָיוּ יִשְׂרָאֵל מְצֻיָּנִים שָׁם:

קדש
ורחץ
כרפס
יחץ
מגיד
רחצה
מוציא
מצה
מרור
כורך
שלחן עורך
צפון
ברך
הלל
נרצה

* Exodus 22:20 as well as many other places.

"...as a small tribe...." *How many? It says: "With seventy souls did your ancestors go down into Mitzraim. And now the Lord your God has put you in a majority above the stars in the sky"* (Deuteronomy 10:22).

BEING

Seventy souls – seventy faces of Torah- seventy nations of the world – seventy ways in – seventy ways out – one for each of us.

"...and there we became a nation...." *From this we learn that Israel remained distinctive there.*

Kadesh
Urḥatz
Karpas
Yaḥatz
Maggid
Raḥtzah
Motzi
Matzah
Maror
Korekh
Shulḥan Orekh
Tzafun
Barekh
Hallel
Nirtzah

DEEPENING

In spite of the temptation to become someone else; in spite of the attraction to don another's mask, to swap persona, to cover up, to disappear, we must stay ourselves, stay who we really are, for our tests are uniquely ours, our life is uniquely ours and God has created us uniquely Hers.

גָּדוֹל, עָצוּם. כְּמָה שֶׁנֶּאֱמַר וּבְנֵי יִשְׂרָאֵל פָּרוּ וַיִּשְׁרְצוּ,
וַיִּרְבּוּ וַיַּעַצְמוּ, בִּמְאֹד מְאֹד, וַתִּמָּלֵא הָאָרֶץ אֹתָם:

BEING

The experience in Mitzraim can be viewed as the birth of a nation. It can also be viewed as the development of a fetus and its eventual birth. The process of spreading out describes cellular division and development of form. As the cells divide, so does the body grow until it fills the entire womb. Then the pressure begins to mount as the womb pushes back creating discomfort for both the container and the contained. When the time is right the unborn "cries out" and the Creator "remembers." Then the Exodus from the confines (Mitzraim) begins. The body prepares itself for the journey. The head descends. The labor pains

וָרָב. כְּמָה שֶׁנֶּאֱמַר רְבָבָה כְּצֶמַח הַשָּׂדֶה נְתַתִּיךְ, וַתִּרְבִּי,
וַתִּגְדְּלִי, וַתָּבוֹאִי בַּעֲדִי עֲדָיִים: שָׁדַיִם נָכֹנוּ, וּשְׂעָרֵךְ צִמֵּחַ,
וְאַתְּ עֵרֹם וְעֶרְיָה: וָאֶעֱבֹר עָלַיִךְ וָאֶרְאֵךְ מִתְבּוֹסֶסֶת בְּדָמָיִךְ
וָאֹמַר לָךְ בְּדָמַיִךְ חֲיִי וָאֹמַר לָךְ בְּדָמַיִךְ חֲיִי:

DEEPENING

An alternative and less positive way of looking at this is by recognizing that the pull into Mitzraim is at first seductive and then repressive. Wealth and power suck us in. Control and manipulation create a false sense of security. And then, just as everything seems to be going our way, just as we seem to be safe, the tentacles entwine and begin to squeeze, as it says....

---

* The full quote from the Prophet (Ezekiel 16:4–10) reads as follows: "...and as for your birth, in the day that you were born your navel (umbilical cord) was not cut, neither were you washed in water to clean you; you were definitely not cleaned (lit. "salted") and you definitely were not swaddled. No eyes pitied you, no compassion was bestowed upon you. On the contrary, you were cast into the open field in all your disgustingness

קדש
ורחץ
כרפס
יחץ
מגיד
רחצה
מוציא
מצה
מרור
כורך
שלחן עורך
צפון
ברך
הלל
נרצה

"...great and powerful...." *As it is said: "And the Children of Israel were fruitful and swarmed and multiplied and became very, very powerful and the land was filled with them"* (Exodus 1:7).

(blows – "*makot*") begin followed by contractions (*Tzirim – Mitzraim*). "How will I get through that tiny gap?" cries the uninitiated. "Just keep going, for I will perform the greatest of miracles," replies the Divine Midwife. The waters break and the crossing through the narrow straits proceeds. With one final push the baby is born. The connection to its birth place, where at first it was so welcome but later became so hostile, is permanently severed – there is no going back that way. A cry of joy is heard. The newborn is fed *mannah* from the breasts of the *Shekhinah*. And what of the "souls that left the Land of Israel and descended into Mitzraim"? This refers to the creative spark of conception that descends from the higher worlds into this world of physical constraint.

"...and numerous [Heb: rav]...." *As it says: "I caused you to become fully grown [Heb: revava] like the vegetation of the field; develop, grow, mature!"** (Ezekiel 16:7).

Kadesh
Urḥatz
Karpas
Yaḥatz
Maggid
Raḥtzah
Motzi
Matzah
Maror
Korekh
Shulḥan Orekh
Tzafun
Barekh
Hallel
Nirtzah

---

on the very day that you were born. And when I passed by you and saw you wallowing in your blood I said to you, 'By your blood may you live!' I said to you, 'By your blood may you live!' I caused you to become fully-grown like the vegetation of the field; develop, grow, mature! Your breasts grew firm and your hair grew thick but still you were naked and bare. Then came the time when I passed by you and saw you and behold it was the time of your fertility; and I spread wings around you covering your nakedness. And I swore a covenant with you,' says the Lord God, 'and you became mine. Then I washed you with water, rinsed away the blood and massaged you with oil...."' The passage goes on to describe the exceedingly generous gifts (perhaps over generous gifts) that were bestowed upon the bride and how her splendor became renowned. But then the inevitable happens: the attractiveness and fame go to her head and she falls victim to her vanity (ego) ("But you trusted in your own beauty....") She becomes ensnared by other suitors, plays the harlot; all that she received so unconditionally she manages to ruin; she even uses her children in her deceit and turns them against their father (lit.: slays them and makes them pass through the fire). How could she forget her origins? This entire passage is a parable describing

וַיָּרֵעוּ אֹתָנוּ הַמִּצְרִים וַיְעַנּוּנוּ. וַיִּתְּנוּ עָלֵינוּ עֲבֹדָה קָשָׁה:

וַיָּרֵעוּ אֹתָנוּ הַמִּצְרִים. כְּמָה שֶׁנֶּאֱמַר הָבָה נִתְחַכְּמָה לוֹ פֶּן יִרְבֶּה, וְהָיָה כִּי תִקְרֶאנָה מִלְחָמָה וְנוֹסַף גַּם הוּא עַל־שֹׂנְאֵינוּ, וְנִלְחַם־בָּנוּ וְעָלָה מִן־הָאָרֶץ:

BEING

One of the critical questions that must be asked is: what was this fight between Pharaoh and Israel really about? Moses had already been informed more or less of all the details about upcoming events during his encounter with God at the Burning Bush (Exodus 3–6). Furthermore, note that Moses never tells Pharaoh: let my people go because enslaving a people is immoral; or: let my people go so that they may be a free people in their own land. What Moses actually proclaims is: "Thus saith the Lord, 'Let my people go that they may serve Me'" (Exodus 7:16). He later adds, "We will go three days into the desert and there we will sacrifice to the Lord our God" (Exodus 8:23). In other words, the entire confrontation is not ostensibly about releasing the slaves from their grueling labor but rather about going into the desert, for a limited period of time only, in order to worship this particular god of ours. One could make the argument that had Moses made the direct plea for the immediate release of all the slaves then the psychological impact of such a demand upon Pharaoh would have been too much and the game would never have even begun. However, something deeper is happening here: the battle is not about the slaves or about the immediate moral

---

the history of Israel and her relationship with God. In many Haggadot the line "...by your blood may you will live..." is transposed and placed at the end of the quote. Thus the blood is no longer the blood of birth but rather the blood shed by a naked, hapless fully-grown virgin enslaved and beaten by cruel slave masters. In this way the prophecy becomes: may this innocent blood that was shed be a sign of the renewal of life (as opposed to: "By blood we fell, by blood we shall arise!"). This transposing of verses was probably edited during one of the darker periods of Jewish history and is another example of the thread of redemptive healing that runs throughout the text.

And the Mitzrim did evil to us and made us suffer and they burdened us with hard labor.

"...and the Mitzrim did evil to us...." *As it says: "Come, let us deal wisely with it [this nation], lest it multiply to such an extent that should we ever be attacked it will join those that hate us and fight against us and drive us from this land"* (Exodus 1:11).

dilemma of slavery [although that is dealt with and codified later; in fact the first laws expounded upon after the ten commandments deal with the issue of slaves and slavery (Exodus 21)]; the battle is a "battle of the gods," or, more precisely, between the Lord God Creator of heaven and earth, and consort to the Children of Israel, and Pharaoh, the godhead of Mitzraim. So, going to "serve the Lord" is what it is all about.*

DEEPENING

We are brought around to face ourselves again and again: whom do we really serve – the Pharaoh within (our ego, our fears, our smallness, our pettiness, our self-righteousness, our ignorance, our earthly duties) or the Lord God?

Kadesh
Urḥatz
Karpas
Yaḥatz
Maggid
Raḥtzah
Motzi
Matzah
Maror
Korekh
Shulḥan Orekh
Tzafun
Barekh
Hallel
Nirtzah

* The commentator Rashi consistently emphasizes how Moses embarrasses Pharaoh by accentuating his mortality and lack of real power: "And the Lord said to Moses: 'Get up early in the morning and present yourself to Pharaoh at the moment that he comes down to the water'" (Exodus 7:15). Rashi: "To ease himself. For he claimed to be a god and asserted therefore that he did not need to ease himself; he used to rise early and go to the Nile and there secretly ease himself.'" Therefore, Moses caught him with his pants down.

וַיְעַנּוּנוּ. כְּמָה שֶׁנֶּאֱמַר וַיָּשִׂימוּ עָלָיו שָׂרֵי מִסִּים, לְמַעַן עַנֹּתוֹ בְּסִבְלֹתָם: וַיִּבֶן עָרֵי מִסְכְּנוֹת לְפַרְעֹה, אֶת־פִּתֹם וְאֶת־רַעַמְסֵס:

BEING

It should be noted that many Egyptian scholars believe that artisans and local labor rather than slaves were responsible for building most of their ancient monuments. They attribute the slave stories, with hundreds of poor souls heaving great stone blocks, to Hollywood dramatization. The Torah version seems to support neither side. The Torah version describes the Hebrews as being involved in building structures not out of quarried stone but from baked mud mixed with straw. The transportation of such bricks did not necessitate large hauling crews and the buildings constructed were not the great, invulnerable pyramids or any of the other magnificent constructs. This didn't make the work any less grueling though, for the mud had to be dug, the mixture mixed, the sludge poured, the kilns worked, the bricks baked, the loads carried and the walls built. But no outstanding edifices remain of our travail. All that work just crumbled into the sand. Oy, the impermanence of our creations over which we work so hard!

וַיִּתְּנוּ עָלֵינוּ עֲבֹדָה קָשָׁה. כְּמָה שֶׁנֶּאֱמַר וַיַּעֲבִדוּ מִצְרַיִם אֶת־בְּנֵי יִשְׂרָאֵל בְּפָרֶךְ:

BEING

The word "*b'farekh*" can also mean "to crumble," the idea being that the purpose of the labor was to crumble the will of the people, to break them spiritually, to reduce them to a pile of humanity. What kind of work can achieve this? Work that is futile, work that has no purpose behind it, work that degrades the creative genius and image of Godliness that we each possess.

DEEPENING

How much effort do we put into our lives! How much of it dissipates into

"...and they oppressed us...." *As it says: "And they imposed taskmasters over them in order to oppress with their sufferings. And they built garrison [or storage] cities for Pharaoh – Pitom and Ramses"* (Exodus 1:11).

DEEPENING

Buddhism* teaches that attachments are the cause of suffering. Attachments in Judaism are synonymous to being enslaved in the House of Bondage. Mitzraim represents everything that enslaves us or that we enslave, everything that we are attached to in the physical, emotional and psychological realms of our lives. It says: "Gods of your masks do not make,"** which is not a commandment that forbids our masks but rather a commandment not to make gods out of them. For instance, money is neutral; it is merely an intermediary in the cycle of bartering. But becoming attached to money, loving money, turning the physical, the impermanent into a god, this is enslavement and bondage. So look inside and see how your inner Pharaoh is making you sweat!

"...and they burdened us with hard labor...." *As it says: "And the Mitzrim worked the Children of Israel harshly"* (Exodus 1:13).

nothing? *Hevel* – vanity. Our egos struggle so hard to keep our heads above water for fear of drowning. When will we realize that we can float? When will we realize that employment as an "*eved HaShem*" – a servant of God – is never soul-crumbling, but rather soul-building?

* Interestingly, the Sanskrit word Nirvana means to "go out" as in the going out or extinguishing of the fine of the desirous ego.

** The literal translation is "Do not make for yourself molten gods" (Exodus 34:17), however the word for molten and the word for mask are synonymous. Interestingly enough, the verses following this command begin a description of the festival cycle starting with Pesaḥ. This verse can therefore be seen as a hint at a festival that will come immediately before Pesaḥ involving masks and their removal – Purim!

וַנִּצְעַק אֶל־יְיָ אֱלֹהֵי אֲבֹתֵינוּ, וַיִּשְׁמַע יְיָ אֶת־קֹלֵנוּ, וַיַּרְא אֶת־עָנְיֵנוּ, וְאֶת־עֲמָלֵנוּ, וְאֶת לַחֲצֵנוּ:

וַנִּצְעַק אֶל־יְיָ אֱלֹהֵי אֲבֹתֵינוּ, כְּמָה שֶׁנֶּאֱמַר וַיְהִי בַיָּמִים הָרַבִּים הָהֵם, וַיָּמָת מֶלֶךְ מִצְרַיִם, וַיֵּאָנְחוּ בְנֵי־יִשְׂרָאֵל מִן־הָעֲבֹדָה וַיִּזְעָקוּ. וַתַּעַל שַׁוְעָתָם אֶל־הָאֱלֹהִים מִן־הָעֲבֹדָה.

BEING

This "crying out" is the turning point of the Haggadah. Up until now we have been going down; suddenly, with one word, everything changes and the ascent begins.

How are we to understand the meaning of this verse: "…and the King of Mitzraim died, and the Children of Israel bent…"? If he died then they should have celebrated. Why did things get worse? Sometimes in our struggle to free ourselves from our Mitzraim, the forces that are entrapping us let go momentarily and then our inner voice is heard saying: "You see it's going to be OK now. We don't have to leave after all. It's safe to stay. The entrapper's gone." And then we relax. And then the "new" king arises with a vengeance. Beware of the wiles of the entrapper.

DEEPENING

Why did it take so long for the children of Israel to be redeemed? For 210 years they were in Mitzraim, about 100 years as slaves. What changed? Did their suffering become too much? Was there a straw that finally broke the camel's back? Maybe or maybe not. But there definitely came the realization that suffering is not a necessity. "I'm not going to take it anymore!"* The internal forces that oppose our desire to escape Mitzraim,

* In the 1976 film *Network*, starring Peter Finch and Faye Dunaway, Finch works as an anchorman for a large television corporation. One day after having concluded the news, he calls the camera to move in close. He proceeds to give an impassioned speech

And we cried out to the Lord the God of our ancestors, and the Lord heard our voice and witnessed our suffering, our toil and our oppression.

"...and we cried out to the Lord the God of our ancestors...." *As it says: "After what seemed like endless days, the King of Mitzraim died. And the Children of Israel* [Israel can be translated us 'straight with/to God'] *bent under the workload and cried out. And their cries ascended to the Lord from the labor"* (Exodus 2:23).

that make us swallow our "crying out," are great and subtle:

"It will be OK."
"It doesn't really hurt – at least not that much."
"I can take it."
"It could be worse."
"At least it can't get any worse."
"I don't deserve better."
"It's my karma/destiny to suffer."
"That's life."

What's your excuse? And how much longer are you going to wait? The turning point between slavery and freedom in the Haggadah pivots upon one expression, "And we cried out." After this the emphasis is on the deliverance. This is the great secret of healing: the healing doesn't come from within – it comes by the grace of God. However, to activate God's grace you have to do something – cry out! God's overflowing love is wanting to become more manifest in our lives. It is we in our arrogance, fear, swollen pride and ignorance who block the flow. Damn your arrogance and cry out! Overcome your fear and cry out! Swallow your pride and cry out! Break through your ignorance and cry out! Just admit

about life and loss: "So I want you to get up now. I want all of you to get up out of your chairs. I want you to get up right now and go to the window, open it and stick your head out and yell, 'I'm mad as hell, and **I'm not going to take this anymore**!'"– Howard Beale (Peter Finch).

וַיִּשְׁמַע יְיָ אֶת קֹלֵנוּ. כְּמָה שֶׁנֶּאֱמַר וַיִּשְׁמַע אֱלֹהִים אֶת־נַאֲקָתָם, וַיִּזְכֹּר אֱלֹהִים אֶת־בְּרִיתוֹ אֶת־אַבְרָהָם, אֶת־יִצְחָק וְאֶת־יַעֲקֹב:

that you are powerless to free yourself from Mitzraim. Just believe that only through a power greater than yourself can redemption occur.* Let go and turn your will and life over to the loving care of God.

Pre-Pesaḥ exercise: Write down your "crying out." It should be addressed to God, for example: "God, please get me out of here!" Use this exclamation as a mantra. Repeat it until the tears flow. Repeat it as if your life depends upon it being heard. Cry it out. Let yourself fall onto your knees. And when you're ready, roll over and lie in a fetal position.

---

* This critical step of "crying out" is paralleled by Step 3 in the Twelve Step Program for abuse recovery. The first three steps are:

1. We admit we are powerless over the source of our bondage (e.g. alcohol) – that our lives have become unmanageable.
2. We come to believe that a Power greater than ourselves can restore us to sanity.
3. We make a decision to turn our will and our life over to the care of God *as we understand God*.

Although the Twelve-Step program of Alcoholics Anonymous was originally designed in the 1930s to help alcoholics overcome their drinking problem, it has evolved into a philosophy and a way of life that teaches people how to be fully human. The remaining nine steps are:

4. We make a searching and fearless moral inventory of ourselves.
5. We admit to God, to ourselves and to another human being the exact nature of our wrongs.
6. We're entirely ready to have God remove all these defects of character.
7. We humbly ask God to remove our shortcomings.
8. We make a list of all persons we had harmed and become willing to make amends to them all.
9. We make direct amends to such people wherever possible, except when to do so would injure them or others.
10. We continue to take personal inventory and when we are wrong, promptly admit it.
11. We seek through prayer and meditation to improve our conscious contact with God, *as we understood God*, praying only for knowledge of God's will for us and power to carry that out.
12. Having had a spiritual awakening as the result of these Steps, we tried to carry this message to those in bondage and to practice these principles in all our affairs.

"...and the Lord heard our voices...." *As it says: "And God heard their moans, and God was reminded of the Divine covenant with Abraham, with Isaac, and with Jacob"* (Exodus 2:23).

You might want to have a blanket available to cover yourself. Allow yourself to be wrapped in the loving arms of the *Shekhinah.**

BEING

In the Garden of Eden story we learn how we lived in intimacy with our Divine Creator. It was a relationship akin to that of lovers walking together in the sunset, enjoying the fragrance and beauty of their natural surroundings. We were fully integrated internally and at one with all of Creation. Our inner female and inner male were perfectly in balance, as were our external relationships between woman and man. And then it went wrong.** And we broke our promises. And we ate of the Tree. And we hid from the presence of our lover and we were embarrassed and ashamed. God said, "If you want to play that game then I'll play too. You hide from me then I'll hide my face from you. And it will seem that I am removed from your life but in truth I will only be hidden. And on the day that you come and search for me I will be there, waiting for you." And so the game continues until we cry out.

Kadesh
Urḥatz
Karpas
Yaḥatz
Maggid
Raḥtzah
Motzi
Matzah
Maror
Korekh
Shulḥan Orekh
Tzafun
Barekh
Hallel
Nirtzah

* The following prayer is appropriate at this stage of the Telling: "God, I offer myself to You, to build me and do with me as You will. Relieve me of the bondage of self, that I may better do Your will. Take away my difficulties, that victory over them may bear witness to those I would help of Your power, Your love and The Way of Life. May I do Your will always!" From www.twelve-step.org.

** This break in the Divine relationship is poetically and erotically described in *Song of Songs*.

וַיַּרְא אֶת־עָנְיֵנוּ. זוֹ פְּרִישׁוּת דֶּרֶךְ אֶרֶץ. כְּמָה שֶׁנֶּאֱמַר וַיַּרְא אֱלֹהִים אֶת בְּנֵי־יִשְׂרָאֵל. וַיֵּדַע אֱלֹהִים.

BEING

This suffering is understood to have involved the denial of sexual intimacy – "knowing" – that Pharaoh imposed upon the men and women of Israel as a method of population control (read: genocide). This could either have occurred by decree, as a result of the exhaustive work or by the fear that newborn males would be condemned to drowning in the River – potent contraceptives all of them.

DEEPENING

It can be said that there are two paths to knowing God:*

1) The way of the intellect, in which the mind attempts to penetrate through the layers of distraction, rising higher and higher towards the Divine throne. Following such an approach, the body is understood as a vessel for the intellect, a donkey for the traveler, and as such must be carefully and properly maintained. It must be fed the most nutritious foods, exercised, given the necessary amount of rest and permitted a minimum amount of sexual activity to satisfy its animal desires. Without this balance the mind might lose its sharpness and the journey fall short of its goal. It's analogous to oiling a machine.**

2) The way of love, in which the whole of one's being – mind, body and spirit – is joined holistically in the dance with God. And this is true not

---

* This insight was given over to me at a crossroads of my life by "a man in the field," Rabbi Steve Wald, in Jerusalem in 1981. We are constantly being sent angels, usually in the form of other human beings, that have critical messages to pass on to us. Most of the time they themselves don't even know the critical nature of their actions and only years later are they informed: "Do you remember that remark you made? Well it changed my life, set me on a new road. I'm so grateful to you." Look back and give thanks to the angels that have come into your life – whether they knew it or not. And then contemplate how many messages you might not have heard or chose to ignore! A Biblical example can be found in the story of Joseph (Genesis 37:15). While looking for his brothers "a man wandering in the field" approaches him....The commentators claim this man to have been the archangel Gabriel. I maintain that it was just a man being acted upon by the archangel Gabriel.

** This way is exemplified by the rationalists – Aristotle and, to a certain degree, Maimonides.

"...and He witnessed our suffering...." *This refers to the separation of the "natural way," as it says: "And God saw the children of Israel and God knew"* (Exodus 2:25).

only of the individual but of all of Creation. Intimacy with God is through relationships: our relationship to ourselves, to our loved ones, to the trees, to the animals, to the planet. Thus, nutritious foods are consumed because we should love our bodies, and concern for the planet displayed because we should love our home. Sexuality is part of the dance; loving intimacy with another evokes and mirrors the intimacy of the Divine with the Divine's Creation. And all of these relationships are reminders and even actualizers for experiencing and knowing the Oneness of all.*

Mitzraim blocks full, loving relationships with others and hence blocks intimacy – "knowing" of God. In Mitzraim, the self acts selfishly out of attachment and fear. Holding on for fear that there may not be enough to go around, whether it is love or bread or status or time. So with such eyes we are not capable of seeing the Divine in the other. With such eyes all we can see is competition for scarce resources, someone to defeat, someone to guard against.

And why is the Divine present in a loving relationship? It is often said that when a man meets a woman and a woman meets a man then two complementary parts are unified back into some archetypal whole.** An alternative view sees a loving relationship as bringing balance to the internal male and female. Moreover such a relationship necessitates a *Tzimtzum* – a contraction – of the ego to make space for the other. It requires a letting go and a letting in. And since this is all true of a loving relationship with the Divine, therefore the loving partner actually becomes a window to the Divine.***

---

* This way is exemplified by Kabbalah and the mystical tradition.

** The Midrash understands that the original Adam was an androgynous being that was later split into separate male and female parts. Kabbalah sees the Divine as possessing both male and female aspects and that since we are created in the image of the Divine then we too must contain the whole.

*** The alternative to a window is a mirror – a glass coated with silver (*kessef* in Hebrew, which also means money) – where all that is seen is one's own reflection. These

וְאֶת־עֲמָלֵנוּ. אֵלּוּ הַבָּנִים. כְּמָה שֶׁנֶּאֱמַר כָּל־הַבֵּן הַיִּלּוֹד הַיְאֹרָה תַּשְׁלִיכֻהוּ, וְכָל־הַבַּת תְּחַיּוּן:

BEING

The Seder night is a *Tikkun* – a Fixing – for the lost children (male and female), for on this night we give central stage to our children to ask and to be answered.*

וְאֶת לַחֲצֵנוּ. זֶה הַדְּחַק. כְּמָה שֶׁנֶּאֱמַר וְגַם־רָאִיתִי אֶת־הַלַּחַץ אֲשֶׁר מִצְרַיִם לֹחֲצִים אֹתָם:

DEEPENING

Being caught in Mitzraim creates terrible pressure on the soul and hence on the entire structure – the intellectual, emotional and physical body. The soul wants to commune with God through the world it is born into, but this channel is blocked. And so the pressure builds up. In chemistry there is a principle called Le Chatelier's Principle** wherein a system at equilibrium will look for means to release pressure should pressure be applied. The same principle occurs in alchemy, the chemistry of

---

thoughts were inspired by Ruth Gan, my beloved wife. Itamar Kagan has pointed out that, looking at someone through a pane of glass when your side is illuminated more brightly than the other side, the glass becomes reflective – you only see yourself, the other side can see you, but you can't see them. And vice-versa. Only by equilibrating the light can you see the other.

* See the commentary on Elijah's cup.

** Le Chatelier's Principle states that if a stress is applied to a system at equilibrium, then the system will readjust, if possible, to reduce the stress (Henry-Louis Le Chatelier, 1850–1936, French chemist and engineer).

קדש
ורחץ
כרפס
יחץ
מגיד
רחצה
מוציא
מצה
מרור
כורך
שלחן עורך
צפון
ברך
הלל
נרצה

***"...and our toil...."** These are our sons. As it says: "Every newborn son shall be cast into the River, while every daughter shall live"* (Exodus 1:22).

DEEPENING

It is on this night that we can start healing the relationship with the drowned-out inner child.

***"...and our oppression...."** This is the stress, as it says: "And I also saw the pressure which Mitzraim imposed upon them"* (Exodus 3:9).

the soul. Ideally, the soul should be in equilibrium between the back-end and the front-end, meaning its connection to its Source along the channel it descended down* (the back end) and the connection to the Source through the actions of its human partner in the natural world** (the front end). When this equilibrium is disrupted and put under stress then the pressure must be released somewhere. Sometimes it's through a breakdown in the physical body like poor health, sometimes through emotional distress and at other times through mental anguish.

* In Kabbalah there are five soul levels that lead back to the source: *Nefesh*, *Neshamah*, *Ruaḥ*, *Ḥayah* and *Yeḥida*.

** A modern source that describes the relationship of the soul to the world can be found in Psychosynthesis, perhaps the most spiritual of the psychological disciplines. As an inclusive approach to human growth, Psychosynthesis dates from 1911 and the early work of Roberto Assagioli, an Italian Psychiatrist. Assagioli maintained that Freud had not given sufficient weight to the "higher" aspects of the human personality, and recognized a need for a more inclusive concept of humanity (www.aap-psychosynthesis.org). A quote from Assagioli seems to sum-up the Pesaḥ process: "From the Eternal/Out of the past/In the present/For the future."

Kadesh
Urḥatz
Karpas
Yaḥatz
Maggid
Raḥtzah
Motzi
Matzah
Maror
Korekh
Shulḥan Orekh
Tzafun
Barekh
Hallel
Nirtzah

וַיּוֹצִיאֵנוּ יְיָ מִמִּצְרַיִם, בְּיָד חֲזָקָה, וּבִזְרֹעַ נְטוּיָה, וּבְמֹרָא גָּדוֹל וּבְאֹתוֹת וּבְמוֹפְתִים:

וַיּוֹצִיאֵנוּ יְיָ מִמִּצְרַיִם. לֹא עַל־יְדֵי מַלְאָךְ, וְלֹא עַל־יְדֵי שָׂרָף, וְלֹא עַל־יְדֵי שָׁלִיחַ. אֶלָּא הַקָּדוֹשׁ בָּרוּךְ הוּא בִּכְבוֹדוֹ וּבְעַצְמוֹ. שֶׁנֶּאֱמַר וְעָבַרְתִּי בְאֶרֶץ מִצְרַיִם בַּלַּיְלָה הַזֶּה, וְהִכֵּיתִי כָל־בְּכוֹר בְּאֶרֶץ מִצְרַיִם, מֵאָדָם וְעַד בְּהֵמָה, וּבְכָל־אֱלֹהֵי מִצְרַיִם אֶעֱשֶׂה שְׁפָטִים אֲנִי יְיָ:

וְעָבַרְתִּי בְאֶרֶץ מִצְרַיִם בַּלַּיְלָה הַזֶּה. אֲנִי וְלֹא מַלְאָךְ. וְהִכֵּיתִי כָל בְּכוֹר בְּאֶרֶץ־מִצְרַיִם. אֲנִי וְלֹא שָׂרָף. וּבְכָל־אֱלֹהֵי מִצְרַיִם אֶעֱשֶׂה שְׁפָטִים. אֲנִי וְלֹא הַשָּׁלִיחַ. אֲנִי יְיָ. אֲנִי הוּא וְלֹא אַחֵר:

And the Lord brought us out of Mitzraim, with a determined hand and an outstretched arm and with great awe and many signs and wonders.

"...and the Lord brought us out of Mitzraim...." *Not by an Angel, not by a Seraf* and not by an Emissary, but the Holy One, Blessed be He, in His Glory and only by Himself, as it says: "And on that night I will pass over the Land of Mitzraim and I will slay every first-born in the Land of Mitzraim, from humans to beasts, and I will judge all the gods of Mitzraim for I am the Lord"* (Exodus 12:12).

"And on that night I will pass over the Land of Mitzraim...." I, and not an Angel.

"...and I will slay every first-born in the Land of Mitzraim...." I, and not a Seraf.

"...and I will judge all the gods of Mitzraim..." I, and not an Emissary. "...for I am the Lord." I, and no other.

Kadesh
Urḥatz
Karpas
Yaḥatz
Maggid
Raḥtzah
Motzi
Matzah
Maror
Korekh
Shulḥan Orekh
Tzafun
Barekh
Hallel
Nirtzah

* *Serafim* (plural for *Seraf*) are of the highest order of angels in Jewish lore. The *Serafim* surround the throne of Glory and unceasingly intone the trisagion ("holy, holy, holy"). They are the angels of Love, of Light and of Fire. Apparently there are four such angels corresponding to the four winds of the world. The *Serafim* have 4 faces and 6 wings as it says in Isaiah 6. (*A Dictionary of Angels*, by G. Davidson).

BEING

Why this emphasis on the fact that it was "I the Lord (YHVH)" that punished Mitzraim and redeemed the Children of Israel rather than some other Heavenly identity? We have already explained that the story of Israel's sojourn, enslavement and release from Mitzraim was a war between the Lord God of the Universe and the deities of Mitzraim ("I will judge all the gods of Mitzraim"). This being so, it was necessary for the final battle to be carried out by the One Himself and no other, otherwise it would be a victory by proxy, thereby defeating the whole purpose of the exercise. On a more spiritual plane, we are taught that angels can perform only one function at a time. Redeeming Israel from the grip of Pharaoh required two attributes: judgment upon Mitzraim for its actions against Israel and, simultaneously, mercy upon Israel for the actions of Mitzraim. This could only be performed by "I the Lord (YHVH)."*

The name of Moses, the servant of God, is only mentioned once in the whole Haggadah. This is somewhat surprising considering the central role he played in the whole drama of the Exodus. This omission is part of the dialectic between Purim and Pesaḥ. In the *Megillat Esther* (the Scroll of Esther), which is read on Purim, the name of God is hidden. We read of a string of coincidences interspersed with human action. God is transcendent; He works subtly behind the scenes to become manifest through human agents who have to make their own decisions and, in the end, fight the good fight; the crown is clearly on the head of Esther and Aḥashverosh; Mordeḥai becomes the hero; the Divine plan remains a mystery until the last moment. Pesaḥ is the very opposite: there is an ordered plan (*Seder*) disclosed before the action starts; God is immanent; the Hand of God is manifest; the people are very passive until the night of Pesaḥ, when all they have to do is slaughter a lamb; Moses and Aaron are direct emissaries speaking only the words that are channeled to them; the crown is clearly on the "head" of the King of kings. To emphasize this direct line of cause and effect, the human agents and heroes are hidden. "I, and not an Angel; I, and not a *Seraf*; I, and not a Messenger; I, and no other."

This is not Moses' story; it is God's story. Let there be no confusion between the messenger and the message!

* Rabbi Joseph Gikatilla, *Gates of Light* (The First Gate). English translation published by Harper Collins, 1994.

DEEPENING

As the *Shekhinah* – the aspect of the Holy One, Blessed be She, that is closest to this dimension of existence – returns from Her exile, so there is a calling out from above* for renewed intimacy between the Creator and the Created. The voice of God can be heard in the "still, small voice" that flows within. We recite daily the *Shemah Yisrael* – Hear, O Israel – but most of us never shut-up long enough to listen. It is said that "after the destruction of the Temple, prophecy was confined to the mouths of children and fools."** This is true, but not in the literal sense. To access the Spirit of Prophecy (meaning to open up a direct line to the Divine) requires bypassing the "sophisticated mind" and entering the "child's mind" or "fool's mind" (or "beginner's mind"). Within this space the *Ruaḥ HaKodesh* – the Holy Spirit – can enter and dance. Looking at the world through the "child's mind" leads to viewing and experiencing the world as an ongoing miracle unfolding from God, as wonder-filled as a young child. It is this experience that is referred to when the Midrash says that when crossing the Reed Sea even (or especially) the handmaiden had a spiritual experience greater than that of the Prophet Ezekiel.*** Input, around which the rational mind cannot create a frame of reference, can take one beyond the intellect to the "beginner's mind." The Festival of Pesaḥ, starting with the Seder night and culminating with the Crossing of the Sea on the Seventh Day, is about re-obtaining that original, lost state of the child where the "mouth of God will speak"**** and we will hear and listen.

Kadesh
Urḥatz
Karpas
Yaḥatz
Maggid
Raḥtzah
Motzi
Matzah
Maror
Korekh
Shulḥan Orekh
Tzafun
Barekh
Hallel
Nirtzah

---

* A useful metaphor for this process is to visualize a magnet that is hovering above a table covered with iron filings. At first the individual pieces of iron lie scattered at random, but as the magnet descends they become magnetically charged and realign themselves to the invisible presence. As the influence of the magnetic flux increases the little filings begin to reach up towards the source of the energy, forming little peaks.

** Talmud Bavli, *Baba Batra* 12a.

*** Yalkut Shimoni, *Beshalaḥ* 244

**** The word Pesaḥ can be translated as meaning *Peh* – mouth, *Saḥ* – speaks. Most commentators understand this as referring to our mouths telling the Telling.

We have now reached the section of the Telling that relates the plagues and miracles that occurred before and during the liberation from Mitzraim. Make sure that your glass is filled for we are about to spill wine. It is a good idea to have the glass resting on a saucer unless the tablecloth will do.

בְּיָד חֲזָקָה. זוֹ הַדֶּבֶר. כְּמָה שֶׁנֶּאֱמַר הִנֵּה
יַד־יְיָ הוֹיָה, בְּמִקְנְךָ אֲשֶׁר בַּשָּׂדֶה, בַּסּוּסִים
בַּחֲמֹרִים בַּגְּמַלִּים, בַּבָּקָר וּבַצֹּאן, דֶּבֶר כָּבֵד
מְאֹד:

וּבִזְרֹעַ נְטוּיָה. זוֹ הַחֶרֶב. כְּמָה שֶׁנֶּאֱמַר
וְחַרְבּוֹ שְׁלוּפָה בְּיָדוֹ, נְטוּיָה עַל־יְרוּשָׁלָיִם:

BEING

The context behind this quote concerns the fall and rise of King David. An angel for the Dark Side tempted him into conducting a census of the people. Against the advice of his councilors he ordered the people counted. God was angry and offered him three alternative punishments: his enemies would be unleashed against him, a famine would strike the land or a pestilence would ravage the land. He chose the third. As the Angel of Death approached Jerusalem with its sword drawn ready to strike, David's eyes were finally opened and he fell upon his face and cried for forgiveness. In His mercy God ordered the angel to sheath its sword and to withdraw.

DEEPENING

What had King David done that was so awful as to warrant such a punishment? And what has this to do with Pesaḥ? The angel tempted David. This was his test. He could have said "No!" He could have withstood

We have now reached the section of the Telling that relates the plagues and miracles that occurred before and during the liberation from Mitzraim. Make sure that your glass is filled for we are about to spill wine. It is a good idea to have the glass resting on a saucer unless the tablecloth will do.

"...with a determined hand...." *This refers to the plague of pestilence, as it says: "Behold the hand of the Lord is presently upon your livestock which is in the field, upon the horses, upon the donkeys, upon the camels, upon the cattle and the sheep; upon them there will be a very severe pestilence"* (Exodus 9:3).

"...and an outstretched arm...." *This refers to the sword, as it says: "...and his drawn sword in his hand stretched out over Jerusalem"*

(Chronicles I 21:16).

the temptation to bolster his ego by counting how many people were in his kingdom or, read another way, how great a king he was! But no! There was a crack, a blind-spot, and the Other Side pried it open and got in. Or rather, David opened the door and it walked right in. Once in, it deafened the king to the wisdom of his advisors. They knew that he was a great king. They knew that counting the people wouldn't make any difference anyway. But David was in doubt – doubt in himself and doubt in God's Glory; doubt that there is nothing greater than resting in God; that being a True King is greater than being a great king. Arrogance – the antithesis of matzah! Arrogance leads to blindness, deafness and forgetfulness. And so he fell. He endangered his life, the lives of his family and the lives of his faithful people. And he sat paralyzed while the angel of death ravaged the land. It was only when it reached Jerusalem that David broke out of his reverie and saw what was happening because of him. What could he do? He did the only thing that can be done. He fell on his face and cried for forgiveness. He threw himself at the Throne of Mercy. He confessed. He offered himself – his own life – in place of the lives of his innocent people. And God heard. And God was moved. And God recalled the angel. And God "shook" His head and "clucked" His tongue at His favorite child.

Kadesh
Urḥatz
Karpas
Yaḥatz
Maggid
Raḥtzah
Motzi
Matzah
Maror
Korekh
Shulḥan Orekh
Tzafun
Barekh
Hallel
Nirtzah

וּבְמֹרָא גָּדֹל. זֶה גִּלּוּי שְׁכִינָה. כְּמָה שֶׁנֶּאֱמַר אוֹ הֲנִסָּה אֱלֹהִים לָבוֹא לָקַחַת לוֹ גוֹי מִקֶּרֶב גּוֹי, בְּמַסֹּת בְּאֹתֹת וּבְמוֹפְתִים וּבְמִלְחָמָה, וּבְיָד חֲזָקָה וּבִזְרוֹעַ נְטוּיָה, וּבְמוֹרָאִים גְּדֹלִים. כְּכֹל אֲשֶׁר־עָשָׂה לָכֶם יְיָ אֱלֹהֵיכֶם בְּמִצְרַיִם, לְעֵינֶיךָ:

BEING

Look around. Do you see the miracles that surround you? Do you see the great wonders of Nature? Do you see the signs that are continuously popping up along your path? Do you see the love that God has for you in your own unique way that distinguishes you from all others? Do you see the outstretched sword that protects you against the enemy? Lift up your eyes and see reality through God's eyes.

+ the pillar by day
a the pillar by night too.

DEEPENING

It is the HaKadosh Barukh Hu that delivers. And when the deliverance occurs His greatness is revealed. Sometimes it's with great drama and sometimes it's quietly, while at other times it happens in the deepest silence. But whichever way it happens the Presence of the *Shekhinah* is experienced and the effect is awesome. The body trembles and the mind is overwhelmed. All remaining ego dissolves. All senses of self – self-importance, self-worth, self-gratification – become senseless. The mind tries to reach out and grasp something, anything, but only finds empty space. Such a great emptiness, so immeasurably large. And it's filled with the Nothingness of Allthingsness. The knees quake and the soul dances. The mouth is dumb and the spirit sings. The eyes close and All is seen. Prepare to praise YAH.

praise you lord. I do   stone

קדש
ורחץ
כרפס
יחץ
מגיד
רחצה
מוציא
מצה
מרור
כורך
שלחן עורך
צפון
ברך
הלל
נרצה

וּבְאֹתוֹת. זֶה הַמַּטֶּה, כְּמָה שֶׁנֶּאֱמַר וְאֶת הַמַּטֶּה הַזֶּה תִּקַּח בְּיָדֶךָ. אֲשֶׁר תַּעֲשֶׂה־בּוֹ אֶת־הָאֹתוֹת.

וּבְמֹפְתִים. זֶה הַדָּם. כְּמָה שֶׁנֶּאֱמַר וְנָתַתִּי מוֹפְתִים בַּשָּׁמַיִם וּבָאָרֶץ:

"...and with great awe...." *This refers to the revealing* [seeing] *of the Holy Spirit* [Shekhinah], *as it says: "Or has God ever tried to go and extricate for himself one nation from the midst of another nation with such trials, such signs and such wonders, and with war and with such a determined hand and with such an outstretched arm and with such great awe at all that the Lord God did for you in Mitzraim in front of your own eyes"* (Exodus 4:33–34).

"...and many signs...." *This refers to the staff, as it says: "And take this staff in your hand and with it you will do signs."* (Exodus 4:17)

"...and wonders...." *This refers to the blood, as it says: "And I will place wonders in the Heavens and the Earth*..."*

DEEPENING

It is said that during the Crossing of the Sea the entire people, from the wisest to the lowest, received an outpouring of the Divine flux to such an extent that their prophetic visions even exceeded that of the Prophet Ezekiel.** In this quote the Prophet Yoel foresees a time wherein a similar course of events will unfold. There will be the external signs of blood, fire and smoke but more than that there will be the internal changes – the Spirit of God will dwell in each person, so that the highest mysteries and deepest secrets will be revealed. Can you imagine how that would unite the generations around the Seder Table? If only we could all share the deepest parts of ourselves without fear of mockery and misunderstanding, knowing that it comes from the Common Source.

* Source: "And afterwards I will pour out my spirit upon all living things; and your sons and daughters shall prophesy; your old men shall dream dreams, your young men shall see visions: also upon the servants and maidservants in those day will I pour out my spirit. And I will exhibit wonders in the heavens and on the earth, blood, fire, and pillars of smoke." Joel 3:1-3

** Yalkut Shimoni: Parshat Beshalaḥ

At the mention of each of these three wonders, a finger is dipped into the wine and a drop spilled over the side of the glass.

דָּם. וָאֵשׁ. וְתִימְרוֹת עָשָׁן:

דָּבָר אַחֵר. בְּיָד חֲזָקָה שְׁתַּיִם. וּבִזְרֹעַ נְטוּיָה שְׁתַּיִם. וּבְמוֹרָא גָּדוֹל שְׁתַּיִם. וּבְאֹתוֹת שְׁתַּיִם. וּבְמוֹפְתִים שְׁתַּיִם:

אֵלּוּ עֶשֶׂר מַכּוֹת שֶׁהֵבִיא הַקָּדוֹשׁ בָּרוּךְ הוּא עַל־הַמִּצְרִים בְּמִצְרַיִם, וְאֵלּוּ הֵן:

At the mention of each of these three wonders, a finger is dipped into the wine and a drop spilled over the side of the glass.

…Blood, and
Fire, and
Pillars of Smoke”
(Joel 3:3).

Another way of understanding these previous phrases is that they allude to the ten plagues:

“…with a determined hand….”

Two plagues!

“…and an outstretched arm….”

Two plagues!

“…and with great awe….”

Two plagues!

“…and many signs….”

Two plagues!

“…and wonders….”

Two plagues!

These are the ten plagues that the Holy One, Blessed be He, brought upon the Mitzrim in Mitzraim, and they are:

Kadesh
Urḥatz
Karpas
Yaḥatz
Maggid
Raḥtzah
Motzi
Matzah
Maror
Korekh
Shulḥan Orekh
Tzafun
Barekh
Hallel
Nirtzah

❧ עֶשֶׂרֶת הַמַּכּוֹת ❧

At the mention of each of these ten plagues, a finger is dipped into the wine and a drop spilled over the side of the glass.

דָּם. צְפַרְדֵּעַ. כִּנִּים. עָרוֹב. דֶּבֶר. שְׁחִין. בָּרָד. אַרְבֶּה. חֹשֶׁךְ. מַכַּת בְּכוֹרוֹת:

BEING

As the Mitzrim drowned in the Sea of Reeds* and the liberated people of Israel sang the song, the Talmud relates** that the Angels also sang until God abruptly stopped them, "My handiwork, my human creatures, are drowning in the sea and you want to sing a song of praise?" People can sing at that moment of liberation since they are so caught up in the moment that they don't have the perspective to see or to empathize with the sufferings of others. And that's OK. But the angels? They surely have the ability to rise above the occasion and have a broader view of cause and effect! So when we spill our wine this year, we are given an opportunity to transcend the narrowness of our human awareness and become like angels – even higher than angels.

DEEPENING

When reading each of the ten plagues, a drop of wine is spilt using one's (little) finger dipped into the cup. This is usually understood to be a symbolic gesture for reducing our level of joy (wine) in recognition of the suffering of the Mitzrim. But honestly, ten drops out of four glasses is hardly a reduction in joy at the death of thousands of Mitzrim! Now take a breath as we look at our own lives. Who have we caused to suffer so that we can be here now, living the life that we are living, at the level of freedom that we have presently chosen, reading these very words? Who has suffered? First of all, our mothers for the discomfort of pregnancy and the pain of birth – the spilt blood. Are you a first-born? If so, then you were the unconscious cause of any suffering endured by your parents when you ended their period of freedom as a pre-parenthood couple (*Makat B'khorot*

קדש
ורחץ
כרפס
יחץ
מגיד
רחצה
מוציא
מצה
מרור
כורך
שלחן עורך
צפון
ברך
הלל
נרצה

---

*   The Hebrew is *Yam Suf* – the Sea of Reeds. It was mistakenly misread as "Red," hence the "Red Sea."

**   Talmud Bavli, *Megillah* 10b

The Ten Plagues

At the mention of each of these ten plagues, a finger is dipped into the wine and a drop spilled over the side of the glass.

Blood, Frogs, Lice, Numerous wild creatures, Livestock plague, Skin boils, Hail, Locusts Darkness, Death of the first-born.

– the death (lit. "blow") of the first-born). The pain we inflicted upon our siblings. The suffering inflicted upon our partners in relationships. The pain inflicted during the ending of a relationship. Even the pain that we inflict upon our own children! What about the pain we inflict upon the planet? What about the pain we have inflicted upon ourselves? Some of this pain is consciously inflicted; some of the pain is unconscious. Many times in order to get out of Mitzraim pain was necessarily inflicted, like being born, like getting divorced. That doesn't mean that we are cruel people, that we hurt for hurt's sake. There was a price to pay in terms of human suffering by coming out of Mitzraim. There was a price to pay in terms of human suffering by coming back to the Land of Israel. This is NOT about guilt! This is about recognizing that there is a price for every step on the journey. This is not about pointing the accusing index finger; this is about opening our hearts to the truth and using the little finger* that points to the Torah when it is held high and open. This is NOT about being sad; it is about being aware in our joy! What is the goal of becoming aware of the pain that we have inflicted along the way? To reduce to zero the pain that we will inflict during the rest of the journey. To move into Messianic consciousness and bring an end to suffering.

There is a connection between Pesaḥ and Tisha B'Av. The first day of Pesaḥ is always the same day of the week as Tisha B'Av (except when the latter is shifted from Shabbat to Sunday). On Pesaḥ we are just becoming aware of the pain inflicted. On Tisha B'Av we grieve for the loss of heart that results from it. And on Yom Kippur we ask for forgiveness for the suffering we have caused.

Kadesh
Urḥatz
Karpas
Yaḥatz
Maggid
Raḥtzah
Motzi
Matzah
Maror
Korekh
Shulḥan Orekh
Tzafun
Barekh
Hallel
Nirtzah

* Each finger is associated with another sefirah (see section 9). The little finger of the right hand is *netzaḥ* identified with Moshe (see Sefer Yetzirah 1:3). It is this finger that we use to point to the Torah as we say: "This is the Torah that Moshe put before the Children of Israel, from the mouth of God to the hand of Moshe." (Daily Siddur)

Three more drops are spilt upon mentioning the following abbreviated forms.

רַבִּי יְהוּדָה הָיָה נוֹתֵן בָּהֶם סִימָנִים:
דְּצַ"ךְ. עֲדַ"שׁ. בְּאַחַ"ב:

The following passages elucidate and embellish the number of miracles that were performed at the Reed Sea over those that took place in Mitzraim. If time is pressing (read: people are getting hungry) then they can be passed over (but read the commentary on regression first). Alternatively, now would be the appropriate time for each participant to relate a miraculous event that occurred in his or her life.

רַבִּי יוֹסֵי הַגְּלִילִי אוֹמֵר: מִנַּיִן אַתָּה אוֹמֵר, שֶׁלָּקוּ הַמִּצְרִים בְּמִצְרַיִם עֶשֶׂר מַכּוֹת, וְעַל הַיָּם לָקוּ חֲמִשִּׁים מַכּוֹת? בְּמִצְרַיִם מַה הוּא אוֹמֵר וַיֹּאמְרוּ הַחַרְטֻמִּם אֶל פַּרְעֹה, אֶצְבַּע אֱלֹהִים הִוא. וְעַל הַיָּם מָה הוּא אוֹמֵר? וַיַּרְא יִשְׂרָאֵל אֶת־הַיָּד הַגְּדֹלָה, אֲשֶׁר עָשָׂה יְיָ בְּמִצְרַיִם, וַיִּירְאוּ הָעָם אֶת־יְיָ. וַיַּאֲמִינוּ בַּייָ, וּבְמשֶׁה עַבְדּוֹ: כַּמָּה לָקוּ בְּאֶצְבַּע, עֶשֶׂר מַכּוֹת: אֱמוֹר מֵעַתָּה, בְּמִצְרַיִם לָקוּ עֶשֶׂר מַכּוֹת, וְעַל הַיָּם לָקוּ חֲמִשִּׁים מַכּוֹת.

BEING

The Red (Reed) Sea is the Sea of Fear.* See it lie before you and know that this is what it is – fear. And when they reached the Sea, Mitzraim (the mind's resistance to change, to freedom) chased after them with 600 armed chariots to bring them back. And they cried. And one man, Naḥshon Ben Aminadav,** began walking into the water. Can you imagine? Panic, fear, hysteria, total loss of faith! And one man began to enter the water. The water came up to his knees, and he continued. The water came up to his waist, and he continued. How they must have cried out to him, "Come back! You don't have to end your life this way! Maybe if we surrender we'll be spared and we can go back to Mitzraim!" And the water came

* "I must not fear. Fear is the mind-killer. Fear is the little-death that brings total obliteration. I will face my fear. I will permit it to pass over me and through me. And when it has gone past I will turn the inner eye to see its path. Where the fear has gone there will be nothing. Only I will remain." – Bene Gesserit's Litany Against Fear from *Dune* by Frank Herbert (Ace Books, 2003).

** This midrash appears in the Talmud Bavli, *Sotah* 37a.

Three more drops are spilt upon mentioning the following abbreviated forms.

Rabbi Yehuda was wont to give them as a mnemonic:
D-Tza-KH
A-Da-Sh
B-A-Ḥa-V

The following passages elucidate and embellish the number of miracles that were performed at the Reed Sea over those that took place in Mitzraim. If time is pressing (read: people are getting hungry) then they can be passed over (but read the commentary on regression first). Alternatively, now would be the appropriate time for each participant to relate a miraculous event that occurred in his or her life.

Rabbi Yosi the Galilean said: "How can one deduce that the Mitzrim in Mitzraim were smitten by ten afflictions whereas by the Sea they were smitten by fifty afflictions? Because in Mitzraim it says: 'And the magicians said to Pharaoh: This is definitely the finger of God!' While at the Sea it says: 'And Israel saw the great hand that the Lord put upon Mitzraim and the people feared the Lord and believed in the Lord and in Moses His servant.** Then, if one finger equals ten afflictions, we must conclude that, since in Mitzraim there were ten afflictions, by the Sea there must have been fifty afflictions."*

up to his chest, to his neck, to his chin, and still he continued. And then the waters reached his lips and began to seep into his mouth. And suddenly the Sea split. And behold lying in front of him was dry land, not muddy, not even a puddle, but dry land. And they walked through the Sea of their Fears as if it never existed. And when they reached the other side the waters closed and their resistance was seen drowning. And at that moment joy welled up in their hearts and they burst forth in song. Do you remember when this happened to you? What was your song?

* Exodus 8:15

** Exodus 14:31. This is said after the waters closed upon the Mitzrim as they chased after the People of Israel.

Kadesh
Urḥatz
Karpas
Yaḥatz
Maggid
Raḥtzah
Motzi
Matzah
Maror
Korekh
Shulḥan Orekh
Tzafun
Barekh
Hallel
Nirtzah

DEEPENING

Regression. It's so easy to fall back into Mitzraim ("just one drink"). The power of habitual ways will fight to get us back into the familiar confinement of prison. In prison there are no homeless, no unemployed, no starving, no taxes and no freedom. It's a known statistic that a large majority of prisoners when paroled, having spent more than a certain time behind bars, will end up back in prison not because they are hardened criminals but because freedom becomes scarier than incarceration. Look what happened the moment the Children of Israel left: the moment they reached the seemingly impenetrable barrier of the Red (Reed) Sea they begged to return to Mitzraim, "Why did you bring us to the desert to die?" At every point in their travels, whenever they faced hardships, they were ready to go back to the Land "of cucumbers, melons, leeks, onions and garlic...."* See how the mind distorts the past? Anything, in order to avoid the insecurity of freedom.** This is especially true when leaving a relationship that doesn't work, whether it's a place of employment or a partner. I know that it's not working; I know staying in the relationship is unhealthy; I know that I've got to get out. But there's so much resistance; it's so scary to be alone again; maybe if I try harder...? And then suddenly it's over. I'm out! I just left and I'm never going back! But I'm so cold and lonely and scared that maybe nobody will care for me again. Maybe we can work it out. Maybe if I go back and we stick to our resolutions and we stop fighting and we start listening to each other and, and.... And we're back together again. But after a few weeks we're back in the same rut. And this time I decide that I'm leaving for good and never coming back! Never...?

קדש
ורחץ
כרפס
יחץ
מגיד
רחצה
מוציא
מצה
מרור
כורך
שלחן עורך
צפון
ברך
הלל
נרצה

* Numbers 11:5 is just one of many examples where the people complained and desired to return.

** *The Insecurity of Freedom* (Schocken, 1987)is the title of one of a collection of essays by the modern day master of Freedom Theology, Abraham Joshua Heschel.

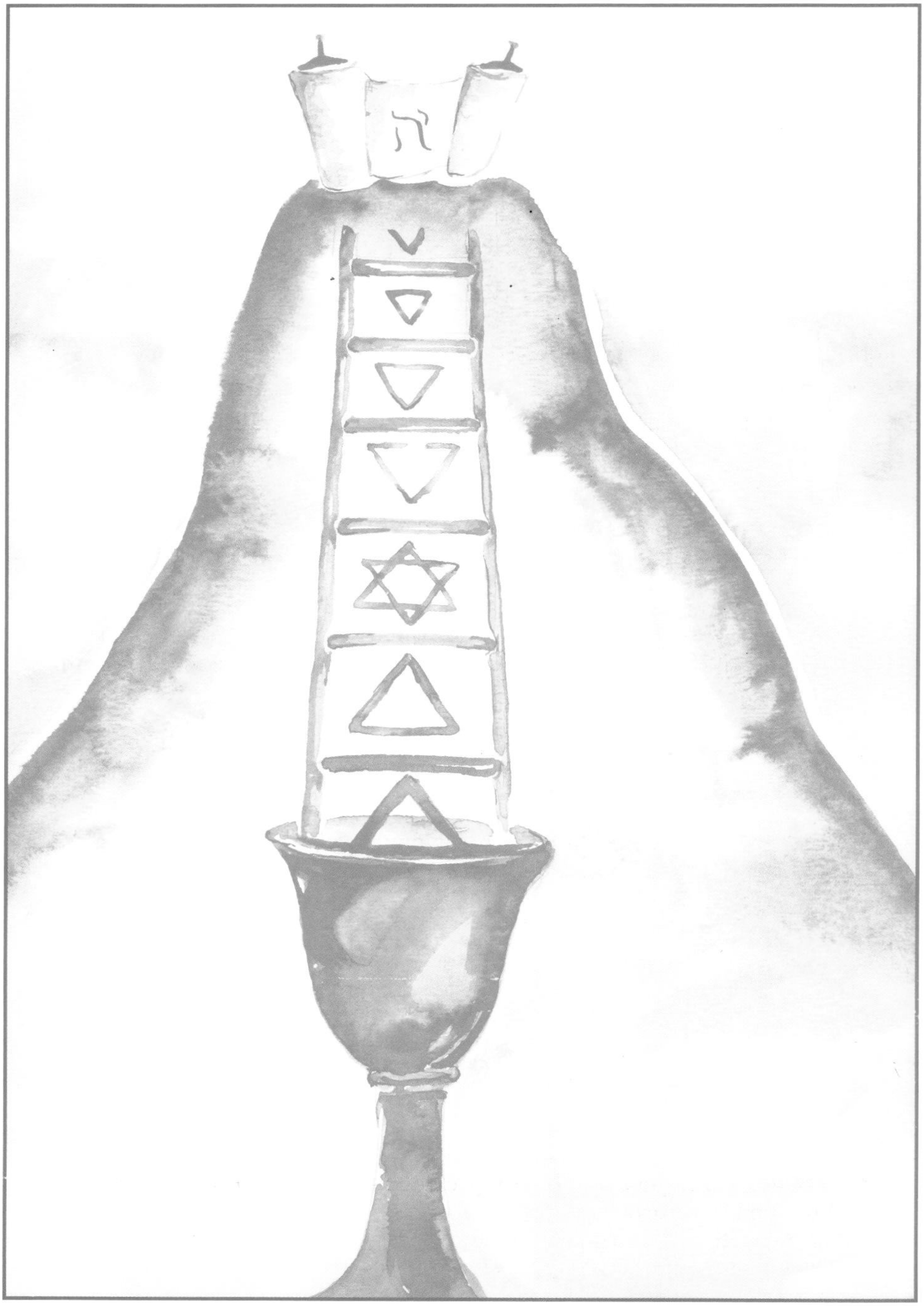
ה

רַבִּי אֱלִיעֶזֶר אוֹמֵר: מִנַּיִן שֶׁכָּל־מַכָּה וּמַכָּה, שֶׁהֵבִיא הַקָּדוֹשׁ בָּרוּךְ הוּא עַל הַמִּצְרִים בְּמִצְרַיִם, הָיְתָה שֶׁל אַרְבַּע מַכּוֹת? שֶׁנֶּאֱמַר יְשַׁלַּח־בָּם חֲרוֹן אַפּוֹ, עֶבְרָה וָזַעַם וְצָרָה, מִשְׁלַחַת מַלְאֲכֵי רָעִים: עֶבְרָה - אַחַת, וָזַעַם - שְׁתַּיִם, וְצָרָה - שָׁלֹשׁ, מִשְׁלַחַת מַלְאֲכֵי רָעִים - אַרְבַּע. אֱמוֹר מֵעַתָּה, בְּמִצְרַיִם לָקוּ אַרְבָּעִים מַכּוֹת, וְעַל הַיָּם לָקוּ מָאתַיִם מַכּוֹת:

רַבִּי עֲקִיבָא אוֹמֵר: מִנַּיִן שֶׁכָּל־מַכָּה וּמַכָּה, שֶׁהֵבִיא הַקָּדוֹשׁ בָּרוּךְ הוּא עַל הַמִּצְרִים בְּמִצְרַיִם, הָיְתָה שֶׁל חָמֵשׁ מַכּוֹת? שֶׁנֶּאֱמַר יְשַׁלַּח־בָּם חֲרוֹן אַפּוֹ, עֶבְרָה וָזַעַם וְצָרָה, מִשְׁלַחַת מַלְאֲכֵי רָעִים. חֲרוֹן אַפּוֹ - אַחַת, עֶבְרָה - שְׁתַּיִם, וָזַעַם - שָׁלֹשׁ, וְצָרָה - אַרְבַּע, מִשְׁלַחַת מַלְאֲכֵי רָעִים - חָמֵשׁ. אֱמוֹר מֵעַתָּה, בְּמִצְרַיִם לָקוּ חֲמִשִּׁים מַכּוֹת, וְעַל הַיָּם לָקוּ חֲמִשִּׁים וּמָאתַיִם מַכּוֹת:

קדש
ורחץ
כרפס
יחץ
מגיד
רחצה
מוציא
מצה
מרור
כורך
שלחן עורך
צפון
ברך
הלל
נרצה

Rabbi Eliezer said: "How can one deduce that each and every affliction that the Holy One, Blessed be He, brought upon the Mitzrim in Mitzraim consisted of four different afflictions? As it says: 'He sent forth against them in His burning anger: wrath, indignation, trouble and a band of fierce angels.' That is: wrath makes one; indignation makes two; trouble makes three; and a band of fierce angels makes four. We must therefore conclude that, since in Mitzraim there were forty afflictions, by the Sea there must have been two hundred afflictions."*

Rabbi Akiva said: "How can one deduce that each and every affliction that the Holy One, Blessed be He, brought upon the Mitzrim in Mitzraim consisted of five different afflictions? As it says: 'He sent forth against them His burning anger, wrath, indignation, trouble and a band of fierce angels.' That is: burning anger makes one; wrath makes two; indignation makes three; trouble makes four; and a band of fierce Angels makes five. We must therefore conclude that, since in Mitzraim there were fifty afflictions, by the Sea there must have been two hundred and fifty afflictions."

* Psalms 78:49

כַּמָּה מַעֲלוֹת טוֹבוֹת לַמָּקוֹם עָלֵינוּ:

אִלּוּ הוֹצִיאָנוּ מִמִּצְרַיִם, וְלֹא עָשָׂה בָהֶם שְׁפָטִים,

דַּיֵּנוּ:

אִלּוּ עָשָׂה בָהֶם שְׁפָטִים, וְלֹא עָשָׂה בֵאלֹהֵיהֶם,

דַּיֵּנוּ:

אִלּוּ עָשָׂה בֵאלֹהֵיהֶם, וְלֹא הָרַג אֶת־בְּכוֹרֵיהֶם,

דַּיֵּנוּ:

אִלּוּ הָרַג אֶת־בְּכוֹרֵיהֶם, וְלֹא נָתַן לָנוּ אֶת־מָמוֹנָם,

דַּיֵּנוּ:

אִלּוּ נָתַן לָנוּ אֶת־מָמוֹנָם, וְלֹא קָרַע לָנוּ אֶת־הַיָּם,

דַּיֵּנוּ:

אִלּוּ קָרַע לָנוּ אֶת־הַיָּם, וְלֹא הֶעֱבִירָנוּ בְתוֹכוֹ בֶּחָרָבָה,

דַּיֵּנוּ:

אִלּוּ הֶעֱבִירָנוּ בְתוֹכוֹ בֶּחָרָבָה, וְלֹא שִׁקַּע צָרֵינוּ בְּתוֹכוֹ,

דַּיֵּנוּ:

אִלּוּ שִׁקַּע צָרֵינוּ בְּתוֹכוֹ,
וְלֹא סִפֵּק צָרְכֵּנוּ בַּמִּדְבָּר אַרְבָּעִים שָׁנָה,

דַּיֵּנוּ:

קדש
ורחץ
כרפס
יחץ
מגיד
רחצה
מוציא
מצה
מרור
כורך
שלחן עורך
צפון
ברך
הלל
נרצה

A 11

Dayeinu* – "It would have been enough, already!"

How many degrees of goodness has the All-Present One bestowed upon us?

If He would have only brought us out of Mitzraim
And not pronounced judgment upon them,
Dayeinu! It would have been enough, already!
If He would have only pronounced judgment upon them
And not brought judgment upon their gods,
Dayeinu! It would have been enough, already!
If He would have only brought judgment upon their gods,
And not slain their first-born,
Dayeinu! It would have been enough, already!
If He would have only slain their first-born,
And not given us their wealth,
Dayeinu! It would have been enough, already!
If He would have only given us their wealth,
And not split the sea,
Dayeinu! It would have been enough, already!
If He would have only split the sea,
And not brought us through it on dry land,
Dayeinu! It would have been enough, already!
If He would have only brought us through it on dry land,
And not drowned our pursuers in it,
Dayeinu! It would have been enough, already!
If He would have only drowned our pursuers in it,
And not supplied us with all our needs in the desert for forty years,
Dayeinu! It would have been enough, already!

Kadesh
Urḥatz
Karpas
Yaḥatz
Maggid
Raḥtzah
Motzi
Matzah
Maror
Korekh
Shulḥan Orekh
Tzafun
Barekh
Hallel
Nirtzah

* For a contemporary version of the Dayeinu by Rabbi Irving Greenberg see: *A Different Night* by Noam Zion and David Dishon (Shalom Hartman Institute, Jerusalem, Israel).

אִלּוּ סִפֵּק צָרְכֵּנוּ בַּמִּדְבָּר אַרְבָּעִים שָׁנָה,
וְלֹא הֶאֱכִילָנוּ אֶת־הַמָּן,

דַּיֵּנוּ:

אִלּוּ הֶאֱכִילָנוּ אֶת־הַמָּן, וְלֹא נָתַן לָנוּ אֶת־הַשַּׁבָּת,

דַּיֵּנוּ:

אִלּוּ נָתַן לָנוּ אֶת־הַשַּׁבָּת, וְלֹא קֵרְבָנוּ לִפְנֵי הַר סִינַי,

דַּיֵּנוּ:

אִלּוּ קֵרְבָנוּ לִפְנֵי הַר סִינַי, וְלֹא נָתַן לָנוּ אֶת־הַתּוֹרָה,

דַּיֵּנוּ:

אִלּוּ נָתַן לָנוּ אֶת־הַתּוֹרָה, וְלֹא הִכְנִיסָנוּ לְאֶרֶץ יִשְׂרָאֵל,

דַּיֵּנוּ:

אִלּוּ הִכְנִיסָנוּ לְאֶרֶץ יִשְׂרָאֵל,
וְלֹא בָנָה לָנוּ אֶת־בֵּית הַבְּחִירָה,

דַּיֵּנוּ:

BEING

The singing of the Dayeinu brings to a close this central part of the Maggid – The Telling – section that started way back with the quotation of the verses from Deuteronomy 26:1–9 that described the going down into Mitzraim, all that happened there and the miraculous deliverance. However the last line of the quotation has not yet been examined: "And He brought us to this Place and gave us this Land, a Land flowing with milk and honey." The concluding stanzas of the Dayeinu will take us there and beyond.

DEEPENING

Dayeinu! Let it suffice! Praise God and be content with the gifts that He has given you. There's always room for more. But right now – Dayeinu! If tomorrow were to be the last day of your life would you be able to praise God for all that you have received up until now? Dayeinu!

Yes 2017 Yes 2018 Here! Y/Y/Y 2019!

קדש
ורחץ
כרפס
יחץ
מגיד
רחצה
מוציא
מצה
מרור
כורך
שלחן עורך
צפון
ברך
הלל
נרצה

If He would have only supplied us with all our needs in the desert for forty years,
And not nourished us with mannah,
Dayeinu! It would have been enough, already!
If He would have only nourished us with mannah,
And not given us the Shabbat,
Dayeinu! It would have been enough, already!
If He would have only given us the Shabbat,
And not brought us near before Mount Sinai,
Dayeinu! It would have been enough, already!
If He would have only brought us near before Mount Sinai,
And not given us the Torah,
Dayeinu! It would have been enough, already!
If He would have only given us the Torah,
And not brought us into the Land of Israel,
Dayeinu! It would have been enough, already!
If He would have only brought us into the Land of Israel,
And not built for us the House of Choseness [the Temple],
Dayeinu! It would have been enough, already!

And yet... And yet... we always want more. More of what? Our soul wants more of the spiritual world; our body wants more of the material world. How can these two desires be reconciled? God does not want to deny us the benefits of living in this world; in fact we are encouraged to pray for our needs. The point is to recognize that everything, everything is from the Source. So Dayeinu can also be read as a question: Dayeinu? No! We want more of You!

There is a great confusion, especially in our times, between our 'needs' and our 'wants'. We are always being persuaded that our wants are really our needs. This is the goal of advertising. It plays into our fear of scarcity, of not having enough, our survivor mentality. It is a very unfriendly way of living on this planet. If only we could remember to make our needs our wants.

עַל אַחַת כַּמָּה וְכַמָּה טוֹבָה כְּפוּלָה וּמְכוּפֶּלֶת לַמָּקוֹם
עָלֵינוּ: שֶׁהוֹצִיאָנוּ מִמִּצְרַיִם, וְעָשָׂה בָּהֶם שְׁפָטִים, וְעָשָׂה
בֵּאלֹהֵיהֶם, וְהָרַג אֶת־בְּכוֹרֵיהֶם, וְנָתַן לָנוּ אֶת־מָמוֹנָם,
וְקָרַע לָנוּ אֶת־הַיָּם, וְהֶעֱבִירָנוּ בְתוֹכוֹ בֶּחָרָבָה, וְשִׁקַּע צָרֵינוּ
בְּתוֹכוֹ, וְסִפֵּק צָרְכֵּנוּ בַּמִּדְבָּר אַרְבָּעִים שָׁנָה, וְהֶאֱכִילָנוּ
אֶת־הַמָּן, וְנָתַן לָנוּ אֶת־הַשַּׁבָּת, וְקֵרְבָנוּ לִפְנֵי הַר סִינַי,
וְנָתַן לָנוּ אֶת־הַתּוֹרָה, וְהִכְנִיסָנוּ לְאֶרֶץ יִשְׂרָאֵל, וּבָנָה לָנוּ
אֶת־בֵּית הַבְּחִירָה, לְכַפֵּר עַל־כָּל־עֲוֹנוֹתֵינוּ:

BEING

The "*House of Choseness*"? What a strange term for the Temple! God opens the door but we have to choose to go in. Then we become chosen. We choose to turn to God and then God will turn to us. But the truth is that we are all chosen already – we just have to act on it.

"*To atone for our misguided ways.*" This is the essence of Judaism: we are human; we know what we should do; we try; we try harder; we somehow don't quite make it; we fall; we recognize our mistakes; we pray for forgiveness; we resolve not to repeat them; we make the necessary changes in our life so as not to fall into the same trap again; we pray for help; we get up and get on with our lives.*

* The central function of the Temple rites was to bring about atonement (at-one-ment or a-tune-ment) for individuals, for communities, for the people and ultimately for the world. This was not done merely by the act of offering up sacrifices of life-giving foods (animals, grain, wine), but by a concerted effort to change (*Teshuvah* – to come around, back onto the true life-path). Atonement and forgiveness are critical for the well-being of the human psyche. As the centrality of Temple worship began to decline, ending with its total destruction, a substitute was sought. The genius of Rabbinic Judaism was that it created a transportable Temple without the blood and fire. The heart became the Holy of Holies, spoken prayers became the sacrifices, every

On each and every one of them how multiple the multitudes of goodness has the All-Present One bestowed upon us:
That he brought us out of Mitzraim;
And pronounced judgment upon them and their gods;
And slew their first-born;
And gave us their wealth;
And split the Sea for us;
And led us through on dry land;
And drowned our pursuers;
And supplied us with all our needs in the desert for forty years;
And nourished us with mannah;
And gave us the Shabbat;
And brought us near before Mount Sinai;
And gave us the Torah;
And brought us into the Land of Israel;
And built for us the House of Choseness
To atone for our misguided ways.

DEEPENING

The story is told* of a Queen who had many children. When they had grown up she called them before her. "My dear children," she announced, "The time has come for you to leave the palace and to find your own paths in life. I pray that you will find adventure, fortune, wisdom and love; that you will learn from your adventures, share your fortunes, listen to your wisdom and be happy in your love." Then, she bade the eldest to approach

individual became a priest, the mealtime table became the altar and the synagogue became the Temple. And we pray that it works!

* From an unpublished collection of short stories by Michael Kagan.

Kadesh
Urḥatz
Karpas
Yaḥatz
Maggid
Raḥtzah
Motzi
Matzah
Maror
Korekh
Shulḥan Orekh
Tzafun
Barekh
Hallel
Nirtzah

פסח מצה ומרור

רַבָּן גַּמְלִיאֵל הָיָה אוֹמֵר: כָּל שֶׁלֹּא אָמַר שְׁלֹשָׁה דְּבָרִים
אֵלוּ בַּפֶּסַח, לֹא יָצָא יְדֵי חוֹבָתוֹ, וְאֵלּוּ הֵן:

פֶּסַח. מַצָּה. וּמָרוֹר:

her. In the privacy of that intimate moment she whispered in his ear, "My beloved son, you are so special to me. In you I can see a reflection of myself. I love you deeply and want only the best for you. Now go and fulfill your life." So saying, she handed him a gift, wrapped up in a way that was perfectly matching his unique character. He graciously accepted the gift. He kissed his mother, the Queen, on her cheek, and, with a tear in his eye and resolution in his heart, he left the palace. "How much she loves me," he thought to himself as he rode away. "Indeed I must be very special to have received such a loving message and such a unique gift." The second child now approached the Queen. In the privacy of that intimate moment she whispered in her ear, "My beloved daughter, you are so special to me.

The roasted bone, the symbolic substitute for the Pascal lamb sacrifice, is pointed to.

פֶּסַח שֶׁהָיוּ אֲבוֹתֵינוּ אוֹכְלִים, בִּזְמַן שֶׁבֵּית הַמִּקְדָּשׁ הָיָה קַיָּם, עַל שׁוּם מָה? עַל שׁוּם שֶׁפָּסַח הַקָּדוֹשׁ בָּרוּךְ הוּא, עַל בָּתֵּי אֲבוֹתֵינוּ בְּמִצְרַיִם, שֶׁנֶּאֱמַר וַאֲמַרְתֶּם זֶבַח פֶּסַח הוּא לַיְיָ, אֲשֶׁר פָּסַח עַל בָּתֵּי בְנֵי יִשְׂרָאֵל בְּמִצְרַיִם, בְּנָגְפּוֹ אֶת־מִצְרַיִם וְאֶת־בָּתֵּינוּ הִצִּיל, וַיִּקֹּד הָעָם וַיִּשְׁתַּחֲווּ:

Pesaḥ, Matzah, Maror

Rabban Gamliel used to say: "Anyone who has not spoken about these three things during Pesaḥ has failed to fulfill his or her requirements, and these are:

***Pesaḥ** – The Sacrifice of the Pascal lamb,*
***Matzah** – The Unleavened Bread, and*
***Maror** – The Bitter Herb.*

In you I can see a reflection of myself. I love you deeply and want only the best for you. Now go and fulfill your life." So saying, she handed her a gift, wrapped up in a way that was perfectly matching her unique character. She graciously accepted the gift. She kissed her mother, the Queen, on her cheek, and, with a tear in her eye and resolution in her heart, she left the palace. "How much she loves me," she thought to herself as she rode away. "Indeed I must be very special to have received such a loving message and such a unique gift." And so it went on from child to child.... (What happened, many years later, when the siblings met up again, you can imagine for yourself.)

Kadesh
Urḥatz
Karpas
Yaḥatz
Maggid
Raḥtzah
Motzi
Matzah
Maror
Korekh
Shulḥan Orekh
Tzafun
Barekh
Hallel
Nirtzah

The roasted bone, the symbolic substitute for the Pascal lamb sacrifice, is pointed to.

For what reason did our ancestors eat the Pascal lamb sacrifice at the time when the Holy Temple was a reality? For the reason that the Holy One, Blessed be He, passed over our ancestors' houses in Mitzraim, as it says: "And you shall tell [your descendents] that it is the Passing-over sacrifice to the Lord, who passed over the houses of the Children of Israel in Mitzraim when he afflicted Mitzraim, but our houses were spared. And when the people [heard this, they] bowed and prostrated themselves in worship"

(Exodus 12:27).

The matzah is held up for all to see.

מַצָּה זוֹ שֶׁאָנוּ אוֹכְלִים, עַל שׁוּם מָה? עַל שׁוּם שֶׁלֹּא הִסְפִּיק בְּצֵקָם שֶׁל אֲבוֹתֵינוּ לְהַחֲמִיץ, עַד שֶׁנִּגְלָה עֲלֵיהֶם מֶלֶךְ מַלְכֵי הַמְּלָכִים, הַקָּדוֹשׁ בָּרוּךְ הוּא, וּגְאָלָם, שֶׁנֶּאֱמַר וַיֹּאפוּ אֶת־הַבָּצֵק אֲשֶׁר הוֹצִיאוּ מִמִּצְרַיִם, עֻגֹת מַצּוֹת, כִּי לֹא חָמֵץ: כִּי גֹרְשׁוּ מִמִּצְרַיִם, וְלֹא יָכְלוּ לְהִתְמַהְמֵהַּ, וְגַם צֵדָה לֹא עָשׂוּ לָהֶם.

BEING

Ḥametz: what is it? It is leavened bread produced by the fermentation of wet flour by yeast enzymes. This reaction releases carbon dioxide gas that causes the dough to swell. Nomadic tribes, like the Bedouins, when not traveling, leave the dough buried in the ground until it has fully fermented. If yeast is not added then the process can take up to three days to complete. In the oven the process is temporarily speeded up until all the enzymes are destroyed and the dough is baked. This is bread – soft, delicious bread. It consists of over 60% empty space produced by a gas that does not sustain human life. Its great volume is an illusion of its true essence. Ḥametz is symbolic of our inflated, swollen egos – mostly hot air.

Matzah: what is it? It is unleavened bread produced by mixing flour and water, but fermentation is prevented by the immediate baking of the dough. It's quick food, easy to prepare. The Bedouins prepare large amounts before traveling because it folds easily, takes up very little room and lasts for a long time. Matzah is what it appears to be – its essence. It is uninflated. It may not be as soft and as tasty as ḥametz but it doesn't need those facades to be what it is. It represents being. It represents being just you, just who you are, with your ego, but an uninflated ego. For after all, the ego is not bad, as it is a necessary part of the interface between the physical world and the spiritual world.

In Israel, the moment the seventh day of Pesaḥ ends, queues begin to gather outside the bakeries. Bread! We must have bread! Can you imagine if the day after Pesaḥ no bread would be available at the supermarket, only matzah! There would be bread riots. I've even witnessed fistfights over the first loaves. If this

The matzah is held up for all to see.

For what reason do we eat this matzah? For the reason that there wasn't enough time for the dough of our ancestors to leaven before the King of kings, Blessed be He, revealed himself to them and delivered them, as it says: "They baked from the dough that they had brought with them out of Mitzraim, unleavened cakes since the dough had not leavened, because they were driven out of Mitzraim and they couldn't delay, nor could they prepare provisions for themselves"

(Exodus 12:39).

is true after only seven days of a strict matzah diet, what was it like after 210 years?

DEEPENING

What is the reason that we eat matzah during Pesaḥ? The immediate answer that is usually given is because the dough did not have time to rise.* However we read that two weeks before the Exodus God tells Moses to prepare the people for a special meal that will take place on the night of the fourteenth of the month: "*And they shall eat the flesh in that night, roasted with fire, and matzot with bitter herbs shall they eat.*" (Exodus 12: 8). Furthermore, "*And this day shall be for you a memorial; and you shall celebrate it as a festival to God throughout your generations; an ordinance forever you will celebrate it. Seven days shall you eat unleavened bread*

Kadesh
Urḥatz
Karpas
Yaḥatz
Maggid
Raḥtzah
Motzi
Matzah
Maror
Korekh
Shulḥan Orekh
Tzafun
Barekh
Hallel
Nirtzah

* "And Mitzraim was urgent upon the people, hastening to send them out of the land; for they said we are dead men. And the people took their dough before it leavened; their kneading troughs being bound up in their outer garments upon their shoulder" (Exodus 12:33–34). And again, "And the children of Israel journeyed from Rameses to Succot.... And they baked unleavened cakes of the dough which they brought forth out of Mitzraim, for it was not leavened; because they were driven out of Mitzraim and could not tarry, neither had they made for themselves any provisions" (Exodus 12: 37–39).

The maror is pointed at or held up for all to see.

מָרוֹר זֶה שֶׁאָנוּ אוֹכְלִים, עַל שׁוּם מַה? עַל שׁוּם שֶׁמֵּרְרוּ הַמִּצְרִים אֶת־חַיֵּי אֲבוֹתֵינוּ בְּמִצְרַיִם, שֶׁנֶּאֱמַר וַיְמָרְרוּ אֶת־חַיֵּיהֶם בַּעֲבֹדָה קָשָׁה, בְּחֹמֶר וּבִלְבֵנִים, וּבְכָל־עֲבֹדָה בַּשָּׂדֶה: אֵת כָּל עֲבֹדָתָם, אֲשֶׁר עָבְדוּ בָהֶם בְּפָרֶךְ.

[matzot]; even from the first day you shall have put away leaven out of your houses..." (Exodus 12:14–15). In other words the instruction to eat matzah and the institutionalization of the matzah festival was proclaimed before the people had even left Mitzraim! It had nothing to do with what came after, whether the dough had time to rise or not. Was that just a coincidence then? The Haggadah gives two explanations for matzah, one at the beginning of the Seder and the other here, just before the Hallel. In the former it says: "*This is the bread of poverty that was eaten by our ancestors in Mitzraim.*" In the latter it states: "*Because the dough of our ancestors did not have time to leaven by the time they were redeemed by the King of kings, the Holy One blessed be He.*" So how can these two views be reconciled? Herein lies the secret of matzah. God instructs Moses to tell the people to prepare themselves for a festive meal of liberation on the night of the fourteenth. So what would have been more suitable to represent true freedom than to eat the liberation meal with proper leavened bread? But God's instructions are clear: the lamb is to be eaten with **unleavened** bread and bitter herbs. Why? Because this meal is to be a *memorial* to the years of slavery, the bitterness of exile, the loss of self-respect, the loss of freedom, the loss of choice and the loss of time. Then the moment of liberation arrives and the Children of Israel leave Mitzraim. And what are they carrying on their shoulders? Their kneading troughs. And what is in the kneading troughs? Unbaked dough. Matzah is the bread of slaves whose egos are forced into constriction, but the desire for bread remains. Which means that even during those frantic moments of packing and loading the donkeys they were still intent on trying to make leavened bread as a symbol of being free! They even went so far as to carry it on their shoulders. Wasn't there anything else more important to carry – maybe their own children? But when they had their first meal stopover, they reached up to remove the fermented dough and,

The maror is pointed at or held up for all to see.

For what reason do we eat this maror? For the reason that the Mitzrim embittered the lives of our ancestors in Mitzraim, as it says: "They embittered their lives with the hard labor of mortar and bricks, and all the toil of the fields; they were worked upon ruthlessly"

(Exodus 1:14).

behold, it hadn't even started swelling!* What they were left with was the same plain, old matzah. How disappointing! And this is one of the uncounted miracles of that period, for leavened bread is just an illusion of freedom. It is the ego wishing to expand and fulfill its desires. It does not and cannot symbolize the true freedom for which God brought us out of Mitzraim. So matzah is both the bread of slavery and poverty, and of the ultimate freedom available to us as servants of God.

BEING

It is said that more than half of the Hebrews living in Mitzraim decided to stay. They had presumably sunk so deep that they could no longer distinguish between slavery and freedom, between illusion and reality.**

The word "ruthless" in English means lacking in compassion. "Ruthful" therefore means full of compassion. Ruth, from the Book of Ruth, was the compassionate one. Shavuot follows Pesaḥ. It is the festival of compassion. It is a milk festival, it is a Mother Earth festival (the wheat harvest), it is a return to Eden festival (the synagogues are filled with greenery), it is a celebration of God's compassion, for He brought us out of Mitzraim, out of the House of Bitterness, and rendezvoused with us in the middle of the desert and betrothed us through the Torah.

---

* During the process of rising the dough needs to be kept at rest otherwise it collapses.

** A vivid and poignant picture of such enslavement mentality is portrayed

בְּכָל־דּוֹר וָדוֹר חַיָּב אָדָם לִרְאוֹת אֶת־
עַצְמוֹ כְּאִלּוּ הוּא יָצָא מִמִּצְרָיִם, שֶׁנֶּאֱמַר
וְהִגַּדְתָּ לְבִנְךָ בַּיּוֹם הַהוּא לֵאמֹר: בַּעֲבוּר זֶה
עָשָׂה יְיָ לִי בְּצֵאתִי מִמִּצְרָיִם. לֹא אֶת־
אֲבוֹתֵינוּ בִּלְבָד גָּאַל הַקָּדוֹשׁ בָּרוּךְ הוּא,
אֶלָּא אַף אוֹתָנוּ גָּאַל עִמָּהֶם, שֶׁנֶּאֱמַר
וְאוֹתָנוּ הוֹצִיא מִשָּׁם, לְמַעַן הָבִיא אוֹתָנוּ
לָתֶת לָנוּ אֶת־הָאָרֶץ אֲשֶׁר נִשְׁבַּע
לַאֲבֹתֵינוּ:

DEEPENING

The Haggadah stipulates that I am to experience the Exodus from Mitzraim as if I myself were in slavery in Mitzraim, as if I myself were redeemed from Mitzraim. How can I experience something that never occurred to me directly? I can't experience someone else's experience – I've never been to Mitzraim; I never went through the Holocaust. While

---

in the film *The Shawshank Redemption* (1994) starring Tim Robbins. "He's just institutionalized.... The man's been in here fifty years, Heywood, fifty years. This is all he knows. In here, he's an important man; he's an educated man. Outside he's nothin' – just a used-up con with arthritis in both hands. Probably couldn't get a library card if he tried...these walls are funny. First you hate 'em, then you get used to 'em. Enough time passes, it gets so you depend on 'em. That's 'institutionalized'.... They send you here for life and that's exactly what they take, the part that counts anyway."

In each and every generation each person is required to see himself as if he had come out of Mitzraim. As it says: "And on that day you will retell to your children, saying: 'We are doing this because of what God did for me when I came out of Mitzraim.'" The Holy One, blessed be He, did not only redeem our ancestors but He also redeemed us with them, as it says: "And he brought* ***us*** *forth from there in order to bring* ***us*** *to the point where He could give* ***us*** *the land that He promised our ancestors"* (Deuteronomy 6:23).

Kadesh
Urhatz
Karpas
Yahatz
Maggid
Rahtzah
Motzi
Matzah
Maror
Korekh
Shulhan Orekh
Tzafun
Barekh
Hallel
Nirtzah

I can hear my father's stories, I cannot experience his pain, his fear, his horror, his helplessness, his loss, his courage, his relief. What I can do is celebrate the fact that he survived. I can appreciate and celebrate the fact that God delivered *them* because if not for that I would not be here today. But what about *me*? While not negating the historical dimension, in order to develop my own relationship with God I must look at my own life's experiences; physically, emotionally and psychologically, using the historical events as archetypes for my own struggles with Mitzraim and my desire to be truly free.

* Exodus 13:8

הלל

As the Maggid – the Telling and Retelling – comes to a culmination we open our hearts and prepare to sing praises to God for giving us, at every moment, the opportunity to become truly free and to receive the gift of the Promised Land. The glasses are topped up, the matzot are covered and everybody raises the second glass in a toast to the Almighty Compassionate One!

לְפִיכָךְ אֲנַחְנוּ חַיָּבִים לְהוֹדוֹת, לְהַלֵּל,
לְשַׁבֵּחַ, לְפָאֵר, לְרוֹמֵם, לְהַדֵּר, לְבָרֵךְ,
לְעַלֵּה וּלְקַלֵּס, לְמִי שֶׁעָשָׂה לַאֲבוֹתֵינוּ וְלָנוּ
אֶת־כָּל־הַנִּסִּים הָאֵלּוּ. הוֹצִיאָנוּ מֵעַבְדוּת
לְחֵרוּת, מִיָּגוֹן לְשִׂמְחָה, וּמֵאֵבֶל לְיוֹם טוֹב,
וּמֵאֲפֵלָה לְאוֹר גָּדוֹל, וּמִשִּׁעְבּוּד לִגְאֻלָּה.
וְנֹאמַר לְפָנָיו שִׁירָה חֲדָשָׁה. הַלְלוּיָהּ:

DEEPENING

Not an old song, not a song from yesterday, for today you are different from before. Notice that you are now different, that new opportunities have opened up, that new potential has arisen, that the mist has cleared by just that much. Now sing your new song.

He's a Waymaker
Total Praise
God of All gods

I Stand
I Stand
I'm in Awe of You

קדש
ורחץ
כרפס
יחץ
מגיד
רחצה
מוציא
מצה
מרור
כורך
שלחן עורך
צפון
ברך
הלל
נרצה

First Part of the Hallel

As the Maggid – the Telling and Retelling – comes to a culmination we open our hearts and prepare to sing praises to God for giving us, at every moment, the opportunity to become truly free and to receive the gift of the Promised Land. The glasses are topped up, the matzot are covered and everybody raises the second glass in a toast to the Almighty Compassionate One!

Consequently, we are surely moved to thank, to praise, to acclaim, to extol, to glorify, to bless, to exalt and to revere the ONE who performed all these miracles on behalf of our ancestors and of ourselves:

He delivered us
from slavery to freedom,
from sorrow to joy,
from grief to festivity,
*from blinding darkness to great light,**
from enslavement to redemption.

And therefore let us sing before Him a New Song:
Praise to YAH – HalleluYAH!

* Alternatively, "from illusion to enlightenment."

The cup is lowered and the matzot are uncovered. The first part of the Hallel – Praise – is recited before the meal. The two psalms recited focus on the theme of slavery to freedom. The rest of the Hallel continues after the meal and focuses on ultimate redemption.

הַלְלוּיָהּ. הַלְלוּ עַבְדֵי יְיָ. הַלְלוּ אֶת־שֵׁם
יְיָ: יְהִי שֵׁם יְיָ מְבֹרָךְ מֵעַתָּה וְעַד עוֹלָם:
מִמִּזְרַח שֶׁמֶשׁ עַד מְבוֹאוֹ. מְהֻלָּל שֵׁם יְיָ:
רָם עַל־כָּל־גּוֹיִם יְיָ. עַל הַשָּׁמַיִם כְּבוֹדוֹ:
מִי כַּייָ אֱלֹהֵינוּ. הַמַּגְבִּיהִי לָשָׁבֶת:
הַמַּשְׁפִּילִי לִרְאוֹת בַּשָּׁמַיִם וּבָאָרֶץ:
מְקִימִי מֵעָפָר דָּל. מֵאַשְׁפֹּת יָרִים אֶבְיוֹן:
לְהוֹשִׁיבִי עִם־נְדִיבִים. עִם נְדִיבֵי עַמּוֹ:
מוֹשִׁיבִי עֲקֶרֶת הַבַּיִת אֵם הַבָּנִים
שְׂמֵחָה. הַלְלוּיָהּ:

The cup is lowered and the matzot are uncovered. The first part of the Hallel – Praise – is recited before the meal. The two psalms recited focus on the theme of slavery to freedom. The rest of the Hallel continues after the meal and focuses on ultimate redemption.

Singing
*Celebrate YAH!**
You who serve YAH! Celebrate Him.
From the dawn's sun's rising –
Onto his homecoming, past the dusk
YAH's repute is constantly celebrated.
YAH transcends
all ethnic national divisions.
Her honored glory is sublime.
Can you peak so high as to
Sit with YAH, our God?
And at the same time
Encompass and scan both
Heaven and Earth?
Getting the poor to stand firm,
Raising from groveling in the dust,
Having dignity in the eyes
Of generous people –
Yes, the people
of one's own population.
Restore Earth our Mother
As the center of Her household
So as to delight in all her children.

(Psalms 113)

* In his translations Reb Zalman prefers to use *YAH* rather than Lord or *HaShem* (The Name). I concur with his opinion that lordship is an unfamiliar concept in our times whereas *YAH*, as in *HalleluYAH* – Praise God – should always be on the tip of our tongues. Furthermore, YAH is the name associated with the Godly attribute of Ḥokhmah, which is the level of greatest expansion and is thus fitting for the Pesah theme of "*from the narrow straits I cried to YAH, from the great expansion YAH answered.*" (Psalm 118). To support this the Talmud states (Eruvin 18b) that: Since the Sanctuary was destroyed it is enough for the world to use only two letters [of the Tetragrammaton].

בְּצֵאת יִשְׂרָאֵל מִמִּצְרָיִם, בֵּית יַעֲקֹב מֵעַם לֹעֵז: הָיְתָה
יְהוּדָה לְקָדְשׁוֹ. יִשְׂרָאֵל מַמְשְׁלוֹתָיו: הַיָּם רָאָה וַיָּנֹס, הַיַּרְדֵּן
יִסֹּב לְאָחוֹר: הֶהָרִים רָקְדוּ כְאֵילִים. גְּבָעוֹת כִּבְנֵי צֹאן: מַה
לְּךָ הַיָּם כִּי תָנוּס. הַיַּרְדֵּן תִּסֹּב לְאָחוֹר: הֶהָרִים תִּרְקְדוּ
כְאֵילִים. גְּבָעוֹת כִּבְנֵי־צֹאן: מִלִּפְנֵי אָדוֹן חוּלִי אָרֶץ. מִלִּפְנֵי
אֱלוֹהַּ יַעֲקֹב: הַהֹפְכִי הַצּוּר אֲגַם־מָיִם. חַלָּמִישׁ לְמַעְיְנוֹ־
מָיִם:

BEING

Praising God is the secret to bringing down the Holy Spirit (*Ruaḥ HaKodesh*).* Everyday, psalms of praise are said before entering the inner sphere of intimate prayer. Praise is compared to a spiritual sword** – it is a powerful tool for the spiritual warrior. Praise is like a spiritual elevator to the Higher Realms.

It is a recommended spiritual practice to praise God. Use your own words. Praising is different from thanking – it is more like complimenting. Praise God for everything.***

DEEPENING

The Haggadah is not just about the Telling of the story; it is not just about connecting with emotions associated with the inner Mitzraim; it is not just about understanding the journey; it is about entering the Divine Presence; it is about unification with the One; it is about bringing Heavenly Jerusalem down and raising up the Earthly Jerusalem so that the two become united. This is the direction that the Haggadah is going to take us in the remaining steps: from praise, into experience, into blessings, into appreciation, into higher praise, into worship, into joy.

---

* This Hallel is dedicated to my holy teacher Matananda Ben Shmuel. She revealed to me the portals of prayer and the paths to God.

** Psalm 147

*** For inspiration see the in Psalm 148, which is also part of the morning service.

Those who strive with God
Find release from their Mitzraim,
From their constricting oppression,
Yes, Jacob's house
From such as malign them.
Thus Jews held Him sacred,
Thus Israel followed His directions.
Why do your oceans recede?
Why do you, Jordan river,
reverse your flow?
Mountains! Why do you frolic
like bucks?
Hills! Why do you skip
like frisky lambs?
For such a people as you,
Oceans recede and make space,
Rivers reverse their flow,
Mountains frolic like bucks,
Hills – like frisky lambs.
Before the Master
Earth becomes receptive.
Yes! Before the God of Jacob,
Who can turn boulders
into wetlands,
Flint into flowing springs.

(Psalms 114)

B-9

Kadesh
Urḥatz
Karpas
Yaḥatz
Maggid
Raḥtzah
Motzi
Matzah
Maror
Korekh
Shulḥan Orekh
Tzafun
Barekh
Hallel
Nirtzah

כוס מרים

The mention of "flowing springs" in the previous psalm is a reference to Miriam's Well, which miraculously provided water for the people of Israel during the entire 40 years of journeying in the desert. In recognition of this understated female contribution to the survival of the Children of Israel, a large (ornamental) cup is filled with (pure) water and placed on the table.

זוֹ כּוֹס מִרְיָם הַנְּבִיאָה. יְהִי רָצוֹן שֶׁנִּזְכֶּה לִשְׁתּוֹת מִמֵּימֵי בְּאֵר
מִרְיָם לִרְפוּאָה וְלִגְאוּלָה. יְהִי רָצוֹן שֶׁנִּלְמַד מִמִּרְיָם וּמִכָּל
הַנָּשִׁים לָצֵאת בְּתֻפִּים וּבִמְחוֹלוֹת אֶל מוּל הַנִּסִּים שֶׁל חַיֵּי
הַיּוֹם יוֹם וְלָשִׁיר לַיְיָ בְּכָל רֶגַע.

This is the Cup of Miriam.
May it be Your will that we continue to drink from the waters of Miriam's Well for healing and for redemption. May we learn from Miriam and all the women that went after her how to step out with timbrels and to dance in celebration for the everyday miracles of life and to sing to the Lord at each moment.

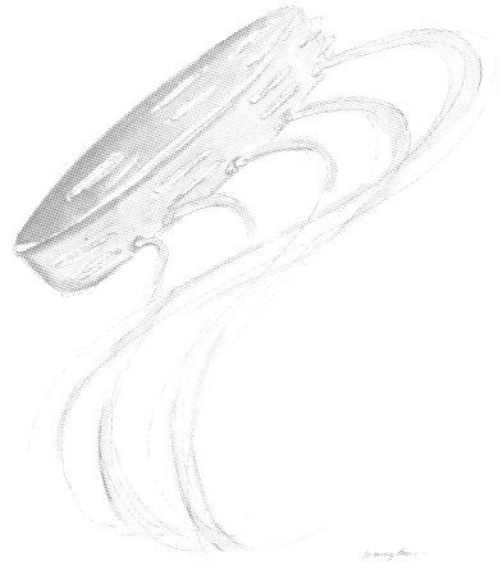

* The ritual of including a cup of water for Miriam to complement the Cup of Elijah is a late 20th Century addition (see www.miriamscup.com). It follows the tradition that has brought us the Haggadah as we presently know it, namely the continual addition of passages down the ages as different communities incorporate their own piece of the Grand Story. This rendition is by Ruth Gan Kagan.

Miriam's Cup

BEING

A midrash teaches us that a miraculous well accompanied the Hebrews throughout their journey in the desert, providing them with water. This well first appears in the story of Hagar (Genesis 21:19) where we find Hagar stranded out in the desert with her son, Ishmael, with no water left to drink. She lifts up her voice and cries. In response (actually, to the cries of her son) her eyes are opened, revealing a well.* The same well was given by God to Miriam, the prophetess, to honor her bravery and devotion to the Children of Israel. Both Miriam and her well were spiritual oases in the desert, sources of sustenance and healing. Her words of comfort gave the Hebrews the faith and confidence to overcome the hardships of the Exodus. We fill Miriam's Cup with water to honor her role in ensuring the survival of the Jewish people. Like Miriam, Jewish women in all generations have been essential for the continuity of our people. As keepers of traditions in the home, women passed down songs and stories, rituals and recipes, from mother to daughter, from generation to generation.**

DEEPENING

In the wake of the crossing of the Reed Sea, the drowning of the Mitzrim cavalry, and the safe deliverance of the Hebrews, a spontaneous song erupts from the mouths of the joyous people. It is led by Moses and answered by the people. The Song of the Sea is introduced by the words: "*I will sing to YHVH...*" (Exodus 15:1). The verb is in the future tense. After the song has been completed the text continues: "*And Miriam the Prophetess, the sister of Aaron, took up the tumbrel in her hand and all the women went out after her with timbrels and with dances. And Miriam sang to them: 'We sing to YHVH...'*" (Exodus 15:21). Present tense! "Now we sing!" Now and not tomorrow. For now is the time to sing to God for now our redemption is upon us. This is the gift and strength of Miriam and the rest of the women.***

---

* Water and woman appear again in the story of Eliezer and Rivka, where the former prays for a sign and the latter pours the water (Genesis 24).

** Adapted from the website: www.miriamscup.com.

*** This beautiful teaching is from Ruth Gan Kagan.

The Maggid section ends with the drinking of the Second Cup of wine. Cover the matzot and, after reciting the blessing over the wine, drink at least half of the cup while reclining.

הִנְנִי מוּכָן וּמְזֻמָּן לְקַיֵּם מִצְוַת כּוֹס שֵׁנִי מֵאַרְבַּע כּוֹסוֹת. לְשֵׁם יִחוּד קוּדְשָׁא בְּרִיךְ הוּא וּשְׁכִינְתֵּיהּ עַל יְדֵי הַהוּא טָמִיר וְנֶעְלָם בְּשֵׁם כָּל יִשְׂרָאֵל:

בָּרוּךְ אַתָּה יְיָ, אֱלֹהֵינוּ מֶלֶךְ הָעוֹלָם, אֲשֶׁר גְּאָלָנוּ וְגָאַל אֶת־אֲבוֹתֵינוּ מִמִּצְרַיִם, וְהִגִּיעָנוּ הַלַּיְלָה הַזֶּה, לֶאֱכָל־בּוֹ מַצָּה וּמָרוֹר. כֵּן, יְיָ אֱלֹהֵינוּ וֵאלֹהֵי אֲבוֹתֵינוּ, יַגִּיעֵנוּ לְמוֹעֲדִים וְלִרְגָלִים אֲחֵרִים, הַבָּאִים לִקְרָאתֵנוּ לְשָׁלוֹם. שְׂמֵחִים בְּבִנְיַן עִירֶךָ, וְשָׂשִׂים בַּעֲבוֹדָתֶךָ, וְנֹאכַל שָׁם מִן הַזְּבָחִים וּמִן הַפְּסָחִים (במוצש״ק אומרים: מִן הַפְּסָחִים וּמִן הַזְּבָחִים), אֲשֶׁר יַגִּיעַ דָּמָם, עַל קִיר מִזְבַּחֲךָ לְרָצוֹן, וְנוֹדֶה לְךָ שִׁיר חָדָשׁ עַל גְּאֻלָּתֵנוּ, וְעַל פְּדוּת נַפְשֵׁנוּ: בָּרוּךְ אַתָּה יְיָ, גָּאַל יִשְׂרָאֵל:

בָּרוּךְ אַתָּה יְיָ, אֱלֹהֵינוּ מֶלֶךְ הָעוֹלָם, בּוֹרֵא פְּרִי הַגָּפֶן:

The *Shekhinah* (the Female Presence of the Divine) is returning. She has been in Exile for so long and now she is returning. Her energy is flowing down and the women are rising up to meet it.* It is the time for men to make way, acknowledge the end of the need to dominate, be acknowledged for having brought us this far and repent for our misogyny. It is time for both men and women to wrap themselves in the *tallit* of the *Shekhinah* so that each individual can be rebalanced, so that each person can heal and be healed.

קדש
ורחץ
כרפס
יחץ
מגיד
רחצה
מוציא
מצה
מרור
כורך
שלחן עורך
צפון
ברך
הלל
נרצה

* This is dedicated to some of the women who taught me so much and brought me so far: Barbara Steinfeld Kagan, Zohar Trifon, Ruth Gan Kagan, Matananda Ben Shmuel and Dori Veness. May their names, deeds and fore-bearing serve as a banner for us all.

TS-10

The Second Cup

The Maggid section ends with the drinking of the Second Cup of wine. Cover the matzot and, after reciting the blessing over the wine, drink at least half of the cup while reclining.

Here I am right now, ready and mindful to participate in the unification of the Transcendent Holy One with the Immanent Shekhinah through the **second** *of the Four Cups.*

Blessed are You, Lord our God, Majesty of the Universe, who redeems us and redeemed our ancestors from Mitzraim, and [by doing so] has brought us to this here night to eat matzah and maror. Yes! Lord, our God and God of our ancestors, may You bring us to future occasions and other festivals in peace, joyous in Your rebuilt city, glad in Your service, and there we will eat of the sacrifices and, particularly, of the Pesaḥ lamb, whose blood will be sprinkled on the walls of Your Altar to be gracefully received; and we thank You with a New Song for our deliverance and for the redemption of our souls. Blessed are You, God, who has delivered Israel.

wow

Blessed are You, Lord our God, Majesty of the Universe, who brings into being the fruit of the vine.

DEEPENING

The Second Cup represents the letter ה (*hey*), the second letter of the Divine Name.* This is in the World of *Beriah* – the World of Intellect, the World of Creation. Through our intellectual processing of the Maggid section of the Haggadah we have opened up the channel for the Divine Energy to flow down as we rise up to meet it.

Stone 2015

Kadesh
Urḥatz
Karpas
Yaḥatz
Maggid
Raḥtzah
Motzi
Matzah
Maror
Korekh
Shulḥan Orekh
Tzafun
Barekh
Hallel
Nirtzah

* See: Introduction User's Manual.

רחצה

The food is almost upon us! Or, by this time, we are almost upon the food! When eating the matzah, followed by eating the bitter herbs (maror) dipped in the sweet ḥaroset, followed by the combination of matzah and maror (Korekh – Hillel's sandwich), do so as a silent meditation. Give yourself time to imbibe the intensity of the matzah and the pungency of the maror. Let your consciousness float. To do this it is important to carefully read the instructions and have what you will need handy so as not to disturb others or yourself.

First there is the ritual washing of the hands. Unlike the previous washing at the beginning of the proceedings this one is said with a blessing. If you have your own set of matzot then it is suggested that you proceed independently at your own pace rather than wait.

Have available enough matzah for the eating of the Matzah and later for the eating of Korekh – the combination of matzah and maror.

Have available the maror and the ḥaroset. The maror is usually of two forms: either freshly grated horseradish (ḥ*azeret*) or a leaf of lettuce that's gone slightly bitter.* A combination is suggested.

It is advisable to read the commentaries below before proceeding.

בָּרוּךְ אַתָּה יְיָ, אֱלֹהֵינוּ מֶלֶךְ הָעוֹלָם, אֲשֶׁר קִדְּשָׁנוּ בְּמִצְוֹתָיו, וְצִוָּנוּ עַל נְטִילַת יָדָיִם:

* The idea behind the use of lettuce for the maror is that what begins growing as something delicious and highly edible turns almost overnight into something inedibly bitter. Thus lettuce becomes an edible metaphor for our stay in Mitzraim: at first we were welcomed and felt at home; later we were scorned and enslaved.

Raḥtza – Second washing of the hands

The food is almost upon us! Or, by this time, we are almost upon the food! When eating the matzah, followed by eating the bitter herbs (maror) dipped in the sweet ḥaroset, followed by the combination of matzah and maror (Korekh – Hillel's sandwich), do so as a silent meditation. Give yourself time to imbibe the intensity of the matzah and the pungency of the maror. Let your consciousness float. To do this it is important to carefully read the instructions and have what you will need handy so as not to disturb others or yourself.

First there is the ritual washing of the hands. Unlike the previous washing at the beginning of the proceedings this one is said with a blessing. If you have your own set of matzot then it is suggested that you proceed independently at your own pace rather than wait.

Have available enough matzah for the eating of the Matzah and later for the eating of Korekh – the combination of matzah and maror.

Have available the maror and the ḥaroset. The maror is usually of two forms: either freshly grated horseradish (*ḥazeret*) or a leaf of lettuce that's gone slightly bitter. A combination is suggested.

It is advisable to read the commentaries below before proceeding.

Blessed are you, Lord our God, Majesty of the Universe, who sanctified us through unification and commanded us to wash [lit.: take] the hands.

Kadesh
Urḥatz
Karpas
Yaḥatz
Maggid
Raḥtzah
Motzi
Matzah
Maror
Korekh
Shulḥan Orekh
Tzafun
Barekh
Hallel
Nirtzah

BEING

The blessing over washing the hands actually reads "*al netilat yadayim.*" The word "*netilah*" is also used in the blessing for shaking the palm branch (*lulav*) on Succot – but what does it mean? In the case of the *lulav* it means the lifting up of the four species together as one. For the washing of the hands it refers to the lifting of a vessel to fill with water to pour over the hands.

DEEPENING

Netilah also means to "cut off." So within this context it suggests the dedication of the hands to Holiness – to detach the hands from the selfish mind and hand them back to their Master.*

* This teaching was brought down by Ayelet Kagan, aged 8 (2002).

מוציא

Remove all two and a half matzot from their coverings. Hold them up and say the two blessings below. Eat about two-thirds of the top matzah in silence, while reclining. Let the images of the evening, of slavery and freedom work through you by the act of imbibing this morphic energy.* It is an eating meditation.

הִנְנִי מוּכָן וּמְזֻמָּן לְקַיֵּם מִצְוַת אֲכִילַת מַצָּה לְשֵׁם יִחוּד קוּדְשָׁא בְּרִיךְ הוּא וּשְׁכִינְתֵּיהּ עַל יְדֵי הַהוּא טָמִיר וְנֶעְלָם בְּשֵׁם כָּל יִשְׂרָאֵל:

בָּרוּךְ אַתָּה יְיָ, אֱלֹהֵינוּ מֶלֶךְ הָעוֹלָם,
הַמּוֹצִיא לֶחֶם מִן הָאָרֶץ:

BEING

The Hebrew word for bread is *LeḤeM*. It shares the same root as the Hebrew word for war - *miLḤaMa*. Therefore the blessing can also be read: "remove war from off the face of the earth."** Furthermore, the word dream – *ḤoLeM* – consists of the same three root letters. So now the blessing can be read as: *"...who removes war from off the face of the earth and allows us to live our deepest dreams."*

מצה

בָּרוּךְ אַתָּה יְיָ, אֱלֹהֵינוּ מֶלֶךְ הָעוֹלָם, אֲשֶׁר קִדְּשָׁנוּ בְּמִצְוֹתָיו
וְצִוָּנוּ עַל אֲכִילַת מַצָּה:

* Rubert Sheldrake in *The Presence of the Past: Morphic Resonance and the Habits of Nature* (Inner Traditions Intl., 1995). Our participating in an ancient ritual allows us to tune in to the morphic field of that original event, causing us to resonate with the past, the present and the future.

** From the wisdom of Ruth Gan Kagan.

קדש
ורחץ
כרפס
יחץ
מגיד
רחצה
מוציא
מצה
מרור
כורך
שלחן עורך
צפון
ברך
הלל
נרצה

A15

Motzi – First blessing over matzah

Remove all two and a half matzot from their coverings. Hold them up and say the two blessings below. Eat about two-thirds of the top matzah in silence, while reclining. Let the images of the evening, of slavery and freedom work through you by the act of imbibing this morphic energy.[9] It is an eating meditation.

Here I am right now, ready and mindful to participate in the unification of the Transcendent Holy One with the Immanent Shekhinah through eating of matzah.

Blessed are You, Lord our God, Majesty of the Universe, who extracts bread from out of the earth.

A16

Matzah – Second blessing over matzah

Blessed are you, Lord our God, Majesty of the Universe, who sanctified us through unification and commanded us to eat matzah.

BEING

What is the difference between matzah and ḥametz? It is the difference between a little bit less than 18 minutes and a little bit more than 18 minutes. Look at the Hebrew: “matzah” is comprised of the letters מ (*mem*), צ (*tzaddik*) and ה (*heh*). “Ḥametz” consists of the letters ח (*ḥet*), מ (*mem*) and צ (*tzaddik*). The difference between these two words is a ה (*heh*) and a ח (*ḥet*). And what’s the difference between theses two letters? The ה (*heh*) is the same as the ח (*ḥet*) except that it has a small opening on its top left. That’s it – just a small gap, no bigger than the eye of a needle. That’s the difference between reality and illusion, between ignorance and enlightenment, between darkness and light, between arrogance and humility, between broken and fixed.

use Alef Bet wheel!

מרור

Take the lettuce leaf, dip it into the haroset and then shake off any excess mixture. Eat without reclining.

הִנְנִי מוּכָן וּמְזֻמָּן לְקַיֵּם מִצְוַת אֲכִילַת מָרוֹר לְשֵׁם יִחוּד קוּדְשָׁא בְּרִיךְ הוּא וּשְׁכִינְתֵּיהּ עַל יְדֵי הַהוּא טָמִיר וְנֶעְלָם בְּשֵׁם כָּל יִשְׂרָאֵל:

בָּרוּךְ אַתָּה יְיָ, אֱלֹהֵינוּ מֶלֶךְ הָעוֹלָם, אֲשֶׁר קִדְּשָׁנוּ בְּמִצְוֹתָיו וְצִוָּנוּ עַל אֲכִילַת מָרוֹר:

DEEPENING

Ḥaroset: where does this come from? Where in the Torah is it mentioned? We have Pesaḥ, maror and matzah but no ḥaroset. It's not mentioned in the Mishnah. It's introduced only in the Gemorah where, amongst other things, one of its powers is to be able to exorcise some strange bug from the head (*Pesaḥim* 127b). Most Haggadot attribute ḥaroset to be a symbol of the clay used to bind the bricks in Mitzraim. Let's go deeper. What are the traditional ingredients of this mixture? Apples, dates, red wine, cinnamon and almonds crushed together to make a paste. It tastes wonderful and is usually eaten by the spoonful. However the instructions in the Haggadah are to dip the maror into the ḥaroset and then shake it off! Meaning, not to eat it! There's no special blessing on the ḥaroset. In fact, it's not meant to be eaten at all. Come and listen. There is a mystical fable that says that King Solomon wrote a book* of all the cures to all the ailments that afflict humankind. It went further than the modern day popular book by Louise Hay** in that it not only attributed the psychosomatic causes of dis-ease but also their spiritual roots. According to the Kabbalistic model the soul is attached to the body by 613 channels of energy. These correspond to the 613 commandments. If any of these passages get blocked then energy can no longer flow freely

* References to this book are found in the Talmud Bavli, *Brachot* 10b, Pesaḥim 56a and Ramban's Introduction to Genesis.

** *Heal Your Body: The Mental Causes for Physical Illness and the Metaphysical Way to Overcome Them* by Louise Hay (Hay House). In this booklet there is listed page after page of illnesses, their psychosomatic origins and healing affirmations.

Maror – Second dipping: bitter herb

Take the lettuce leaf, dip it into the ḥaroset and then shake off any excess mixture. Eat without reclining.

Here I am right now, ready and mindful to participate in the unification of the Transcendent Holy One with the Immanent Shekhinah through eating of maror.

Blessed are you, Lord our God, Majesty of the Universe, who sanctified us through unification and commanded us to eat maror.

from the spiritual realms into the psychological, emotional and physical bodies. The symptoms of such clogged light arteries are sickness. The cure lies in the *mitzvah* (commandment or connector). So the book consisted of lists and lists of ailments: when feeling ill they just looked up the problem in the Book of Shlomo (*shalem* – wholeness, holistic) and followed the corresponding instructions. However the book began to be misused. Prayers for well-being became obsolete. People relied on the book almost like magic. So the wise King hid all copies of the book and in its stead he wrote the Song of Songs within which all the cures are present but hidden as allegories. And what is the theme of this book? Love. It is the love song between lovers which is an allegory of God's love for Creation. It is for this reason that it is read during Pesaḥ. Love – the cure-all for all dis-ease. Apples, dates, red wine, cinnamon and almonds – the ingredients of ḥaroset – all feature in the Song. When the ḥaroset is eaten the Song is being tasted. And since the Song is love, the ḥaroset becomes a powerful love potion. It is so strong in fact, all that is needed is just to dip the maror, the bitterness, into the love potion for the pain to be neutralized. Just a touch, a homeopathic whisper. It's an energetic remedy for all dis-ease – God's Love cures all!

The ḥaroset is the secret of the Haggadah. Love is the secret of Life.*

Kadesh
Urḥatz
Karpas
Yaḥatz
Maggid
Raḥtzah
Motzi
Matzah
Maror
Korekh
Shulḥan Orekh
Tzafun
Barekh
Hallel
Nirtzah

* See *Love is Letting Go of Fear* by Gerald Jampolsky (Celestial Arts, 1988).

כורך

Take the bottom matzah (or, if you don't have your own individual set, from a common pool) and prepare a sandwich with the lettuce or ḥazeret (freshly grated horseradish). There are some opinions that suggest adding a touch of ḥaroset as well. The following is recited and the sandwich is eaten while reclining.

זֵכֶר לְמִקְדָּשׁ כְּהִלֵּל: כֵּן עָשָׂה הִלֵּל בִּזְמַן שֶׁבֵּית הַמִּקְדָּשׁ הָיָה קַיָּם. הָיָה כּוֹרֵךְ פֶּסַח מַצָּה וּמָרוֹר וְאוֹכֵל בְּיַחַד. לְקַיֵּם מַה שֶּׁנֶּאֱמַר: עַל־מַצּוֹת וּמְרֹרִים יֹאכְלֻהוּ:

DEEPENING

The Holy Temple was a witness to reality – True Reality. What is True Reality? It is that all is One, all is God. As it was stated earlier, this is the underlying theme of the Haggadah, for what is True Freedom? It is to be free from illusions. What illusions? That I and Thou, me and it, he and she, up and down, good and evil...really exist. This duality of existence is our daily experience but that doesn't mean that it is True. An illustration is brought from the very configuration of the Temple itself. Within the Holy of Holies lay the Holy Container upon which stood the three dimensional representation of two angels – the *Keruvim* (Cherubim). Precise instructions were given in Exodus 25:18 as to how these two shapes were to be constructed. The Holy Container was overlaid with a thick gold covering. The *Keruvim* were formed by beating the underside of the gold sheet until two lumps emerged. When enough material had been pounded out from the underside the details were carved out from the outer side.* Thus, even though the two appear as separate, they are

קדש
ורחץ
כרפס
יחץ
מגיד
רחצה
מוציא
מצה
מרור
כורך
שלחן עורך
צפון
ברך
הלל
נרצה

* It must have looked a little bit like the descriptions of the emergence of the Universe from the Big Bang: before the beginning there was a uniform Nothing; then a random fluctuation in the Nothing accelerated and expanded becoming the Something. Allthings come from the Nothing.

Korekh – The Sandwich* of Hillel

Take the bottom matzah (or, if you don't have your own individual set, from a common pool) and prepare a sandwich with the lettuce or ḥazeret (freshly grated horseradish). There are some opinions that suggest adding a touch of ḥaroset as well. The following is recited and the sandwich is eaten while reclining.

In memory of the Holy Temple according to Hillel.

This is what Hillel used to do during the era that the House of Sanctification existed: he would combine the Pascal lamb with the matzah and the maror and eat them in oneness in order to fulfill what is said: "You shall eat it [the lamb] on matzot and maror"

(Numbers 9:11).

in fact one.** The same is true for the construction of the Holy Menorah – this too was fashioned from one piece of gold.

This recognition of the Oneness is the main leitmotiv in the songs that conclude the evening's journey: "*One kid goat bought for two coins,*" and "*Who knows one – One is the Lord who is in both the Heavens and the Earth (the two)*".

Kadesh
Urḥatz
Karpas
Yaḥatz
Maggid
Raḥtzah
Motzi
Matzah
Maror
Korekh
Shulḥan Orekh
Tzafun
Barekh
Hallel
Nirtzah

---

* For an interesting comparison of Hillel's Sandwich and the sounds of the Shofar see Section Yaḥatz.

** Another representation to illustrate this principle is inspired by Edwin Abbott's *Flatland – A Romance of Many Dimensions*. Imagine a two-dimensional world existing in a penetrable plane. A hand with outstretched fingers begins to descend though this plane. A two dimensional being living in the plane will first see four seemingly separate rings appear (fingers). Of course this being cannot look "up" and therefore cannot realize the common source of these shapes. As the hand continues to penetrate into the plane, the rings will fluctuate slightly in circumference until a fatter fifth circle (thumb) will suddenly appear some distance from the others. A little after that, the four original circles will seem to coalesce into a sausage shape (knuckles). A little later the fifth circle will also converge and the sausage will then turn into a much larger circle (wrist). If only the two dimensional being could transcend his plane of existence and witness the unity behind the separateness of its reality!

שולחן עורך

Eat with mindfulness, gratitude and joy, for the manner in which you consume will affect the unification of the Holy Name, the י (*yod* from the First Cup) and the ה (*hey* from the Second Cup) with the ו (*vav* from the Third Cup) and the ה (*hey* from the Fourth Cup).

צפון

It is now time to conclude the meal with the eating of the Afikoman. If each participant had his or her own set of matzot then the two-thirds piece that was separated at the beginning should be recovered. At least half a slice of matzah should be eaten while leaning. If the facilitator of the Seder is the only one with a set of matzot then more pieces should be distributed to the other participants. By this time the Afikoman should have disappeared and will need to be ransomed back in order to conclude the Seder.

הִנְנִי מוּכָן וּמְזֻמָּן לְקַיֵּם מִצְוַת אֲכִילַת הָאֲפִיקוֹמָן זֵכֶר לְקָרְבַּן פֶּסַח הַנֶּאֱכָל עַל הַשּׂוֹבַע.

DEEPENING

The Afikoman is "stolen" by the children and then ransomed back, for it is only the children that have the ability to bring the final healing. They have not yet lost the gift of prophecy. They are still connected. They will redeem us. And what is true of our children is true of our inner child.

The child stands before us with the Afikoman in his hand, a big grin on his or her face and asks, "What is it worth to you? What are you prepared to pay for your healing – for everything has a price." The Afikoman is usually under-priced.

A19

✺ Shulḥan Orekh – The Meal ✺

Eat with mindfulness, gratitude and joy, for the manner in which you consume will affect the unification of the Holy Name, the ' (*yod* from the First Cup) and the ה (*hey* from the Second Cup) with the ו (*vav* from the Third Cup) and the ה (*hey* from the Fourth Cup).

"Become a person for whom satisfying the needs of the body is a spiritual experience. Some people eat to have the strength to study Torah. Others, more spiritually awakened, study Torah in order to learn how to eat."

(Reb Naḥman of Bratzlav)

3 hrs to here!

13 - 15

✺ Tzafun – The Afikoman* ✺

It is now time to conclude the meal with the eating of the Afikoman. If each participant had his or her own set of matzot then the two-thirds piece that was separated at the beginning should be recovered. At least half a slice of matzah should be eaten while leaning. If the facilitator of the Seder is the only one with a set of matzot then more pieces should be distributed to the other participants. By this time the Afikoman should have disappeared and will need to be ransomed back in order to conclude the Seder.

Kadesh

Urḥatz

Karpas

Yaḥatz

Maggid

Raḥtzah

Motzi

Matzah

Maror

Korekh

Shulḥan Orekh

Tzafun

Barekh

Hallel

Nirtzah

Here I am right now, ready and mindful to participate in the unification through the eating of the Afikoman which is in remembrance of the Pascal lamb sacrifice that was eaten in a satiated state.

---

*   The requirement is that the Afikoman be consumed before midnight, where midnight is defined as half way between nightfall and first light. However Rav Soloveitchik *z"l* gave an opinion that, for the sake of deepening one's awareness of the meaning of the evening, this deadline can be extended.

ברך

שִׁיר הַמַּעֲלוֹת בְּשׁוּב יְיָ אֶת שִׁיבַת צִיּוֹן הָיִינוּ כְּחֹלְמִים:
אָז יִמָּלֵא שְׂחוֹק פִּינוּ וּלְשׁוֹנֵנוּ רִנָּה
אָז יֹאמְרוּ בַגּוֹיִם הִגְדִּיל יְיָ לַעֲשׂוֹת עִם אֵלֶּה:
הִגְדִּיל יְיָ לַעֲשׂוֹת עִמָּנוּ הָיִינוּ שְׂמֵחִים:
שׁוּבָה יְיָ אֶת שְׁבִיתֵנוּ כַּאֲפִיקִים בַּנֶּגֶב:
הַזֹּרְעִים בְּדִמְעָה בְּרִנָּה יִקְצֹרוּ: הָלוֹךְ יֵלֵךְ וּבָכֹה נֹשֵׂא מֶשֶׁךְ
הַזָּרַע בֹּא יָבֹא בְרִנָּה נֹשֵׂא אֲלֻמֹּתָיו:

המזמן אומר:

רַבּוֹתַי נְבָרֵךְ.

המסובין:

יְהִי שֵׁם יְיָ מְבוֹרָךְ מֵעַתָּה וְעַד עוֹלָם.

המזמן:

יְהִי שֵׁם יְיָ מְבוֹרָךְ מֵעַתָּה וְעַד עוֹלָם.
בִּרְשׁוּת מָרָנָן וְרַבָּנָן וְרַבּוֹתַי,
נְבָרֵךְ (בעשרה: אֱלֹהֵינוּ) שֶׁאָכַלְנוּ מִשֶּׁלוֹ.

המסובין:

בָּרוּךְ (אֱלֹהֵינוּ) שֶׁאָכַלְנוּ מִשֶּׁלוֹ וּבְטוּבוֹ חָיִינוּ.

המזמן:

בָּרוּךְ (אֱלֹהֵינוּ) שֶׁאָכַלְנוּ מִשֶּׁלוֹ וּבְטוּבוֹ חָיִינוּ.

בָּרוּךְ הוּא וּבָרוּךְ שְׁמוֹ:

B-16 (6 min!) long

Barekh – Blessing the Source of our Food

A Reaching Up Song: *We dream**
how God will bring us back to Zion.
Then shall we laugh again.
Then shall we sing again.
Then people will say:
"How great it is!
Look at what God has done for them!
If God had done the same for us,
We too would be glad."

Oh God! Why don't You bring us back?
As you bring back water
To the dried-up Negev streams?

Yes, we will trust. We sowed with tears,
We will reap with song.

Those who go, casting out seeds.
Sometimes feel like weeping.
Yet on they go, always trusting,
That they shall come back singing.
Bearing in the harvest sheaves. (Psalms 126)

Invitation and Consent

Leader

Ḥaverai n'va-rekh.
Friends, let us give praise.

Response

Y'hi sheym YAH m'vorakh me'ata v'ad olam.
Barukh [Eloheynu] sh'akhalnu mi-shelo.
Barukh [Eloheynu] sh'akhalnu mi-shelo uv'tuvo ḥayinu.
Barukh Hu/Brukhah Hi, u'varukh sh'mo/sh'mah!

May God's name be praised, now and forever.
With your consent, friends:
Let us praise our God,
whose food we have eaten.

Leader

Barukh [Eloheynu] sh'akhalnu mi-shelo uv'tuvo ḥayinu.

Praised be our God
of whose abundance we have eaten
and by whose goodness we live.

Together

Barukh hu, u'varukh sh'mo.
Praised be God and praised be God's name.

* An alternative translation reads: "When God will return us to Zion it will be like a dream." There are at least two ways to understand this sentiment: either the return itself will seem like a dream or the return means that I am now truly awake and have left the dream world of temporary illusions. In this second reading, the preferred from a Holistic Judaism perspective, Zion represents full God-consciousness. This is the theme of the film *The Matrix.*

Kadesh
Urḥatz
Karpas
Yaḥatz
Maggid
Raḥtzah
Motzi
Matzah
Maror
Korekh
Shulḥan Orekh
Tzafun
Barekh
Hallel
Nirtzah

בָּרוּךְ אַתָּה יְיָ, אֱלֹהֵינוּ מֶלֶךְ הָעוֹלָם, הַזָּן אֶת
הָעוֹלָם כֻּלּוֹ בְּטוּבוֹ בְּחֵן בְּחֶסֶד וּבְרַחֲמִים.
הוּא נוֹתֵן לֶחֶם לְכָל בָּשָׂר כִּי לְעוֹלָם חַסְדּוֹ.
וּבְטוּבוֹ הַגָּדוֹל תָּמִיד לֹא חָסַר לָנוּ,
וְאַל יֶחְסַר לָנוּ מָזוֹן לְעוֹלָם וָעֶד.
בַּעֲבוּר שְׁמוֹ הַגָּדוֹל, כִּי הוּא אֵל זָן וּמְפַרְנֵס
לַכֹּל וּמֵטִיב לַכֹּל,
וּמֵכִין מָזוֹן לְכָל בְּרִיּוֹתָיו אֲשֶׁר בָּרָא.
(כָּאָמוּר, פּוֹתֵחַ אֶת יָדֶךָ וּמַשְׂבִּיעַ לְכָל חַי רָצוֹן.)
בָּרוּךְ אַתָּה יְיָ, הַזָּן אֶת הַכֹּל:

Thanking God for the Food and its Nourishment

Praise, yes, praise is Yours, Oh God.
Ruler of all time and space
Who every day invites the world
to the feast of love, goodness and compassion.

You feed us and You sustain us
and the whole world
with Your goodness
Your grace and compassion.
Food You provide for all Your creatures
Whom You love so abundantly.

And because You are so good to us,
We have never lacked sustenance in the past
And we trust that we will never lack food in the future.
This You do for Your own repute
That You may be known as:
The One who sustains.
The One who supports.
The One who provides food for each creature's needs.
You know well what each one needs.
For You did create us all.

Therefore do we praise and thank You,
The One who nourishes all.

Barukh attah YAH, hazzan et hakkol.

Kadesh
Urḥatz
Karpas
Yaḥatz
Maggid
Raḥtzah
Motzi
Matzah
Maror
Korekh
Shulḥan Orekh
Tzafun
Barekh
Hallel
Nirtzah

נוֹדֶה לְּךָ יְיָ אֱלֹהֵינוּ עַל שֶׁהִנְחַלְתָּ לַאֲבוֹתֵינוּ
אֶרֶץ חֶמְדָּה טוֹבָה וּרְחָבָה,
וְעַל שֶׁהוֹצֵאתָנוּ יְיָ אֱלֹהֵינוּ מֵאֶרֶץ מִצְרַיִם,
וּפְדִיתָנוּ מִבֵּית עֲבָדִים,
וְעַל בְּרִיתְךָ שֶׁחָתַמְתָּ בִּבְשָׂרֵנוּ וְעַל תּוֹרָתְךָ שֶׁלִּמַּדְתָּנוּ,
וְעַל חֻקֶּיךָ שֶׁהוֹדַעְתָּנוּ וְעַל חַיִּים חֵן וָחֶסֶד שֶׁחוֹנַנְתָּנוּ,
וְעַל אֲכִילַת מָזוֹן שָׁאַתָּה זָן וּמְפַרְנֵס אוֹתָנוּ תָּמִיד,
בְּכָל יוֹם וּבְכָל עֵת וּבְכָל שָׁעָה:

Thanking God for the Exodus, the Torah, the Holy Land – and for the Joy of Eating:

We thank You, YAH, our God,
because you settled our ancestors
in a land desirable and good and wide.

You extricated us, YAH our God,
from the straits and narrow places of Mitzraim,
and freed us from being at home in servitude.

We thank You for the promise sealed in our flesh,
For the Torah teaching which You impart to us,
For the rules You made us know;
for life,
for beauty,
for love,
with which you are generous.

And we thank You for the joy of eating
which You grant us
while You nurture us,
every day, every moment.

וְעַל הַכֹּל יְיָ אֱלֹהֵינוּ אֲנַחְנוּ מוֹדִים לָךְ,
וּמְבָרְכִים אוֹתָךְ,
יִתְבָּרַךְ שִׁמְךָ בְּפִי כָּל חַי תָּמִיד
לְעוֹלָם וָעֶד.
כַּכָּתוּב,
וְאָכַלְתָּ וְשָׂבָעְתָּ, וּבֵרַכְתָּ אֶת יְיָ אֱלֹהֶיךָ
עַל הָאָרֶץ הַטֹּבָה אֲשֶׁר נָתַן לָךְ.
בָּרוּךְ אַתָּה יְיָ, עַל הָאָרֶץ וְעַל הַמָּזוֹן:

Thanking God for the Good Earth and Her Produce

For all this, Our God.
We worship and thank You.
Whose Name is praised
By ever new expressions of life.

We do this to fulfill Your command, which states:
"Eat your fill, praising YAH, your God,
for the earthy goodness which God so freely gave to you."

Therefore we say:
Praise to You YAH
for the Earth and for her food.

Barukh attah YAH al ha'aretz v'al hamazzon.

רַחֵם נָא, יְיָ אֱלֹהֵינוּ,
עַל יִשְׂרָאֵל עַמֶּךָ,
וְעַל יְרוּשָׁלַיִם עִירֶךָ,
וְעַל צִיּוֹן מִשְׁכַּן כְּבוֹדֶךָ, וְעַל מַלְכוּת בֵּית דָּוִד
מְשִׁיחֶךָ,
וְעַל הַבַּיִת הַגָּדוֹל וְהַקָּדוֹשׁ שֶׁנִּקְרָא שִׁמְךָ עָלָיו.
אֱלֹהֵינוּ, אָבִינוּ, רְעֵנוּ, זוּנֵנוּ, פַּרְנְסֵנוּ, וְכַלְכְּלֵנוּ,
וְהַרְוִיחֵנוּ,
וְהַרְוַח לָנוּ יְיָ אֱלֹהֵינוּ מְהֵרָה מִכָּל צָרוֹתֵינוּ,
וְנָא עַל תַּצְרִיכֵנוּ,
יְיָ אֱלֹהֵינוּ, לֹא לִידֵי מַתְּנַת בָּשָׂר וָדָם,
וְלֹא לִידֵי הַלְוָאָתָם.
כִּי אִם לְיָדְךָ הַמְּלֵאָה, הַפְּתוּחָה, הַקְּדוֹשָׁה וְהָרְחָבָה,
שֶׁלֹּא נֵבוֹשׁ וְלֹא נִכָּלֵם לְעוֹלָם וָעֶד:

קדש
ורחץ
כרפס
יחץ
מגיד
רחצה
מוציא
מצה
מרור
כורך
שלחן עורך
צפון
ברך
הלל
נרצה

As a Mother Wombs
Her Children in Mercy

Have pity, Oh God, on
Israel Your people,
Jerusalem Your city,
Zion Your glory's shrine
and on David's messianic world order.

And pity the Holy House
The Temple of Grandeur
Where it was so easy
To call upon You.

Our God, Source of our being,
Mother, Father, Provider, Sustainer,
You nourish and support us,
Yet still allow us our independence.

God, keep us free from needs that enslave us.
Permit us not to depend
on gifts, handouts or loans.
For even when others offer help,
what they give is little
and the indignity is great.

But may we only rely
On Your full, broadly open hand,
So we never lose self-respect,
Nor suffer shame or disgrace.

Kadesh
Urḥatz
Karpas
Yaḥatz
Maggid
Raḥtzah
Motzi
Matzah
Maror
Korekh
Shulḥan Orekh
Tzafun
Barekh
Hallel
Nirtzah

On Shabbat

רְצֵה וְהַחֲלִיצֵנוּ יְיָ אֱלֹהֵינוּ בְּמִצְוֹתֶיךָ
וּבְמִצְוַת יוֹם הַשְּׁבִיעִי,
הַשַּׁבָּת הַגָּדוֹל וְהַקָּדוֹשׁ הַזֶּה. כִּי
יוֹם זֶה גָּדוֹל וְקָדוֹשׁ הוּא לְפָנֶיךָ,
לִשְׁבָּת בּוֹ וְלָנוּחַ בּוֹ בְּאַהֲבָה כְּמִצְוַת רְצוֹנֶךָ.
וּבִרְצוֹנְךָ הָנִיחַ לָנוּ,
יְיָ אֱלֹהֵינוּ, שֶׁלֹּא תְהֵא צָרָה וְיָגוֹן וַאֲנָחָה
בְּיוֹם מְנוּחָתֵנוּ.
וְהַרְאֵנוּ יְיָ אֱלֹהֵינוּ בְּנֶחָמַת צִיּוֹן עִירֶךָ,
וּבְבִנְיַן יְרוּשָׁלַיִם עִיר קָדְשֶׁךָ,
כִּי אַתָּה הוּא בַּעַל הַיְשׁוּעוֹת וּבַעַל הַנֶּחָמוֹת:

We Also Give Thanks for the Shabbat's Rest

On Shabbat

In commanding us You share Your will with us.
In commanding us You impart in us the strength to fulfill the commandment.
We thank You for the commandment of the seventh day,
the great Shabbat, the holy Shabbat,
this Shabbat.
A great day it is, holy it is, a day in which we live Your Presence.
We rest on it; we relax on it,
according to Your will.
On this day of rest – may there be no pain,
no worry, no anguish, stress or sighing.

On this Shabbat day open our eyes to the vision for the consolation of Zion,
and the upbuilding of Jerusalem, Your holy city.
For You are the Source of liberation and consolation.

אֱלֹהֵינוּ וֵאלֹהֵי אֲבוֹתֵינוּ, יַעֲלֶה וְיָבֹא וְיַגִּיעַ,
וְיֵרָאֶה, וְיֵרָצֶה, וְיִשָּׁמַע, וְיִפָּקֵד,
וְיִזָּכֵר זִכְרוֹנֵנוּ וּפִקְדוֹנֵנוּ,
וְזִכְרוֹן אֲבוֹתֵינוּ, וְזִכְרוֹן מָשִׁיחַ בֶּן דָּוִד עַבְדֶּךָ,
וְזִכְרוֹן יְרוּשָׁלַיִם עִיר קָדְשֶׁךָ,
וְזִכְרוֹן כָּל עַמְּךָ בֵּית יִשְׂרָאֵל לְפָנֶיךָ,
לִפְלֵיטָה לְטוֹבָה לְחֵן וּלְחֶסֶד וּלְרַחֲמִים,
לְחַיִּים וּלְשָׁלוֹם בְּיוֹם חַג הַמַּצּוֹת הַזֶּה.
זָכְרֵנוּ יְיָ אֱלֹהֵינוּ בּוֹ לְטוֹבָה.
וּפָקְדֵנוּ בוֹ לִבְרָכָה.
וְהוֹשִׁיעֵנוּ בוֹ לְחַיִּים.
וּבִדְבַר יְשׁוּעָה וְרַחֲמִים,
חוּס וְחָנֵּנוּ וְרַחֵם עָלֵינוּ וְהוֹשִׁיעֵנוּ, כִּי אֵלֶיךָ עֵינֵינוּ,
כִּי אֵל מֶלֶךְ חַנּוּן וְרַחוּם אָתָּה:

We Celebrate the Holy Season

Our God and God of our ancestors,
May this prayer we offer to You,
Rise and come and reach You.
Be noted and accepted
and heard by You;
Be remembered and acted upon:
As You become aware of us,
As You remember us.
You remembered our parents.
You will remember the Messiaḥ, David's heir,
You are mindful of Jerusalem Your city.
You are mindful of Israel Your people.
Allow them all to find their way
To Goodness, to grace, to kindness
To mercy, to life and to peace.
On this Pesaḥ
Think well of this day
Be mindful on it for our blessing,
Grant us the good life on it.
And as concerns such matters as salvation and mercy
Pity us, be kind; save us, be gentle,
For our eyes look to You –
Divine, Majestic One,
Who is also Kind and Gentle.

וּבְנֵה יְרוּשָׁלַיִם עִיר הַקֹּדֶשׁ
בִּמְהֵרָה בְיָמֵינוּ.
בָּרוּךְ אַתָּה יְיָ, בּוֹנֵה בְרַחֲמָיו יְרוּשָׁלָיִם.
אָמֵן:

קדש
ורחץ
כרפס
יחץ
מגיד
רחצה
מוציא
מצה
מרור
כורך
שלחן עורך
צפון
ברך
הלל
נרצה

We Remember Others as We Remember Jerusalem

We ate and drank
Yet we forget not
that there is exile, destruction,
famine, fear and want.
Please, forget us not,
But in remembering us, remember all in want.
Make this world a place of holiness,
Now in our lifetime, as You rebuild Jerusalem.
Praised are You, YAH
Who in building up mercy
Builds Jerusalem.

Barukh attah YAH, boneh b'raḥamav Yerushalayim:
Amen – do as we believe!

בָּרוּךְ אַתָּה יְיָ אֱלֹהֵינוּ מֶלֶךְ הָעוֹלָם,
הָאֵל אָבִינוּ, מַלְכֵּנוּ, אַדִּירֵנוּ,
בּוֹרְאֵנוּ, גּוֹאֲלֵנוּ, יוֹצְרֵנוּ,
קְדוֹשֵׁנוּ קְדוֹשׁ יַעֲקֹב,
רוֹעֵנוּ רוֹעֵה יִשְׂרָאֵל.
הַמֶּלֶךְ הַטּוֹב וְהַמֵּטִיב לַכֹּל,
שֶׁבְּכָל יוֹם וָיוֹם הוּא הֵטִיב,
הוּא מֵטִיב, הוּא יֵיטִיב לָנוּ. הוּא גְּמָלָנוּ,
הוּא גוֹמְלֵנוּ, הוּא יִגְמְלֵנוּ לָעַד,
לְחֵן וּלְחֶסֶד וּלְרַחֲמִים וּלְרֶוַח הַצָּלָה וְהַצְלָחָה,
בְּרָכָה וִישׁוּעָה, נֶחָמָה,
פַּרְנָסָה וְכַלְכָּלָה, וְרַחֲמִים,
וְחַיִּים וְשָׁלוֹם, וְכָל טוֹב,
וּמִכָּל טוּב לְעוֹלָם אַל יְחַסְּרֵנוּ:

קדש
ורחץ
כרפס
יחץ
מגיד
רחצה
מוציא
מצה
מרור
כורך
שלחן עורך
צפון
ברך
הלל
נרצה

We Thank You for Thanksgiving and for All that You Are To Us

Praise, yea praise to You, Oh God.
Source of our being
Merciful Mother, Mighty Father;
Powerful Ruler, Redeeming Creator;
Holy Artist, Jacob's Sanctifier;
Guiding Shepherd, Israel's Shepherd;
Sovereign who is good to all.
In Your goodness You do not discriminate.
Doing good day by day
according to that day's needs.
So You did act out of goodness in the past,
And so will You deal with us in the future.
You give of Your Self. You gave of Your Self
freely and completely, kindly and mercifully,
generously and abundantly.
To save us, to prosper us, to bless us,
to redeem us, to console us,
to sustain and support us –
in mercy, life and in goodness,
while not diminishing the good You hold in
store for us
for eternity.

Kadesh
Urḥatz
Karpas
Yaḥatz
Maggid
Raḥtzah
Motzi
Matzah
Maror
Korekh
Shulḥan Orekh
Tzafun
Barekh
Hallel
Nirtzah

הָרַחֲמָן, הוּא יִמְלוֹךְ עָלֵינוּ לְעוֹלָם וָעֶד.
הָרַחֲמָן, הוּא יִתְבָּרַךְ בַּשָּׁמַיִם וּבָאָרֶץ.
הָרַחֲמָן, הוּא יִשְׁתַּבַּח לְדוֹר דּוֹרִים,
וְיִתְפָּאַר בָּנוּ לָעַד וּלְנֵצַח נְצָחִים,
וְיִתְהַדַּר בָּנוּ לָעַד וּלְעוֹלְמֵי עוֹלָמִים.
הָרַחֲמָן, הוּא יְפַרְנְסֵנוּ בְּכָבוֹד.
הָרַחֲמָן, הוּא יִשְׁבּוֹר עֻלֵּנוּ מֵעַל צַוָּארֵנוּ
וְהוּא יוֹלִיכֵנוּ קוֹמְמִיּוּת לְאַרְצֵנוּ.
הָרַחֲמָן, הוּא יִשְׁלַח לָנוּ בְּרָכָה מְרֻבָּה בַּבַּיִת הַזֶּה,
וְעַל שֻׁלְחָן זֶה שֶׁאָכַלְנוּ עָלָיו.
הָרַחֲמָן, הוּא יִשְׁלַח לָנוּ אֶת אֵלִיָּהוּ הַנָּבִיא זָכוּר לַטּוֹב,
וִיבַשֶּׂר לָנוּ בְּשׂוֹרוֹת טוֹבוֹת יְשׁוּעוֹת וְנֶחָמוֹת.

הָרַחֲמָן, הוּא יְבָרֵךְ אֶת (אָבִי מוֹרִי) בַּעַל הַבַּיִת הַזֶּה,
וְאֶת (אִמִּי מוֹרָתִי) בַּעֲלַת הַבַּיִת הַזֶּה,
אוֹתָם וְאֶת בֵּיתָם וְאֶת זַרְעָם וְאֶת כָּל אֲשֶׁר לָהֶם.

(אם הוא סמוך על שלחן עצמו אומר:)
הָרַחֲמָן, הוּא יְבָרֵךְ אוֹתִי
(וְאָבִי וְאִמִּי וְאִשְׁתִּי/וּבַעְלִי וְזַרְעִי וְאֶת כָּל אֲשֶׁר לִי)

אוֹתָנוּ וְאֶת כָּל אֲשֶׁר לָנוּ,
כְּמוֹ שֶׁנִּתְבָּרְכוּ אֲבוֹתֵינוּ,
אַבְרָהָם יִצְחָק וְיַעֲקֹב:
בַּכֹּל, מִכֹּל, כֹּל.
כֵּן יְבָרֵךְ אוֹתָנוּ כֻּלָּנוּ יַחַד.
בִּבְרָכָה שְׁלֵמָה, וְנֹאמַר אָמֵן:

We Pray for the Messianic Age and Times of Peace Invocations for the Future:

Haraḥaman Hu....

Kind-hearted One! Rule over us always.

Caring One! Be involved with our heaven and on our earth.
Feeling One!
You who are praised from one generation to the next,
Take pride in us always.
May our lives honor You in this world and in the next.

Merciful One! Grant us an honorable livelihood.

Warm-hearted One! Break the restraints that make us strangers,
lead us home with dignity.

Generous One! Send abundant blessing
to this home and to this table.

One who grants pleasant surprises!
Send Elijah the prophet, of the blessed memory,
to bring us good news of liberation and consolation.

Compassionate One!
Bless and protect all of us, our loved ones and our families,
our endeavors and our possessions.
May we all be blessed
like Abraham – with everything;
like Sarah – with faithfulness;
like Isaac – by everyone;
like Jacob – in every way;
like Raḥel – with warmth;
like Leah – with love.
And to all this, let us say – Amen!

בַּמָּרוֹם יְלַמְּדוּ עֲלֵיהֶם וְעָלֵינוּ זְכוּת,
שֶׁתְּהֵא לְמִשְׁמֶרֶת שָׁלוֹם,
וְנִשָּׂא בְרָכָה מֵאֵת יְיָ וּצְדָקָה מֵאֱלֹהֵי יִשְׁעֵנוּ,
וְנִמְצָא חֵן וְשֵׂכֶל טוֹב בְּעֵינֵי אֱלֹהִים וְאָדָם:

On Shabbat add:

הָרַחֲמָן, הוּא יַנְחִילֵנוּ יוֹם שֶׁכֻּלּוֹ שַׁבָּת וּמְנוּחָה לְחַיֵּי הָעוֹלָמִים.

הָרַחֲמָן, הוּא יַנְחִילֵנוּ יוֹם שֶׁכֻּלּוֹ טוֹב.

הָרַחֲמָן,
הוּא יְזַכֵּנוּ לִימוֹת הַמָּשִׁיחַ וּלְחַיֵּי הָעוֹלָם הַבָּא.
מִגְדּוֹל יְשׁוּעוֹת מַלְכּוֹ,
וְעֹשֶׂה חֶסֶד לִמְשִׁיחוֹ לְדָוִד וּלְזַרְעוֹ עַד עוֹלָם:
עֹשֶׂה שָׁלוֹם בִּמְרוֹמָיו,
הוּא יַעֲשֶׂה שָׁלוֹם עָלֵינוּ וְעַל כָּל יִשְׂרָאֵל,
וְאִמְרוּ אָמֵן:

קדש
ורחץ
כרפס
יחץ
מגיד
רחצה
מוציא
מצה
מרור
כורך
שלחן עורך
צפון
ברך
הלל
נרצה

Sublime One!

Interpret our act as prompted by
good intentions, as an act of
surrender, worthy of blessing from You.

And even if we are not deemed worthy,
then accept our act of thanksgiving
as a kind favor on Your part. Oh Helping God!

May we ever be found pleasant and wise
by You God
and by all our fellow human beings.

Compassionate One! Help us
so that we may be worthy of being alive
when the Messiah time finally arrives.
Grant strength and loving-kindness
to the Messiah,
to David's descendants, to the very ends of time.
Oh God! We know that You can make peace on high –
That is not too difficult.
Grant peace to us and to all Israel –
That is more difficult:
Grant us peace!

יְראוּ אֶת יְיָ קְדֹשָׁיו,
כִּי אֵין מַחְסוֹר לִירֵאָיו:
כְּפִירִים רָשׁוּ וְרָעֵבוּ,
וְדוֹרְשֵׁי יְיָ לֹא יַחְסְרוּ כָל טוֹב:
הוֹדוּ לַייָ כִּי טוֹב,
כִּי לְעוֹלָם חַסְדּוֹ:
פּוֹתֵחַ אֶת יָדֶךָ וּמַשְׂבִּיעַ לְכָל חַי רָצוֹן:
בָּרוּךְ הַגֶּבֶר אֲשֶׁר יִבְטַח בַּייָ,
וְהָיָה יְיָ מִבְטַחוֹ:
נַעַר הָיִיתִי גַם זָקַנְתִּי
וְלֹא רָאִיתִי צַדִּיק נֶעֱזָב,
וְזַרְעוֹ מְבַקֶּשׁ לָחֶם:
יְיָ עֹז לְעַמּוֹ יִתֵּן,
יְיָ יְבָרֵךְ אֶת עַמּוֹ בַשָּׁלוֹם:

We Encourage One Another Before Leaving the Table:

Fear Our God, you who make God holy!
Fearing only God, what will you lack?
Those who are self-sufficient, like young lions,
May starve in relying on their own strength.
But those who seek Only God
Shall not lack all that is good.
Give thanks to God who is so good,
Whose kindness is ever aware
of the needs of the world.
Blessed are they who trust in God,
For God will ever be their protector.
I was young, now I'm old
yet never saw a Tzaddik so forsaken
that their child seeks only bread.
How can this be? How could this happen?
Surely blessings will be heaped on those
who are really righteous, fair and just.
May what we ate be a source of satisfaction;
What we drank, a source of health;
What we left, a source of blessing.
According to Scripture:
"The host set food before them, they ate and left enough for others,
As God has spoken."
God will surely give strength to our people,
God will bless our folk with SHALOM!

Kadesh
Urḥatz
Karpas
Yaḥatz
Maggid
Raḥtzah
Motzi
Matzah
Maror
Korekh
Shulḥan Orekh
Tzafun
Barekh
Hallel
Nirtzah

הִנְנִי מוּכָן וּמְזֻמָּן לְקַיֵּם מִצְוַת כּוֹס שְׁלִישִׁי מֵאַרְבַּע כּוֹסוֹת. לְשֵׁם יִחוּד קוּדְשָׁא בְּרִיךְ הוּא וּשְׁכִינְתֵּיהּ
עַל יְדֵי הַהוּא טָמִיר וְנֶעְלָם בְּשֵׁם כָּל יִשְׂרָאֵל:

בָּרוּךְ אַתָּה יְיָ, אֱלֹהֵינוּ מֶלֶךְ הָעוֹלָם, בּוֹרֵא פְּרִי הַגָּפֶן:

DEEPENING

The Third Cup represents the letter ו (*vav*), the third letter in the Divine Name. This is the World of *Yetzirah*, the World of Formation and Emotion. We have eaten and feel satisfied; we have eaten of the goodness of God's bounty and have taken delight in its variety; we have given thanks and rejoiced in our good fortune.

כוס אליהו הנביא

The Fourth Cup is poured for everyone.
A large cup is also filled to the brim and placed on the table next to the Cup of Miriam. This is the Cup of Elijah the Prophet.
The front door of the house is opened.
All stand and make the following declarations:

הָרַחֲמָן הוּא יִשְׁלַח לָנוּ בִּמְהֵרָה אֶת אֵלִיָּהוּ הַנָּבִיא זָכוּר לַטּוֹב, וִיבַשֶּׂר לָנוּ בְּשׂוֹרוֹת טוֹבוֹת, יְשׁוּעוֹת וְנֶחָמוֹת. כָּאָמוּר: הִנֵּה אָנֹכִי שֹׁלֵחַ לָכֶם אֵת אֵלִיָּה הַנָּבִיא לִפְנֵי בּוֹא יוֹם יְיָ הַגָּדוֹל וְהַנּוֹרָא: וְהֵשִׁיב לֵב אָבוֹת עַל בָּנִים וְלֵב בָּנִים עַל אֲבוֹתָם:

DEEPENING

The Cup of Eliyahu (Elijah) the Prophet holds a mystical fascination over children's imaginations and is a central feature of the Seder table. What is it doing here? The source comes from a dispute in the Talmud regarding

קדש
ורחץ
כרפס
יחץ
מגיד
רחצה
מוציא
מצה
מרור
כורך
שלחן עורך
צפון
ברך
הלל
נרצה

The Third Cup

*Here I am right now, ready and mindful to participate in the unification of the Transcendent Holy One with the Immanent Shekhinah through the **third** of the Four Cups.*

Blessed are You, Lord our God, Majesty of the Universe, who brings into being the fruit of the vine.

The Cup of Elijah the Prophet

The Fourth Cup is poured for everyone.
A large cup is also filled to the brim and placed on the table next to the Cup of Miriam. This is the Cup of Elijah the Prophet.
The front door of the house is opened.
All stand and make the following declarations:

May the All Merciful One send us the Prophet Elijah, may his memory be a blessing, to bring us good tidings, redemption and comfort, as it is written: "Behold! I am sending to you Elijah the Prophet, before the Lord's great and awesome day. And he shall return the hearts of the parents to their children and return the hearts of the children to their parents"

(Malakhi 3:24).

the levels of redemption that we are to celebrate with the drinking of wine. The levels appear as separate expressions in Exodus 6:6–8: "*Therefore say to the Children of Israel, I am the Lord, and I will **extricate** you from under the burdens of Mitzraim, and I will **deliver** you out of their bondage, and I will **redeem** you with an outstretched arm, and with great judgments. And I will **take** you to me for a people…and I will **bring** you into the land….*" Is the last promise part of the drama of the Exodus or not? The answer is left undecided until the arrival of Eliyahu, the herald of the Messiah, who will resolve all disputes. Thus, in the meantime,

Kadesh
Urḥatz
Karpas
Yaḥatz
Maggid
Raḥtzah
Motzi
Matzah
Maror
Korekh
Shulḥan Orekh
Tzafun
Barekh
Hallel
Nirtzah

✥ שְׁפֹךְ חֲמָתְךָ ✥

שְׁפֹךְ חֲמָתְךָ אֶל־הַגּוֹיִם אֲשֶׁר לֹא יְדָעוּךָ, וְעַל־מַמְלָכוֹת אֲשֶׁר בְּשִׁמְךָ לֹא קָרָאוּ: כִּי אָכַל אֶת־יַעֲקֹב וְאֶת־נָוֵהוּ הֵשַׁמּוּ: שְׁפֹךְ־עֲלֵיהֶם זַעְמֶךָ, וַחֲרוֹן אַפְּךָ יַשִּׂיגֵם תִּרְדֹּף בְּאַף וְתַשְׁמִידֵם מִתַּחַת שְׁמֵי יְיָ:

we drink Four Cups and leave a fifth one undrunk on the table. Is that all? Listen, for here lies a great secret. The importance of Eliyahu at the Seder table can be attributed to our deepest slavery – our slavery to our family dramas. The Seder, this inter-generational gathering, brings out all the worst – and best – memories of family inter-actions. The family drama – the most insidious of all slaveries – is ever present. The voices of our fathers; the voices of our mothers; the voices of our siblings; our own voices as children; they are all present at the Seder table, whether in actuality or as memories, and they are all still there pulling us this way and that. And the Seder table, like everything else mentioned here, is only an encapsulation, a microcosm of our lives. The manner in which we then relate to our children and partners is therefore influenced by these voices, which conjure up such deep emotions. The Messiah, the great healing, will come when we can open our hearts to our parents and when we can, as parents, open our hearts to our children. To hear them and to be heard by them. To love them and to be loved by them.

This inter-generational healing can be visualized in the letter aleph א – the first letter of the name "Eliyahu." The diagonal line represents us, the upper hook is our hand reaching up to our grandparents (past generation) and the lower hook is our hand reaching down to our children (future generation).

Between the Third Cup and the Fourth Cup comes Eliyahu, the Prophet. He represents the covenant between the Creator and the Created. He will repair the rift between the ו (vav) and the ה (heh) of the Divine Name, the male and female aspects of ourselves, our species and the cosmos.

קדש
ורחץ
כרפס
יחץ
מגיד
רחצה
מוציא
מצה
מרור
כורך
שלחן עורך
צפון
ברך
הלל
נרצה

We express our anxieties and trepidation about those now involved in evil. We ask God to deal with them accordingly and hope we ourselves will be spared confrontation.

Pour Out Your Wrath

"Pour out Your fury upon the nations which are ignorant of You and upon the regimes that do not invoke Your Name; for they devoured Jacob and destroyed his home" (Psalms 79:6–7).

(Some Sephardic texts stop here.)

"Pour out Your wrath upon them and may Your burning fury overcome them" (Psalms 69:25).

"Pursue them in rage and destroy them from under the Lord's Heavens" (Lamentations 3:66).

BEING

It should be remembered that Elijah was a fire-brand prophet, a zealous advocate for the Lord. At one point he arrives at Mount Ḥorev forlorn, wanting to die for having apparently failed in stopping the evil Queen Jezabel and the spread of idolatry.* God brings about a storm and announces to the Prophet: "I am not in the storm." He then brings an earthquake and again announces: "I am not in the earthquake." And then comes a great fire: "I am not in the fire." And then silence, and in the silence comes The Voice saying: "I am in the sounds of silence." Elijah later undergoes a fiery transformation as he is borne Heavenward by a blazing chariot. From then onwards he is known as the messenger of peace and healing.

It is also traditionally accepted that Elijah was the reincarnation of Pinḥas,** who had very similar personality traits – being over-zealous for God and then receiving the "correcting" (*Tikkun*) blessing of Peace.

This passage, "Pour out Your Fury," was introduced into the Haggadah during the times of the Crusades that decimated Jewish communities across Europe. Also, since Pesaḥ and Easter usually coincide, this "Night of Watching" was also the night of anti-Jewish pogroms.*** So the opening of the door was an act of defiance and courage, of protest and freedom.

Kadesh
Urḥatz
Karpas
Yaḥatz
Maggid
Raḥtzah
Motzi
Matzah
Maror
Korekh
Shulḥan Orekh
Tzafun
Barekh
Hallel
Nirtzah

When should we give up our anger and when should we not?

There is a Talmudic tale about how once Rabbi Meir prayed for the death of two troublesome thieves in the community. His wife, the learned Bruria, urged him to pray instead for the removal of wickedness. He did, and the thieves repented.

שפך אהבתך

שְׁפֹךְ אַהֲבָתְךָ עַל הַגּוֹיִים אֲשֶׁר יְדָעוּךָ
וְעַל מַמְלָכוֹת אֲשֶׁר בְּשִׁמְךָ קוֹרְאִים
בִּגְלַל חֲסָדִים שֶׁהֵם עוֹשִׂים עִם יַעֲקֹב
וּמְגִנִּים עַל עַמְּךָ יִשְׂרָאֵל מִפְּנֵי אוֹכְלֵיהֶם.
יִזְכּוּ לִרְאוֹת בְּסֻכַּת בְּחִירֶיךָ
וְלִשְׂמֹחַ בְּשִׂמְחַת גּוֹיֶיךָ.

Pour out Your love on the nations that know You and on the kingdoms that call upon Your Name for the loving-kindness that they perform with Jacob and their defense of the People of Israel in the face of those that would devour them. May they be privileged to see the Succah of peace spread for Your chosen ones and rejoice in the joy of Your nations.

קדש
ורחץ
כרפס
יחץ
מגיד
רחצה
מוציא
מצה
מרור
כורך
שלחן עורך
צפון
ברך
הלל
נרצה

---

anticipation of violent attacks by their normally peaceful neighbors (Jack Kagan and Dov Cohen: *Surviving the Holocaust with the Jewish Russian Partisans*, Vallentine Mitchell, 2001).

Pour Out Your Love*

DEEPENING

What an incredible contrast these two images present! We open the door to let Elijah the Prophet, the harbinger of peace, enter, and at the same time we let our anger out and call for the destruction of our enemies and the enemies of God. How can we explain this dichotomy?

Look at the way the Psalmist recommends dealing with our anger, for we cannot and must not deny our anger. Anger management involves expressing our anger and then handing it over to God. Let the Lord of Justice, the Lover of Righteousness, do what has to be done. It is not for us to wreak revenge upon the ignorant. Holding on to anger is another attachment, another Mitzraim. Those who "call upon the Name of God" are called upon to detach from their anger and by doing so become transformed into God's Peacemakers.

We were abused in every generation – Mitzraim being the archetype – but the Torah teaches us that we must transcend the "normal" or human response of revenge. Mitzraim received the karmic response directly from the Holy One Blessed be She. We are not to hate the Mitzrim for what they did to us, but rather must rise up into a state of compassion for the blindness of God's shadows.

Kadesh
Urḥatz
Karpas
Yaḥatz
Maggid
Raḥtzah
Motzi
Matzah
Maror
Korekh
Shulḥan Orekh
Tzafun
Barekh
Hallel
Nirtzah

* This remarkable passage, which is quoted in the Haggadah entitled *A Different Night*, by Noam Zion and David Dishon, is said to have first appeared in a medieval (1521) Ashkenazi Haggadah from Worms. This inclusion may have been due to the fact that there is known to have been contact at that time between Jewish and Christian mystics. See for instance: *Rosicrucian Enlightenment* by Frances Amelia Yates (Routledge Classics).

הלל

Fill the Fourth Cup and sing God's praises with all your heart and soul.

לֹא לָנוּ יְיָ לֹא לָנוּ כִּי לְשִׁמְךָ תֵּן כָּבוֹד,
עַל חַסְדְּךָ עַל אֲמִתֶּךָ:
לָמָּה יֹאמְרוּ הַגּוֹיִם, אַיֵּה נָא אֱלֹהֵיהֶם:
וֵאלֹהֵינוּ בַשָּׁמָיִם כֹּל אֲשֶׁר חָפֵץ עָשָׂה:
עֲצַבֵּיהֶם כֶּסֶף וְזָהָב,
מַעֲשֵׂה יְדֵי אָדָם:
פֶּה לָהֶם וְלֹא יְדַבֵּרוּ עֵינַיִם לָהֶם וְלֹא יִרְאוּ:
אָזְנַיִם לָהֶם וְלֹא יִשְׁמָעוּ,
אַף לָהֶם וְלֹא יְרִיחוּן:
יְדֵיהֶם וְלֹא יְמִישׁוּן,
רַגְלֵיהֶם וְלֹא יְהַלֵּכוּ,
לֹא יֶהְגּוּ בִּגְרוֹנָם:
כְּמוֹהֶם יִהְיוּ עֹשֵׂיהֶם,
כֹּל אֲשֶׁר בֹּטֵחַ בָּהֶם:
יִשְׂרָאֵל בְּטַח בַּייָ עֶזְרָם וּמָגִנָּם הוּא:
בֵּית אַהֲרֹן בִּטְחוּ בַייָ,
עֶזְרָם וּמָגִנָּם הוּא:
יִרְאֵי יְיָ בִּטְחוּ בַייָ, עֶזְרָם וּמָגִנָּם הוּא:

קדש
ורחץ
כרפס
יחץ
מגיד
רחצה
מוציא
מצה
מרור
כורך
שלחן עורך
צפון
ברך
הלל
נרצה

A 29

Hallel – Praising the Lord

Fill the Fourth Cup and sing God's praises with all your heart and soul.

Don't do it for us,
YAH, not only for us.
But to Your character give the glory
For Your kindness and
Your integrity.
Let not detractors mock us,
saying: "Where is your God?"
Our heavenly God
Does everything as He pleases.

They who get depressed over
Money and gold,
That they have forged
with their hands –
They have mouths that do not speak.
They have eyes that fail to see.
Their ears hear no music.
They are not able to enjoy
good scent.
Hands they have
and never really touching.
Feet that get them nowhere.
Throats that do not sing.
Merely toiling, they are like robots,
Not trustworthy at all.

But Israel, trusting God,
Finds help and protection in Her.
Aaron's house, trusting God,
Finds help and protection in Him.
They, who are awed by God
And trusting God,
Find help and protection in Her.

יְיָ זְכָרָנוּ יְבָרֵךְ,
יְבָרֵךְ אֶת בֵּית יִשְׂרָאֵל,
יְבָרֵךְ אֶת בֵּית אַהֲרֹן:
יְבָרֵךְ יִרְאֵי יְיָ,
הַקְּטַנִּים עִם הַגְּדֹלִים:
יֹסֵף יְיָ עֲלֵיכֶם,
עֲלֵיכֶם וְעַל בְּנֵיכֶם:
בְּרוּכִים אַתֶּם לַייָ,
עֹשֵׂה שָׁמַיִם וָאָרֶץ:
הַשָּׁמַיִם שָׁמַיִם לַייָ,
וְהָאָרֶץ נָתַן לִבְנֵי אָדָם:
לֹא הַמֵּתִים יְהַלְלוּ יָהּ,
וְלֹא כָּל יֹרְדֵי דוּמָה:
וַאֲנַחְנוּ נְבָרֵךְ יָהּ,
מֵעַתָּה וְעַד עוֹלָם, הַלְלוּיָהּ:

קדש
ורחץ
כרפס
יחץ
מגיד
רחצה
מוציא
מצה
מרור
כורך
שלחן עורך
צפון
ברך
הלל
נרצה

YAH, be mindful of us.
Bless us.
Bless the house of Israel,
Bless the house of Aaron.
Bless those awed by You.
Both the little with the big.
Keep us and our children
growing in blessing.
And we, with the grace of the God
Who fashions Heaven and Earth,
Will bless all of you.

While Heaven is God's Heaven,
Earth is for the children
of the soil.

Being dead
we cannot celebrate YAH,
Or being downcast and speechless.
Yes! We will bless YAH
in the Now,
As well as in the long run.

Celebrate YAH!

אָהַבְתִּי כִּי יִשְׁמַע יְיָ,
אֶת קוֹלִי תַּחֲנוּנָי:
כִּי הִטָּה אָזְנוֹ לִי וּבְיָמַי אֶקְרָא:
אֲפָפוּנִי חֶבְלֵי מָוֶת,
וּמְצָרֵי שְׁאוֹל מְצָאוּנִי צָרָה וְיָגוֹן אֶמְצָא:
וּבְשֵׁם יְיָ אֶקְרָא,
אָנָּה יְיָ מַלְּטָה נַפְשִׁי:
חַנּוּן יְיָ וְצַדִּיק,
וֵאלֹהֵינוּ מְרַחֵם:
שֹׁמֵר פְּתָאִים יְיָ דַּלּוֹתִי וְלִי יְהוֹשִׁיעַ:
שׁוּבִי נַפְשִׁי לִמְנוּחָיְכִי,
כִּי יְיָ גָּמַל עָלָיְכִי:
כִּי חִלַּצְתָּ נַפְשִׁי מִמָּוֶת אֶת עֵינִי מִן דִּמְעָה,
אֶת רַגְלִי מִדֶּחִי:
אֶתְהַלֵּךְ לִפְנֵי יְיָ,
בְּאַרְצוֹת הַחַיִּים:
הֶאֱמַנְתִּי כִּי אֲדַבֵּר,
אֲנִי עָנִיתִי מְאֹד:
אֲנִי אָמַרְתִּי בְחָפְזִי כָּל הָאָדָם כֹּזֵב:

I hope that YAH hears
my pleading voice.
You have inclined Your ear to me
The days I called before.
Then I was enveloped
by the threat of death.
The demons of Hell had attacked me.
I found only hurt and pain.
I called out for YAH:
"Please, YAH, free my soul,
Being gracious and caring!"
Our God showed mercy
to a poor fool like me
He gave protection.
Soul of mine – be at rest!
YAH has been kind to you.
You have released my life from death,
My eyes from weeping,
My feet from faltering.
Now I can walk before YAH
among the living on the land.
Being greatly chastened,
I have come to faith –
Instead of blaming people,
Calling them all deceivers.

מָה אָשִׁיב לַייָ,
כָּל תַּגְמוּלוֹהִי עָלָי:
כּוֹס יְשׁוּעוֹת אֶשָּׂא,
וּבְשֵׁם יְיָ אֶקְרָא:
נְדָרַי לַייָ אֲשַׁלֵּם,
נֶגְדָה נָּא לְכָל עַמּוֹ:
יָקָר בְּעֵינֵי יְיָ הַמָּוְתָה לַחֲסִידָיו:
אָנָּה יְיָ כִּי אֲנִי עַבְדֶּךָ אֲנִי עַבְדְּךָ,
בֶּן אֲמָתֶךָ פִּתַּחְתָּ לְמוֹסֵרָי:
לְךָ אֶזְבַּח זֶבַח תּוֹדָה וּבְשֵׁם יְיָ אֶקְרָא:
נְדָרַי לַייָ אֲשַׁלֵּם נֶגְדָה נָּא לְכָל עַמּוֹ:
בְּחַצְרוֹת בֵּית יְיָ בְּתוֹכֵכִי יְרוּשָׁלָיִם הַלְלוּיָהּ:

What can I offer to YAH
for all the kindness
You have given me as a gift?
Let me raise the redeeming chalice
and invoke YAH's Name.
Thus will I pay my debt
In front of all Your people.
The death of the devout
is too expensive in YAH's view.
Please, YAH!
I want to serve You
as my mother serves You.
You have freed me from my bondage.
No slaughter but thanksgiving
do I offer to You.
Thus do I pay my debt
in front of all His people
who are gathered in His courts,
YAH's Jerusalem home.
HalleluYAH! Celebrate YAH!

(Psalms 116)

הַלְלוּ אֶת יְיָ כָּל גּוֹיִם,
שַׁבְּחוּהוּ כָּל הָאֻמִּים:
כִּי גָבַר עָלֵינוּ חַסְדּוֹ,
וֶאֱמֶת יְיָ לְעוֹלָם הַלְלוּיָהּ:

הוֹדוּ לַייָ כִּי טוֹב,
כִּי לְעוֹלָם חַסְדּוֹ:
יֹאמַר נָא יִשְׂרָאֵל,
כִּי לְעוֹלָם חַסְדּוֹ:
יֹאמְרוּ נָא בֵית אַהֲרֹן,
כִּי לְעוֹלָם חַסְדּוֹ:
יֹאמְרוּ נָא יִרְאֵי יְיָ,
כִּי לְעוֹלָם חַסְדּוֹ:

קדש
ורחץ
כרפס
יחץ
מגיד
רחצה
מוציא
מצה
מרור
כורך
שלחן עורך
צפון
ברך
הלל
נרצה

All You nations Celebrate YAH!
All peoples praise Her.
Overwhelming us
with Her Grace and His Truth.
In time and eternity.
HalleluYAH! (Psalms 117)

YAH is good! Thank Him!
He is kind to all the world's beings.
Israel! Say it out loud;
He is kind to all the world's beings.
Aaron's kin! Say it in public!
He is kind to all the world's beings.
You who are in awe of YAH! Proclaim it!
He is kind to all the world's beings.

מִן הַמֵּצַר קָרָאתִי יָּהּ,
עָנָנִי בַמֶּרְחָב יָהּ:
יְיָ לִי לֹא אִירָא,
מַה יַּעֲשֶׂה לִי אָדָם:
יְיָ לִי בְּעֹזְרָי,
וַאֲנִי אֶרְאֶה בְשֹׂנְאָי:
טוֹב לַחֲסוֹת בַּייָ,
מִבְּטֹחַ בָּאָדָם:
טוֹב לַחֲסוֹת בַּייָ מִבְּטֹחַ בִּנְדִיבִים:
כָּל גּוֹיִם סְבָבוּנִי בְּשֵׁם יְיָ כִּי אֲמִילַם:
סַבּוּנִי גַם סְבָבוּנִי בְּשֵׁם יְיָ כִּי אֲמִילַם:
סַבּוּנִי כִדְבֹרִים דֹּעֲכוּ כְּאֵשׁ קוֹצִים,
בְּשֵׁם יְיָ כִּי אֲמִילַם:
דָּחֹה דְחִיתַנִי לִנְפֹּל,
וַייָ עֲזָרָנִי:
עָזִּי וְזִמְרָת יָהּ, וַיְהִי לִי לִישׁוּעָה:

I called on You in my distress.
You, YAH, answered me with largesse.
As long as YAH is my support
what can mere mortals do to me?
Help me, YAH,
through those who help me.
Then I can see to my foes.
Better to trust You, YAH,
Than to rely on dole from the wealthy.
Though racists want to trap me,
Just by invoking YAH,
I will disperse them.
Though they besiege me,
Just by invoking YAH,
I will disperse them.
Like stinging wasps
they want to attack me,
Like a fire of thorns
they wish to scorch me.
Just by invoking YAH
I will disperse them.
They shove me to make me fall,
YAH comes to my aid.
My forceful song is YAH.
That was what saved me.

קוֹל רִנָּה וִישׁוּעָה בְּאָהֳלֵי צַדִּיקִים,
יְמִין יְיָ עֹשָׂה חָיִל:
יְמִין יְיָ רוֹמֵמָה, יְמִין יְיָ עֹשָׂה חָיִל:
לֹא אָמוּת כִּי אֶחְיֶה, וַאֲסַפֵּר מַעֲשֵׂי יָהּ:
יַסֹּר יִסְּרַנִּי יָּהּ, וְלַמָּוֶת לֹא נְתָנָנִי:
פִּתְחוּ לִי שַׁעֲרֵי צֶדֶק, אָבֹא בָם אוֹדֶה יָהּ:
זֶה הַשַּׁעַר לַייָ, צַדִּיקִים יָבֹאוּ בוֹ:
אוֹדְךָ כִּי עֲנִיתָנִי, וַתְּהִי לִי לִישׁוּעָה:
אוֹדְךָ כִּי עֲנִיתָנִי, וַתְּהִי לִי לִישׁוּעָה:
אֶבֶן מָאֲסוּ הַבּוֹנִים, הָיְתָה לְרֹאשׁ פִּנָּה:
אֶבֶן מָאֲסוּ הַבּוֹנִים, הָיְתָה לְרֹאשׁ פִּנָּה:
מֵאֵת יְיָ הָיְתָה זֹּאת, הִיא נִפְלָאת בְּעֵינֵינוּ:
מֵאֵת יְיָ הָיְתָה זֹּאת, הִיא נִפְלָאת בְּעֵינֵינוּ:
זֶה הַיּוֹם עָשָׂה יְיָ, נָגִילָה וְנִשְׂמְחָה בוֹ:
זֶה הַיּוֹם עָשָׂה יְיָ, נָגִילָה וְנִשְׂמְחָה בוֹ:

קדש
ורחץ
כרפס
יחץ
מגיד
רחצה
מוציא
מצה
מרור
כורך
שלחן עורך
צפון
ברך
הלל
נרצה

A happy chant of being saved
echoes through
the dwellings of the just.
YAH's right arm is like an army.
Like an army, YAH's right arm
overcomes all.
I will not die!
I will live
to tell of YAH's works.
Though YAH chastens me,
He did not deliver me to death.
Gates! Open wide to fairness.
Entering them I give thanks to YAH.
Truly this is YAH's gate,
The virtuous gain entrance to it.

Repeat two times

I thank You – You did answer me.
In humbling me You saved my life.

Repeat two times

I, who was cast aside
like an unwieldy boulder,
am now made the cap stone.

Repeat two times

This was YAH's doing.
I am still surprised and amazed.

Repeat two times

This sure is the very day
that YAH has done it.
Come let us now all
delight and rejoice.

Kadesh
Urḥatz
Karpas
Yaḥatz
Maggid
Raḥtzah
Motzi
Matzah
Maror
Korekh
Shulḥan Orekh
Tzafun
Barekh
Hallel
Nirtzah

אָנָּא יְיָ הוֹשִׁיעָה נָּא.

אָנָּא יְיָ הוֹשִׁיעָה נָּא.

אָנָּא יְיָ הַצְלִיחָה נָּא.

אָנָּא יְיָ הַצְלִיחָה נָּא:

בָּרוּךְ הַבָּא בְּשֵׁם יְיָ,

בֵּרַכְנוּכֶם מִבֵּית יְיָ:

בָּרוּךְ הַבָּא בְּשֵׁם יְיָ,

בֵּרַכְנוּכֶם מִבֵּית יְיָ:

אֵל יְיָ וַיָּאֶר לָנוּ,

אִסְרוּ חַג בַּעֲבֹתִים עַד קַרְנוֹת הַמִּזְבֵּחַ:

אֵל יְיָ וַיָּאֶר לָנוּ,

אִסְרוּ חַג בַּעֲבֹתִים עַד קַרְנוֹת הַמִּזְבֵּחַ:

אֵלִי אַתָּה וְאוֹדֶךָּ אֱלֹהַי אֲרוֹמְמֶךָּ:

אֵלִי אַתָּה וְאוֹדֶךָּ אֱלֹהַי אֲרוֹמְמֶךָּ:

הוֹדוּ לַיְיָ כִּי טוֹב,   כִּי לְעוֹלָם חַסְדּוֹ:

הוֹדוּ לַיְיָ כִּי טוֹב, כִּי לְעוֹלָם חַסְדּוֹ

Oh, YAH! Do help us!
Oh, YAH! Do help us!

Oh, YAH! Let us succeed!
Oh, YAH! Let us succeed!

Repeat two times

As you come in YAH's Name,
we greet and bless you
from YAH's home.

Repeat two times

YAH enlightens us mightily.
Let us decorate His altar with myrtles,
attached to the corners of His shrine.

Repeat two times

I am grateful that You are my God,
Oh exalted Divine One.

Repeat two times

YAH is good! Thank Him!
He is kind to all the world's beings.

יְהַלְלוּךָ יְיָ אֱלֹהֵינוּ כָּל מַעֲשֶׂיךָ,
וַחֲסִידֶיךָ צַדִּיקִים עוֹשֵׂי רְצוֹנֶךָ,
וְכָל עַמְּךָ בֵּית יִשְׂרָאֵל בְּרִנָּה יוֹדוּ וִיבָרְכוּ וִישַׁבְּחוּ וִיפָאֲרוּ
וִירוֹמְמוּ וְיַעֲרִיצוּ וְיַקְדִּישׁוּ וְיַמְלִיכוּ אֶת שִׁמְךָ מַלְכֵּנוּ, תָּמִיד.
כִּי לְךָ טוֹב לְהוֹדוֹת וּלְשִׁמְךָ נָאֶה לְזַמֵּר,
כִּי מֵעוֹלָם וְעַד עוֹלָם אַתָּה אֵל:

It's late and you're tired. You're satiated with food, wine and good Torah and all you want to do now is go to sleep. Hang on a bit longer, for the best is yet to come. Worship! Sing the Songs, the Holy Songs! (But if you want to skip then jump down to the drinking of the Fourth Cup.)

הוֹדוּ לַיְיָ כִּי טוֹב,
כִּי לְעוֹלָם חַסְדּוֹ:
הוֹדוּ לֵאלֹהֵי הָאֱלֹהִים,
כִּי לְעוֹלָם חַסְדּוֹ:
הוֹדוּ לַאֲדֹנֵי הָאֲדֹנִים,
כִּי לְעוֹלָם חַסְדּוֹ:
לְעֹשֵׂה נִפְלָאוֹת גְּדֹלוֹת לְבַדּוֹ,
כִּי לְעוֹלָם חַסְדּוֹ:
לְעֹשֵׂה הַשָּׁמַיִם בִּתְבוּנָה,
כִּי לְעוֹלָם חַסְדּוֹ:
לְרוֹקַע הָאָרֶץ עַל הַמָּיִם,
כִּי לְעוֹלָם חַסְדּוֹ:
לְעֹשֵׂה אוֹרִים גְּדֹלִים,
כִּי לְעוֹלָם חַסְדּוֹ:

All Your creation celebrates You YAH, our God
Your devout ones, Tzaddikim, who do what You order
All Your people, the family of God-wrestlers
In song offer gratitude, always worshipping, acclaiming,
Adoring, dignifying, honoring, holding Your Name sacred and regal.
Being grateful to You is so good
Singing paeans to Your renown is our pleasure
In all universes You are God.

(Psalms 118)

It's late and you're tired. You're satiated with food, wine and good Torah and all you want to do now is go to sleep. Hang on a bit longer, for the best is yet to come. Worship! Sing the Songs, the Holy Songs! (But if you want to skip then jump down to the drinking of the Fourth Cup.)

Give thanks to YAH for all the goodness
He is kind to all the world's beings.
Give thanks to the God of gods
He is kind to all the world's beings.
Give thanks to the Master of masters
He is kind to all the world's beings.
For doing great wonders on His own
He is kind to all the world's beings.
For making the heavens with understanding
He is kind to all the world's beings.
For spreading out the Earth on the waters
He is kind to all the world's beings.
For producing great illuminations
He is kind to all the world's beings.
The sun to dominate during the day
He is kind to all the world's beings.
The moon and the stars to dominate at night
He is kind to all the world's beings.
For punishing Mitzraim through their firstborn
He is kind to all the world's beings.

אֶת הַשֶּׁמֶשׁ לְמֶמְשֶׁלֶת בַּיּוֹם,
כִּי לְעוֹלָם חַסְדּוֹ:
אֶת הַיָּרֵחַ וְכוֹכָבִים לְמֶמְשְׁלוֹת בַּלָּיְלָה,
כִּי לְעוֹלָם חַסְדּוֹ:
לְמַכֵּה מִצְרַיִם בִּבְכוֹרֵיהֶם,
כִּי לְעוֹלָם חַסְדּוֹ:
וַיּוֹצֵא יִשְׂרָאֵל מִתּוֹכָם,
כִּי לְעוֹלָם חַסְדּוֹ:
בְּיָד חֲזָקָה וּבִזְרוֹעַ נְטוּיָה,
כִּי לְעוֹלָם חַסְדּוֹ:
לְגֹזֵר יַם סוּף לִגְזָרִים,
כִּי לְעוֹלָם חַסְדּוֹ:
וְהֶעֱבִיר יִשְׂרָאֵל בְּתוֹכוֹ,
כִּי לְעוֹלָם חַסְדּוֹ:
וְנִעֵר פַּרְעֹה וְחֵילוֹ בְיַם סוּף,
כִּי לְעוֹלָם חַסְדּוֹ:
לְמוֹלִיךְ עַמּוֹ בַּמִּדְבָּר,
כִּי לְעוֹלָם חַסְדּוֹ:
לְמַכֵּה מְלָכִים גְּדֹלִים,
כִּי לְעוֹלָם חַסְדּוֹ:
וַיַּהֲרֹג מְלָכִים אַדִּירִים,
כִּי לְעוֹלָם חַסְדּוֹ:
לְסִיחוֹן מֶלֶךְ הָאֱמֹרִי,
כִּי לְעוֹלָם חַסְדּוֹ:
וּלְעוֹג מֶלֶךְ הַבָּשָׁן,
כִּי לְעוֹלָם חַסְדּוֹ:
וְנָתַן אַרְצָם לְנַחֲלָה,
כִּי לְעוֹלָם חַסְדּוֹ:
נַחֲלָה לְיִשְׂרָאֵל עַבְדּוֹ,
כִּי לְעוֹלָם חַסְדּוֹ:
שֶׁבְּשִׁפְלֵנוּ זָכַר לָנוּ,
כִּי לְעוֹלָם חַסְדּוֹ:
וַיִּפְרְקֵנוּ מִצָּרֵינוּ,
כִּי לְעוֹלָם חַסְדּוֹ:
נֹתֵן לֶחֶם לְכָל בָּשָׂר,
כִּי לְעוֹלָם חַסְדּוֹ:
הוֹדוּ לְאֵל הַשָּׁמָיִם,
כִּי לְעוֹלָם חַסְדּוֹ:

קדש
ורחץ
כרפס
יחץ
מגיד
רחצה
מוציא
מצה
מרור
כורך
שלחן עורך
צפון
ברך
הלל
נרצה

And for extracting Israel from amongst them
He is kind to all the world's beings.
With a determined hand and an outstretched arm
He is kind to all the world's beings.
For dividing the Reed Sea into pathways
He is kind to all the world's beings.
And for bringing Israel across through them
He is kind to all the world's beings.
And for shaking Pharaoh and his army into the Reed Sea
He is kind to all the world's beings.
For leading His people into the wilderness
He is kind to all the world's beings.
And for smiting great kings
He is kind to all the world's beings.
And for killing mighty kings
He is kind to all the world's beings.
For Siḥon, king of the Amorites
He is kind to all the world's beings.
And for Og, king of Bashan
He is kind to all the world's beings.
And for giving their land to inherit
He is kind to all the world's beings.
A heritage to Israel His servant
He is kind to all the world's beings.
For remembering us when we were down
He is kind to all the world's beings.
And for breaking us out from our narrow constraints
He is kind to all the world's beings.
For providing food to all flesh
He is kind to all the world's beings.
Thanks to God of the Heavens
He is kind to all the world's beings.

(Psalms 136)

נִשְׁמַת כָּל חַי תְּבָרֵךְ
אֶת שִׁמְךָ יְיָ אֱלֹהֵינוּ.
וְרוּחַ כָּל בָּשָׂר,
תְּפָאֵר וּתְרוֹמֵם זִכְרְךָ מַלְכֵּנוּ תָּמִיד,
מִן הָעוֹלָם וְעַד הָעוֹלָם אַתָּה אֵל.
וּמִבַּלְעָדֶיךָ אֵין לָנוּ מֶלֶךְ גּוֹאֵל וּמוֹשִׁיעַ,
פּוֹדֶה וּמַצִּיל וּמְפַרְנֵס (וְעוֹנֶה) וּמְרַחֵם,
בְּכָל עֵת צָרָה וְצוּקָה.
אֵין לָנוּ מֶלֶךְ (עוֹזֵר וְסוֹמֵךְ) אֶלָּא אָתָּה:
אֱלֹהֵי הָרִאשׁוֹנִים וְהָאַחֲרוֹנִים,
אֱלוֹהַּ כָּל בְּרִיּוֹת, אֲדוֹן כָּל תּוֹלָדוֹת,
הַמְהֻלָּל (בְּכֹל) בְּרֹב הַתִּשְׁבָּחוֹת,
הַמְנַהֵג עוֹלָמוֹ בְּחֶסֶד וּבְרִיּוֹתָיו בְּרַחֲמִים.
וַיְיָ (עֵר, הִנֵּה) לֹא יָנוּם וְלֹא יִישָׁן,
הַמְעוֹרֵר יְשֵׁנִים וְהַמֵּקִיץ נִרְדָּמִים,
(מְחַיֶּה מֵתִים וְרוֹפֵא חוֹלִים,
פּוֹקֵחַ עִוְרִים וְזוֹקֵף כְּפוּפִים) וְהַמֵּשִׂיחַ אִלְּמִים,
וְהַמַּתִּיר אֲסוּרִים, וְהַסּוֹמֵךְ נוֹפְלִים,
וְהַזּוֹקֵף כְּפוּפִים,
(וְהַמְפַעֲנֵחַ נֶעְלָמִים) וּלְךָ לְבַדְּךָ אֲנַחְנוּ מוֹדִים.

Worship

Nishmat

All breathing life
adores Your Name
YAH, Our God -
All flesh alive
is raised to ecstasy
each time we become aware of You!
Beyond endless Time and Space that's vast
You are Divine
Only You are the One who
ultimately extricates and frees,
ransoms, saves and sustains us
and cares when we are in distress.
You, You alone secure our lives.

You are ultimate Cause and ultimate Effect,
Source of all Creation,
You manifest in all birthing,
In every compliment it is You we praise.
You manage Your Universe with kindness
and compassion to all beings within it.

YAH, ever awake and ever alert!
You rouse us from the deepest sleep,
You give words to the speechless,
You release the imprisoned,
You support the stumbling,
You give dignity to the downtrodden.
Every appreciation we offer is Yours.

(וְ)אִלּוּ פִינוּ מָלֵא שִׁירָה כַּיָּם,
וּלְשׁוֹנֵנוּ רִנָּה כַּהֲמוֹן גַּלָּיו,
וְשִׂפְתוֹתֵינוּ שֶׁבַח כְּמֶרְחֲבֵי רָקִיעַ,
וְעֵינֵינוּ מְאִירוֹת כַּשֶּׁמֶשׁ וְכַיָּרֵחַ,
וְיָדֵינוּ פְרוּשׂוֹת כְּנִשְׁרֵי שָׁמָיִם,
וְרַגְלֵינוּ קַלּוֹת כָּאַיָּלוֹת,
אֵין (אָנוּ) אֲנַחְנוּ מַסְפִּיקִים,
לְהוֹדוֹת לְךָ יְיָ אֱלֹהֵינוּ וֵאלֹהֵי אֲבוֹתֵינוּ,
וּלְבָרֵךְ אֶת שְׁמֶךָ (שִׁמְךָ מַלְכֵּנוּ) עַל אַחַת מֵאָלֶף אֶלֶף אַלְפֵי
אֲלָפִים וְרִבֵּי רְבָבוֹת פְּעָמִים, הַטּוֹבוֹת,
שֶׁעָשִׂיתָ עִם אֲבוֹתֵינוּ וְעִמָּנוּ.

(מִלְּפָנִים) מִמִּצְרַיִם גְּאַלְתָּנוּ יְיָ אֱלֹהֵינוּ,
וּמִבֵּית עֲבָדִים פְּדִיתָנוּ, בְּרָעָב זַנְתָּנוּ, וּבְשָׂבָע כִּלְכַּלְתָּנוּ,
מֵחֶרֶב הִצַּלְתָּנוּ,
וּמִדֶּבֶר מִלַּטְתָּנוּ,
וּמֵחֳלָיִם רָעִים וְרַבִּים וְנֶאֱמָנִים דִּלִּיתָנוּ:
עַד הֵנָּה עֲזָרוּנוּ רַחֲמֶיךָ,
וְלֹא עֲזָבוּנוּ חֲסָדֶיךָ (יְיָ אֱלֹהֵינוּ)
וְאַל תִּטְּשֵׁנוּ יְיָ אֱלֹהֵינוּ לָנֶצַח.

If ocean-full our mouth were with music,
Our tongues singing like the ceaseless surf,
Our lips praising You to the skies,
Our eyes blazing like sun and moon,
Our arms spread like soaring eagles,
Our legs sprinting like those of deer,
We could not thank You enough,
YAH! Our God, our ancestors' God!
Neither could we celebrate by naming
The times exceeding millions
The places exceeding billions
The favors You did for our ancestors and for us.

YAH! Oh God! From oppression
You redeemed us.
Now we can never be at home in slavery –
During famines You fed us enough to live on,
You shielded us from wars and plagues,
From diseases of body and mind You pulled us through.
To this moment Your caring helped us
We never lacked Your kindness.
Please don't ever abandon us God!

Kadesh
Urḥatz
Karpas
Yaḥatz
Maggid
Raḥtzah
Motzi
Matzah
Maror
Korekh
Shulḥan Orekh
Tzafun
Barekh
Hallel
Nirtzah

עַל כֵּן אֵבָרִים שֶׁפִּלַּגְתָּ בָּנוּ,
וְרוּחַ וּנְשָׁמָה שֶׁנָּפַחְתָּ בְּאַפֵּינוּ,
וְלָשׁוֹן אֲשֶׁר שַׂמְתָּ בְּפִינוּ,
הֵן הֵם יוֹדוּ וִיבָרְכוּ וִישַׁבְּחוּ וִיפָאֲרוּ וִירוֹמְמוּ וְיַעֲרִיצוּ
וְיַקְדִּישׁוּ וְיַמְלִיכוּ אֶת שִׁמְךָ מַלְכֵּנוּ (תָּמִיד),
כִּי כָל פֶּה לְךָ יוֹדֶה,
וְכָל לָשׁוֹן לְךָ תִשָּׁבַע (וְכָל עַיִן לְךָ תְצַפֶּה),
וְכָל בֶּרֶךְ לְךָ תִכְרַע,
וְכָל קוֹמָה לְפָנֶיךָ תִשְׁתַּחֲוֶה,
וְכָל לְבָבוֹת יִירָאוּךָ,
וְכָל קֶרֶב וּכְלָיוֹת יְזַמְּרוּ לִשְׁמֶךָ.
כַּדָּבָר שֶׁכָּתוּב, כָּל עַצְמוֹתַי תֹּאמַרְנָה יְיָ מִי כָמוֹךָ.
מַצִּיל עָנִי מֵחָזָק מִמֶּנּוּ, וְעָנִי וְאֶבְיוֹן מִגֹּזְלוֹ.

(שַׁוְעַת עֲנִיִּים אַתָּה תִשְׁמַע צַעֲקַת הַדַּל תַּקְשִׁיב וְתוֹשִׁיעַ) מִי יִדְמֶה לָּךְ,
וּמִי יִשְׁוֶה לָּךְ וּמִי יַעֲרָךְ לָךְ:
הָאֵל הַגָּדוֹל הַגִּבּוֹר וְהַנּוֹרָא,
אֵל עֶלְיוֹן קֹנֵה שָׁמַיִם וָאָרֶץ:
נְהַלֶּלְךָ וּנְשַׁבֵּחֲךָ וּנְפָאֶרְךָ וּנְבָרֵךְ אֶת־שֵׁם קָדְשֶׁךָ. כָּאָמוּר,
לְדָוִד, בָּרְכִי נַפְשִׁי אֶת יְיָ,
וְכָל קְרָבַי אֶת שֵׁם קָדְשׁוֹ:

DEEPENING

This prayer – "All Breathing Life" – is one of the most beautiful prayers in our entire liturgy.* It is a sublime example of worship prayer. It follows praise, it is born out of praise – it is worship. And what is left of us lies prostrate on the floor as our souls expand outwards and upwards, backwards and upwards, reaching up higher and higher to touch and be touched by the Source of All Life.

* The origins of this prayer go back to at least Talmudic times. It is first referred to in the Talmud Bavli *Pesaḥim* 118a.

Our limbs want each to thank You!
The air of each breath You breathed into us,
Their very substance bless with gratitude with praise and celebration,
Honoring that exalted Holiness,
So majestic, that is Your fame!
Our speech is appreciation,
Our expression an oath of loyalty,
Our attitude surrender,
Our stance before You obedience,
Our feelings overwhelming awe,
Our inners singing scales of Your Names,
As it is written:
"All my very essence exclaims:
'YAH! Who's like You?' You inspire the gentle to stand up to the bully,
The poor disempowered to stand up to the thug.

No other can claim to be what You are;
No other can pretend to be the Great God,
The Mighty, The Awesome, The God Most High,
Yet nesting in Heavens and Earth!
So we will keep celebrating and delighting and blessing Your Holy Name with David:
"YAH! Breathes my soul out to You,
All my inners pulse with You!"

הָאֵל בְּתַעֲצֻמוֹת עֻזֶּךָ,
הַגָּדוֹל בִּכְבוֹד שְׁמֶךָ.
הַגִּבּוֹר לָנֶצַח וְהַנּוֹרָא בְּנוֹרְאוֹתֶיךָ.
הַמֶּלֶךְ הַיּוֹשֵׁב עַל כִּסֵּא רָם וְנִשָּׂא:

שׁוֹכֵן עַד, מָרוֹם וְקָדוֹשׁ שְׁמוֹ:
וְכָתוּב, רַנְּנוּ צַדִּיקִים בַּיְיָ, לַיְשָׁרִים נָאוָה תְהִלָּה.
בְּפִי יְשָׁרִים תִּתְהַלָּל.
וּבְדִבְרֵי צַדִּיקִים תִּתְבָּרַךְ. וּבִלְשׁוֹן חֲסִידִים תִּתְרוֹמָם.
וּבְקֶרֶב קְדוֹשִׁים תִּתְקַדָּשׁ:

וּבְמַקְהֲלוֹת רִבְבוֹת עַמְּךָ בֵּית יִשְׂרָאֵל,
בְּרִנָּה יִתְפָּאֵר שִׁמְךָ מַלְכֵּנוּ,
בְּכָל דּוֹר וָדוֹר, שֶׁכֵּן חוֹבַת כָּל הַיְצוּרִים,
לְפָנֶיךָ יְיָ אֱלֹהֵינוּ,
וֵאלֹהֵי אֲבוֹתֵינוּ,
לְהוֹדוֹת לְהַלֵּל לְשַׁבֵּחַ לְפָאֵר לְרוֹמֵם
לְהַדֵּר לְבָרֵךְ לְעַלֵּה וּלְקַלֵּס,
עַל כָּל דִּבְרֵי שִׁירוֹת וְתִשְׁבְּחוֹת דָּוִד בֶּן יִשַׁי עַבְדְּךָ מְשִׁיחֶךָ:

Ha'El

Potent God Force!
Magnanimous in Glory,
Ever-prevailing.
Awesome Mystery!
Majestic One, who presides over all destiny!

Shokhein Ad

Eternal Shekhinah, Holy Beyond,
Saints sing YAH!
In harmony with decent folks;
Good people exalt You,
Saints are Your blessing,
Devotees sanctify You.

And You delight in our inner Holiness.
Wherever crowds are gathered,
Generation after generation,
The house of Israel,
The people of Your flock
Sing to You,
Adoring Your Name
– Oh, our Prince.

God, our parents' God!
All creatures are committed
to be grateful, celebrate and praise,
to exalt, worship and glorify,
to bless, esteem and adore,
Beyond all the songs and tributes of David,
Your empowered servant.

Kadesh
Urḥatz
Karpas
Yaḥatz
Maggid
Raḥtzah
Motzi
Matzah
Maror
Korekh
Shulḥan Orekh
Tzafun
Barekh
Hallel
Nirtzah

(וּבְכֵן) **יִשְׁתַּבַּח** שִׁמְךָ לָעַד מַלְכֵּנוּ,
הָאֵל הַמֶּלֶךְ הַגָּדוֹל וְהַקָּדוֹשׁ בַּשָּׁמַיִם וּבָאָרֶץ.
כִּי לְךָ נָאֶה, יְיָ אֱלֹהֵינוּ וֵאלֹהֵי אֲבוֹתֵינוּ (לְעוֹלָם וָעֶד):
שִׁיר וּשְׁבָחָה, הַלֵּל וְזִמְרָה,
עֹז וּמֶמְשָׁלָה,
נֶצַח, גְּדֻלָּה וּגְבוּרָה,
תְּהִלָּה וְתִפְאֶרֶת, קְדֻשָּׁה וּמַלְכוּת.
בְּרָכוֹת וְהוֹדָאוֹת מֵעַתָּה וְעַד עוֹלָם
(אַתָּה אֵל). בָּרוּךְ אַתָּה יְיָ,
אֵל מֶלֶךְ גָּדוֹל (וּמְהֻלָּל) בַּתִּשְׁבָּחוֹת,
אֵל הַהוֹדָאוֹת, אֲדוֹן הַנִּפְלָאוֹת,
הַבּוֹחֵר בְּשִׁירֵי זִמְרָה,
מֶלֶךְ (יָחִיד) אֵל חֵי הָעוֹלָמִים:

קדש
ורחץ
כרפס
יחץ
מגיד
רחצה
מוציא
מצה
מרור
כורך
שלחן עורך
צפון
ברך
הלל
נרצה

Yishtabaḥ

Your Name be praised, always,
Majestic One.
Powerful and gentle Source,
Making Heaven and Earth sacred.
It is our pleasure to dedicate to You,
Our God and Our parents' God,
Time and again:
Music and Celebration,
Jubilation and Symphony,
Fortissimo, Anthem,
Victory March, Largo Forte,
Paean and Hymn,
Sanctus and Maestoso,
Laudo and Aria,
Celebrating Your Divine reputation
in every realm.
We worship You YAH,
Generous, Great, Regal One
Who is the One
to whom we offer all these.

God whom we appreciate,
Source of all wonder,
Fountain of all souls
Author of all that happens,
Who delights in music and chant,
Origin of Unity.
You are the Life
that flows through all the worlds.
Amen.

הִנְנִי מוּכָן וּמְזֻמָּן לְקַיֵּם מִצְוַת כּוֹס רְבִיעִי מֵאַרְבַּע כּוֹסוֹת. לְשֵׁם יִחוּד קוּדְשָׁא בְּרִיךְ הוּא וּשְׁכִינְתֵּיהּ
עַל יְדֵי הַהוּא טָמִיר וְנֶעְלָם בְּשֵׁם כָּל יִשְׂרָאֵל:

בָּרוּךְ אַתָּה יְיָ, אֱלֹהֵינוּ מֶלֶךְ הָעוֹלָם, בּוֹרֵא פְּרִי הַגָּפֶן:

DEEPENING

This cup represents the World of *Assiyah* – the World of Physicality, which is the letter ה – the final letter in the Divine Name. While we have been given the opportunity to ascend to the heights of *Atzilut* – the World of Spiritual Existence – so we have created a channel for the Divine energy to descend into this World of Doing. This is expressed so beautifully in the next section – the Conclusion, in which we dance for Jerusalem – the Heavenly Jerusalem meeting the Earthly Jerusalem. May we all be privileged to dance there together next year.

good place to show the merging star!

Blessing after drinking wine:

בָּרוּךְ אַתָּה יְיָ, אֱלֹהֵינוּ מֶלֶךְ הָעוֹלָם, עַל הַגֶּפֶן וְעַל פְּרִי הַגֶּפֶן, וְעַל תְּנוּבַת הַשָּׂדֶה, וְעַל אֶרֶץ חֶמְדָּה טוֹבָה וּרְחָבָה, שֶׁרָצִיתָ וְהִנְחַלְתָּ לַאֲבוֹתֵינוּ, לֶאֱכוֹל מִפִּרְיָהּ וְלִשְׂבּוֹעַ מִטּוּבָהּ. רַחֵם נָא יְיָ אֱלֹהֵינוּ עַל יִשְׂרָאֵל עַמֶּךָ, וְעַל יְרוּשָׁלַיִם עִירֶךָ, וְעַל צִיּוֹן מִשְׁכַּן כְּבוֹדֶךָ, וְעַל מִזְבְּחֶךָ וְעַל הֵיכָלֶךָ. וּבְנֵה יְרוּשָׁלַיִם עִיר הַקֹּדֶשׁ בִּמְהֵרָה בְיָמֵינוּ, וְהַעֲלֵנוּ לְתוֹכָהּ, וְשַׂמְּחֵנוּ בְּבִנְיָנָהּ, וְנֹאכַל מִפִּרְיָהּ, וְנִשְׂבַּע מִטּוּבָהּ, וּנְבָרֶכְךָ עָלֶיהָ בִּקְדֻשָּׁה וּבְטָהֳרָה. (בשבת: וּרְצֵה וְהַחֲלִיצֵנוּ בְּיוֹם הַשַּׁבָּת הַזֶּה) וְשַׂמְּחֵנוּ בְּיוֹם חַג הַמַּצּוֹת הַזֶּה. כִּי אַתָּה יְיָ טוֹב וּמֵטִיב לַכֹּל, וְנוֹדֶה לְּךָ עַל הָאָרֶץ וְעַל פְּרִי הַגָּפֶן. בָּרוּךְ אַתָּה יְיָ, עַל הָאָרֶץ וְעַל פְּרִי הַגָּפֶן (בארץ ישראל: גַּפְנָהּ):

קדש
ורחץ
כרפס
יחץ
מגיד
רחצה
מוציא
מצה
מרור
כורך
שלחן עורך
צפון
ברך
הלל
נרצה

B-21

Fourth Cup

The Fourth Cup is drunk while leaning.

Here I am right now, ready and mindful to participate in the unification of the Transcendent Holy One with the Immanent Shekhinah through the ***fourth*** *of the Four Cups.*

Blessed are You, Lord our God, Majesty of the Universe, who brings into being the fruit of the vine.

Blessing after drinking wine:

Blessed are You, Lord our God, Majesty of the Universe, for the vine and for the fruit of the vine and for produce of the field, and for the beautiful, good and expansive land, which You willed as an inheritance to our ancestors to eat of its fruit and to be satisfied with its bounty. Oh Lord our God, have compassion upon us, upon Israel Your people, upon Jerusalem Your City, upon Zion the indwelling of Your Presence, upon Your altar and upon Your Temple. And rebuild the Holy City of Jerusalem speedily in our time, and bring us up into it to be joyous in its reestablishment and we will eat of her fruit and be satisfied through her bounty. And we will pour blessings upon You in Holiness and in Purity

[On Shabbat add: *May You desire our release on this Shabbat day*]

And You will make us rejoice on this Festival of Matzot, because You are the Lord that is Good and bestows Good to all, and we give thanks to You for the Land and for the fruits of the vine:

Blessed are You, Lord, for the Land and for the fruits of her vines

נִרְצָה

חֲסַל סִדּוּר פֶּסַח כְּהִלְכָתוֹ,
כְּכָל מִשְׁפָּטוֹ וְחֻקָּתוֹ.
כַּאֲשֶׁר זָכִינוּ
לְסַדֵּר אוֹתוֹ,
כֵּן נִזְכֶּה לַעֲשׂוֹתוֹ.
זָךְ שׁוֹכֵן מְעוֹנָה,
קוֹמֵם קְהַל
עֲדַת מִי מָנָה.
קָרֵב נַהֵל נִטְעֵי כַנָּה,
פְּדוּיִם לְצִיּוֹן בְּרִנָּה.

לְשָׁנָה הַבָּאָה בִּירוּשָׁלָיִם:

B-22

Nirtzah – And in conclusion…

We conclude the Seder ritual as a rite,
As we understood it and as it was beyond our understanding.
Just as we were blessed to experience it,
May we be blessed to realize it.
Ominous One, who dwells on High,
Raise us up, as a nation of renown.
May You soon gather Your beloved throng,
Redeemed we come to Zion, singing You our song.

NEXT YEAR IN JERUSALEM

NEXT YEAR IN THE REBUILT JERUSALEM

NEXT YEAR IN EARTHLY JERUSALEM –

A REFLECTION OF THE HEAVENLY JERUSALEM

Play Jerusalem (T.18 Revivaltime CD) and wind w M. Sklar El Shaddai! CD.

B-25
B-26

The following song is sung on the first night of Pesaḥ only. If you don't want to say them all, then choose your favorites.

וּבְכֵן "וַיְהִי בַּחֲצִי הַלַּיְלָה"

אָז רוֹב נִסִּים הִפְלֵאתָ בַּלַּיְלָה, בְּרֹאשׁ אַשְׁמוּרוֹת זֶה הַלַּיְלָה,
גֵּר צֶדֶק נִצַּחְתּוֹ כְּנֶחֱלַק לוֹ לַיְלָה, וַיְהִי בַּחֲצִי הַלַּיְלָה.
דַּנְתָּ מֶלֶךְ גְּרָר בַּחֲלוֹם הַלַּיְלָה, הִפְחַדְתָּ אֲרַמִּי בְּאֶמֶשׁ לַיְלָה,
וַיָּשַׂר יִשְׂרָאֵל לְמַלְאָךְ וַיּוּכַל לוֹ לַיְלָה, וַיְהִי בַּחֲצִי הַלַּיְלָה.
זֶרַע בְּכוֹרֵי פַתְרוֹס מָחַצְתָּ בַּחֲצִי הַלַּיְלָה, חֵילָם לֹא מָצְאוּ בְּקוּמָם בַּלַּיְלָה, טִיסַת נְגִיד חֲרֹשֶׁת סִלִּיתָ בְכוֹכְבֵי לַיְלָה,
וַיְהִי בַּחֲצִי הַלַּיְלָה.
יָעַץ מְחָרֵף לְנוֹפֵף אִוּוּי הוֹבַשְׁתָּ פְגָרָיו בַּלַּיְלָה, כָּרַע בֵּל וּמַצָּבוֹ בְּאִישׁוֹן לַיְלָה, לְאִישׁ חֲמוּדוֹת נִגְלָה רָז חֲזוֹת לַיְלָה, וַיְהִי בַּחֲצִי הַלַּיְלָה.
מִשְׁתַּכֵּר בִּכְלֵי קֹדֶשׁ נֶהֱרַג בּוֹ בַּלַּיְלָה, נוֹשַׁע מִבּוֹר אֲרָיוֹת פּוֹתֵר בִּעֲתוּתֵי לַיְלָה, שִׂנְאָה נָטַר אֲגָגִי וְכָתַב סְפָרִים בַּלַּיְלָה,
וַיְהִי בַּחֲצִי הַלַּיְלָה.
עוֹרַרְתָּ נִצְחֲךָ עָלָיו בְּנֶדֶד שְׁנַת לַיְלָה, פּוּרָה תִדְרוֹךְ לְשׁוֹמֵר מַה מִּלַּיְלָה,
צָרַח כַּשּׁוֹמֵר וְשָׂח אָתָא בֹקֶר וְגַם לַיְלָה, וַיְהִי בַּחֲצִי הַלַּיְלָה.
קָרֵב יוֹם אֲשֶׁר הוּא לֹא יוֹם וְלֹא לַיְלָה, רָם הוֹדַע כִּי לְךָ הַיּוֹם אַף לְךָ הַלַּיְלָה, שׁוֹמְרִים הַפְקֵד לְעִירְךָ כָּל הַיּוֹם וְכָל הַלַּיְלָה,
תָּאִיר כְּאוֹר יוֹם חֶשְׁכַת לַיְלָה, וַיְהִי בַּחֲצִי הַלַּיְלָה.

The following song is sung on the first night of Pesaḥ only. If you don't want to say them all, then choose your favorites.

Light in the Middle of Darkness

And it came to pass at midnight!
Then, in times of old, You performed many wonders by night,
At the beginning of the watches of this night.
The righteous convert [Abraham], You gave victory by dividing for him the night.
And it came to pass at midnight!

You judged the king of Gerar [Avimelekh] in a dream at night.
You frightened the Aramean [Lavan] in the dark of the night.
Yisrael fought an angel and overcame him at night.
And it came to pass at midnight!

You stilled the firstborn of Patros [Mitzraim] at midnight.
They did not find their host upon arising at night.
The army of the prince of Ḥaroshet [Sisera], You swept away with the stars of the night.
And it came to pass at midnight!

The blasphemer [Sanḥeirev] planned to raise his hand against Jerusalem, but You turned them into dry corpses in the night.
Bel with its pedestal was overturned in the darkness of the night.
To the man You delighted in [Daniel] was revealed the secret of the visions of the night.
And it came to pass at midnight!

He who became drunk from the holy vessels [Belshazzar] was killed that very night.
Saved from the lions' den was he [Daniel] who interpreted the horrors of the night.
The Aggagi [Haman] nursed hatred and wrote edicts by night.
And it came to pass at midnight!

You began Your victory over him with disturbing [Aḥashverosh's] sleep at night.
Trample the winepress for those who ask the watchman, "What will come of the night?"
He will shout like a watchman, and say: "Morning shall came and also night."
And it came to pass at midnight!

Bring close the Day [the Messiah] that is neither day nor night.
Exalted One, make known that Yours is the day and Yours is also the night.
Appoint guards for Your city, all day and all night.
Brighten like the light of the day the darkness of night.
And it came to pass at midnight!

The following song is sung in place of the previous one on the second Seder night.

וּבְכֵן וַאֲמַרְתֶּם זֶבַח פֶּסַח:

אֹמֶץ גְּבוּרוֹתֶיךָ הִפְלֵאתָ בַּפֶּסַח: בְּרֹאשׁ כָּל מוֹעֲדוֹת נִשֵּׂאתָ פֶּסַח:
גִּלִּיתָ לְאֶזְרָחִי חֲצוֹת לֵיל פֶּסַח: וַאֲמַרְתֶּם זֶבַח פֶּסַח:
דְּלָתָיו דָּפַקְתָּ כְּחוֹם הַיּוֹם בַּפֶּסַח: הִסְעִיד נוֹצְצִים עֻגוֹת מַצּוֹת בַּפֶּסַח:
וְאֶל הַבָּקָר רָץ זֵכֶר לְשׁוֹר עֵרֶךְ פֶּסַח: וַאֲמַרְתֶּם זֶבַח פֶּסַח:
זוֹעֲמוּ סְדוֹמִים וְלוֹהֲטוּ בָּאֵשׁ בַּפֶּסַח: חֻלַּץ לוֹט מֵהֶם וּמַצּוֹת אָפָה בְּקֵץ
פֶּסַח: טִאטֵאתָ אַדְמַת מוֹף וְנוֹף בְּעָבְרְךָ בַּפֶּסַח:
וַאֲמַרְתֶּם זֶבַח פֶּסַח:
יָהּ רֹאשׁ כָּל הוֹן מָחַצְתָּ בְּלֵיל שִׁמּוּר פֶּסַח: כַּבִּיר עַל בֵּן בְּכוֹר פָּסַחְתָּ
בְּדַם פֶּסַח: לְבִלְתִּי תֵּת מַשְׁחִית לָבֹא בִּפְתָחַי בַּפֶּסַח:
וַאֲמַרְתֶּם זֶבַח פֶּסַח:
מְסֻגֶּרֶת סֻגָּרָה בְּעִתּוֹתֵי פֶּסַח: נִשְׁמְדָה מִדְיָן בִּצְלִיל שְׂעוֹרֵי עֹמֶר פֶּסַח:
שֹׂרְפוּ מִשְׁמַנֵּי פּוּל וְלוּד בִּיקַד יְקוֹד פֶּסַח:
וַאֲמַרְתֶּם זֶבַח פֶּסַח:
עוֹד הַיּוֹם בְּנֹב לַעֲמֹד עַד גָּעָה עוֹנַת פֶּסַח: פַּס יַד כָּתְבָה לְקַעֲקֵעַ צוּל
בַּפֶּסַח: צָפֹה הַצָּפִית עָרוֹךְ הַשֻּׁלְחָן בַּפֶּסַח: וַאֲמַרְתֶּם זֶבַח פֶּסַח:
קָהָל כִּנְּסָה הֲדַסָּה צוֹם לְשַׁלֵּשׁ בַּפֶּסַח: רֹאשׁ מִבֵּית רָשָׁע מָחַצְתָּ בְּעֵץ
חֲמִשִּׁים בַּפֶּסַח: שְׁתֵּי אֵלֶּה רֶגַע תָּבִיא לְעוּצִית בַּפֶּסַח:
תָּעֹז יָדְךָ תָּרוּם יְמִינְךָ כְּלֵיל הִתְקַדֵּשׁ חַג פֶּסַח:
וַאֲמַרְתֶּם זֶבַח פֶּסַח:

The following song is sung in place of the previous one on the second Seder night.

Coming Closer* on Pesaḥ

And you shall say: This is the Pesaḥ sacrifice.
You displayed Your mighty powers wondrously on Pesaḥ.
Above all seasons of delight You elevated Pesaḥ.
You revealed the Exodus to the
Easterner [Abraham] at the midnight of Pesaḥ.

And you shall say: This is the Pesaḥ sacrifice.

You knocked at his door in the heat of the day on Pesaḥ.
He gave the angels cakes of matzah to dine on during Pesaḥ.
He ran to the herd, harbinger of the sacrificial feast of the Pesaḥ.

And you shall say: This is the Pesaḥ sacrifice.

The Sodomites provoked and were burned up with fire on Pesaḥ.
Lot was rescued from them and he baked matzot at the end of Pesaḥ.
You swept the ground of Moph and Noph [Mitzraim]
when You passed though on Pesaḥ.

And you shall say: This is the Pesaḥ sacrifice.

God, You stilled the head of every firstborn on the watchful night of Pesaḥ.
Powerful One, You skipped over Your firstborn
by merit of the blood of Pesaḥ.
So as not to let the Destroyer enter my threshold on Pesaḥ.

And you shall say: This is the Pesaḥ sacrifice.

The besieged city [Jericho] was besieged at the time of Pesaḥ.
Midian was destroyed [by Gideon] through a barley cake
from the Omer Offering of Pesaḥ.
The mighty nobles of Pul and Lud [Assyria] were burnt
in a great conflagration on Pesaḥ.

And you shall say: This is the Pesaḥ sacrifice.

Still today [Sanḥeirev] would be standing at Nov
until the time came for Pesaḥ.
A hand inscribed the destruction of Tzul [Babylon] on Pesaḥ.
As the watch was set and the table spread on Pesaḥ.

And you shall say: This is the Pesaḥ sacrifice.

Hadassah [Esther] assembled a congregation
for a three-day fast on Pesaḥ.
The head of the wicked clan [Haman] You crushed
through a gallows of fifty cubits, on Pesaḥ.
Double will You bring in an instant upon Utzis [Edom] on Pesaḥ.
Let Your hand be strengthened and Your right arm be uplifted,
as on that night when You made holy the festival of Pesaḥ.

And you shall say: This is the Pesaḥ sacrifice.

---

* The word "sacrifice" in Hebrew is "*korban*," which actually means to come close. By letting go of what one holds close, one comes closer to God. This is exemplified by Abraham's willingness to let go of his son, his only son, the son he loved – Isaac.

2019

כִּי לוֹ נָאֶה, כִּי לוֹ יָאֶה:

אַדִּיר בִּמְלוּכָה, בָּחוּר כַּהֲלָכָה, גְּדוּדָיו יֹאמְרוּ לוֹ: לְךָ וּלְךָ, לְךָ כִּי לְךָ,
לְךָ אַף לְךָ, לְךָ יְיָ הַמַּמְלָכָה, **כִּי לוֹ נָאֶה כִּי לוֹ יָאֶה.**

דָּגוּל בִּמְלוּכָה, הָדוּר כַּהֲלָכָה, וָתִיקָיו יֹאמְרוּ לוֹ: לְךָ וּלְךָ, לְךָ כִּי לְךָ,
לְךָ אַף לְךָ, לְךָ יְיָ הַמַּמְלָכָה, **כִּי לוֹ נָאֶה, כִּי לוֹ יָאֶה.**

זַכַּאי בִּמְלוּכָה, חָסִין כַּהֲלָכָה, טַפְסְרָיו יֹאמְרוּ לוֹ: לְךָ וּלְךָ, לְךָ כִּי לְךָ,
לְךָ אַף לְךָ, לְךָ יְיָ הַמַּמְלָכָה, **כִּי לוֹ נָאֶה, כִּי לוֹ יָאֶה.**

יָחִיד בִּמְלוּכָה, כַּבִּיר כַּהֲלָכָה, לִמּוּדָיו יֹאמְרוּ לוֹ: לְךָ וּלְךָ, לְךָ כִּי לְךָ,
לְךָ אַף לְךָ, לְךָ יְיָ הַמַּמְלָכָה, **כִּי לוֹ נָאֶה, כִּי לוֹ יָאֶה.**

מָרוֹם בִּמְלוּכָה, נוֹרָא כַּהֲלָכָה, סְבִיבָיו יֹאמְרוּ לוֹ: לְךָ וּלְךָ, לְךָ כִּי לְךָ,
לְךָ אַף לְךָ, לְךָ יְיָ הַמַּמְלָכָה, **כִּי לוֹ נָאֶה, כִּי לוֹ יָאֶה.**

עָנָיו בִּמְלוּכָה, פּוֹדֶה כַּהֲלָכָה, צַדִּיקָיו יֹאמְרוּ לוֹ: לְךָ וּלְךָ, לְךָ כִּי לְךָ,
לְךָ אַף לְךָ, לְךָ יְיָ הַמַּמְלָכָה, **כִּי לוֹ נָאֶה, כִּי לוֹ יָאֶה.**

קָדוֹשׁ בִּמְלוּכָה, רַחוּם כַּהֲלָכָה, שִׁנְאַנָּיו יֹאמְרוּ לוֹ: לְךָ וּלְךָ, לְךָ כִּי לְךָ,
לְךָ אַף לְךָ, לְךָ יְיָ הַמַּמְלָכָה, **כִּי לוֹ נָאֶה, כִּי לוֹ יָאֶה.**

תַּקִּיף בִּמְלוּכָה, תּוֹמֵךְ כַּהֲלָכָה, תְּמִימָיו יֹאמְרוּ לוֹ: לְךָ וּלְךָ, לְךָ כִּי לְךָ,
לְךָ אַף לְךָ, לְךָ יְיָ הַמַּמְלָכָה, **כִּי לוֹ נָאֶה, כִּי לוֹ יָאֶה.**

Praise Only the One

Mighty in Kingship, perfectly distinguished, His companies say to Him:
to You and again to You;
to You, yes to You;
to You, only to You;
You, God, are the Sovereign.
To Him [praise] is becoming; to Him [praise] is fitting.
Renowned in Kingship, perfectly glorious, His faithful say to Him:
to You and again to You;
to You, yes to You;
to You, only to You;
You, God, are the Sovereign.
To Him [praise] is becoming; to Him [praise] is fitting.
Worthy in Kingship, perfectly immune, His princes say to Him:
to You and again to You;
to You, yes to You;
to You, only to You;
You, God, are the Sovereign.
To Him [praise] is becoming; to Him [praise] is fitting.
Unique in Kingship, perfectly powerful, His learned ones say to Him:
to You and again to You;
to You, yes to You;
to You, only to You;
You, God, are the Sovereign.
To Him [praise] is becoming; to Him [praise] is fitting.
Commanding in Kingship, perfectly awesome,
His surrounding [angels] say to Him:
to You and again to You;
to You, yes to You;
to You, only to You;
You, God, are the Sovereign.
To Him [praise] is becoming; to Him [praise] is fitting.
Modest in Kingship, perfectly the Redeemer, His legions say to Him:
to You and again to You;
to You, yes to You;
to You, only to You;
You, God, are the Sovereign.
To Him [praise] is becoming; to Him [praise] is fitting.
Holy in Kingship, perfectly merciful, His snow-white angels say to Him:
to You and again to You;
to You, yes to You;
to You, only to You;
You, God, are the Sovereign.
To Him [praise] is becoming; to Him [praise] is fitting.
Resolute in Kingship, perfectly supportive, His perfect ones say to Him:
to You and again to You;
to You, yes to You;
to You, only to You;
You, God, are the Sovereign.
To Him [praise] is becoming; to Him [praise] is fitting.

אַדִּיר הוּא

אַדִּיר הוּא, יִבְנֶה בֵיתוֹ בְּקָרוֹב,
בִּמְהֵרָה בִּמְהֵרָה בְּיָמֵינוּ בְּקָרוֹב.
אֵל בְּנֵה, אֵל בְּנֵה, בְּנֵה בֵיתְךָ בְּקָרוֹב.

בָּחוּר הוּא, גָּדוֹל הוּא, דָּגוּל
הוּא, יִבְנֶה בֵיתוֹ בְּקָרוֹב, בִּמְהֵרָה בִּמְהֵרָה בְּיָמֵינוּ בְּקָרוֹב.
אֵל בְּנֵה, אֵל בְּנֵה, בְּנֵה בֵיתְךָ בְּקָרוֹב.

הָדוּר הוּא, וָתִיק הוּא, זַכַּאי הוּא, חָסִיד הוּא,
יִבְנֶה בֵיתוֹ בְּקָרוֹב, בִּמְהֵרָה בִּמְהֵרָה בְּיָמֵינוּ בְּקָרוֹב.
אֵל בְּנֵה, אֵל בְּנֵה, בְּנֵה בֵיתְךָ בְּקָרוֹב.

טָהוֹר הוּא, יָחִיד הוּא, כַּבִּיר הוּא, לָמוּד הוּא, מֶלֶךְ הוּא,
נוֹרָא הוּא, סַגִּיב הוּא, עִזּוּז הוּא, פּוֹדֶה הוּא, צַדִּיק הוּא,
יִבְנֶה בֵיתוֹ בְּקָרוֹב, בִּמְהֵרָה בִּמְהֵרָה בְּיָמֵינוּ בְּקָרוֹב.
אֵל בְּנֵה, אֵל בְּנֵה, בְּנֵה בֵיתְךָ בְּקָרוֹב.

קָדוֹשׁ הוּא, רַחוּם הוּא, שַׁדַּי הוּא, תַּקִּיף הוּא,
יִבְנֶה בֵיתוֹ בְּקָרוֹב, בִּמְהֵרָה בִּמְהֵרָה בְּיָמֵינוּ בְּקָרוֹב.
אֵל בְּנֵה, אֵל בְּנֵה, בְּנֵה בֵיתְךָ בְּקָרוֹב.

May God Build His Vessel Anew

He is mighty.
May He soon build His House, speedily, yes speedily, in our days, soon.
God, build! God, build! Build Your House soon!

He is distinguished,
He is great,
He is renowned.
May He soon build His House, speedily, yes speedily, in our days, soon.
God, build! God, build! Build Your House soon!

He is glorious,
He is faithful,
He is worthy,
He is gracious.
May He soon build His House, speedily, yes speedily, in our days, soon.
God, build! God, build! Build Your House soon!

He is pure,
He is unique,
He is powerful,
He is majestic,
He is awesome,
He is sublime,
He is all-powerful,
He is the Redeemer,
He is righteous.
May He soon build His House, speedily, yes speedily, in our days, soon.
God, build! God, build! Build Your House soon!
He is holy,
He is merciful,
He is Almighty,
He is forceful.

May He soon build His House, speedily, yes speedily, in our days, soon.
God, build! God, build! Build Your House soon!

A suggested and enjoyable way to sing the following song is to have each number sung by different participants according to their ascending ages. Thus the youngest around the table takes the role of "one," the next in line takes "two," and so on. The refrain: "In heaven and on earth" is sung by all the participants together.

אֶחָד מִי יוֹדֵעַ? אֶחָד אֲנִי יוֹדֵעַ: אֶחָד אֱלֹהֵינוּ שֶׁבַּשָּׁמַיִם וּבָאָרֶץ.

שְׁנַיִם מִי יוֹדֵעַ? שְׁנַיִם אֲנִי יוֹדֵעַ:
שְׁנֵי לֻחוֹת הַבְּרִית,
אֶחָד אֱלֹהֵינוּ שֶׁבַּשָּׁמַיִם וּבָאָרֶץ.

שְׁלֹשָׁה מִי יוֹדֵעַ? שְׁלֹשָׁה אֲנִי יוֹדֵעַ: שְׁלֹשָׁה אָבוֹת,
שְׁנֵי לֻחוֹת הַבְּרִית,
אֶחָד אֱלֹהֵינוּ שֶׁבַּשָּׁמַיִם וּבָאָרֶץ.

אַרְבַּע מִי יוֹדֵעַ? אַרְבַּע אֲנִי יוֹדֵעַ:
אַרְבַּע אִמָּהוֹת, שְׁלֹשָׁה אָבוֹת,
שְׁנֵי לֻחוֹת הַבְּרִית,
אֶחָד אֱלֹהֵינוּ שֶׁבַּשָּׁמַיִם וּבָאָרֶץ.

חֲמִשָּׁה מִי יוֹדֵעַ? חֲמִשָּׁה אֲנִי יוֹדֵעַ:
חֲמִשָּׁה חוּמְשֵׁי תוֹרָה,
אַרְבַּע אִמָּהוֹת, שְׁלֹשָׁה אָבוֹת,
שְׁנֵי לֻחוֹת הַבְּרִית,
אֶחָד אֱלֹהֵינוּ שֶׁבַּשָּׁמַיִם וּבָאָרֶץ.

A suggested and enjoyable way to sing the following song is to have each number sung by different participants according to their ascending ages. Thus the youngest around the table takes the role of "one," the next in line takes "two," and so on. The refrain: "In heaven and on earth" is sung by all the participants together.

Who Knows No-thing?

Who knows one? I know one:
One is our God, who is in Heaven and on Earth.

Who knows two? I know two:
two are the Tablets of the Covenant;
One is our God, who is in Heaven and on Earth.

Who knows three? I know three:
three are the Patriarchs;
two are the Tablets of the Covenant;
One is our God, who is in Heaven and on Earth.

Who knows four? I know four:
four are the Matriarchs;
three are the Patriarchs;
two are the Tablets of the Covenant;
One is our God, who is in Heaven and on Earth.

Who knows five? I know five:
five are the Books of the Torah;
four are the Matriarchs;
three are the Patriarchs;
two are the Tablets of the Covenant;
One is our God, who is in Heaven and on Earth.

שִׁשָּׁה מִי יוֹדֵעַ? שִׁשָּׁה אֲנִי יוֹדֵעַ:
שִׁשָּׁה סִדְרֵי מִשְׁנָה,
חֲמִשָּׁה חוּמְשֵׁי תוֹרָה,
אַרְבַּע אִמָּהוֹת, שְׁלֹשָׁה אָבוֹת,
שְׁנֵי לֻחוֹת הַבְּרִית,
אֶחָד אֱלֹהֵינוּ שֶׁבַּשָּׁמַיִם וּבָאָרֶץ.

שִׁבְעָה מִי יוֹדֵעַ? שִׁבְעָה אֲנִי יוֹדֵעַ:
שִׁבְעָה יְמֵי שַׁבַּתָּא, שִׁשָּׁה סִדְרֵי מִשְׁנָה,
חֲמִשָּׁה חוּמְשֵׁי תוֹרָה,
אַרְבַּע אִמָּהוֹת, שְׁלֹשָׁה אָבוֹת,
שְׁנֵי לֻחוֹת הַבְּרִית,
אֶחָד אֱלֹהֵינוּ שֶׁבַּשָּׁמַיִם וּבָאָרֶץ.

שְׁמוֹנָה מִי יוֹדֵעַ? שְׁמוֹנָה אֲנִי יוֹדֵעַ:
שְׁמוֹנָה יְמֵי מִילָה, שִׁבְעָה יְמֵי שַׁבַּתָּא,
שִׁשָּׁה סִדְרֵי מִשְׁנָה, חֲמִשָּׁה חוּמְשֵׁי תוֹרָה,
אַרְבַּע אִמָּהוֹת, שְׁלֹשָׁה אָבוֹת,
שְׁנֵי לֻחוֹת הַבְּרִית,
אֶחָד אֱלֹהֵינוּ שֶׁבַּשָּׁמַיִם וּבָאָרֶץ.

Who knows six? I know six:
six are the Orders of the Mishnah;
five are the Books of the Torah;
four are the Matriarchs;
three are the Patriarchs;
two are the Tablets of the Covenant;
One is our God, who is in Heaven and on Earth.

Who knows seven? I know seven:
seven are the days of the week;
six are the Orders of the Mishnah;
five are the Books of the Torah;
four are the Matriarchs;
three are the Patriarchs;
two are the Tablets of the Covenant;
One is our God, who is in Heaven and on Earth.

Who knows eight? I know eight:
eight are the days to circumcision;
seven are the days of the week;
six are the Orders of the Mishnah;
five are the Books of the Torah;
four are the Matriarchs;
three are the Patriarchs;
two are the Tablets of the Covenant;
One is our God, who is in Heaven and on Earth.

תִּשְׁעָה מִי יוֹדֵעַ? תִּשְׁעָה אֲנִי יוֹדֵעַ:
תִּשְׁעָה יַרְחֵי לֵדָה, שְׁמוֹנָה יְמֵי מִילָה,
שִׁבְעָה יְמֵי שַׁבַּתָּא, שִׁשָּׁה סִדְרֵי מִשְׁנָה,
חֲמִשָּׁה חוּמְשֵׁי תוֹרָה,
אַרְבַּע אִמָּהוֹת, שְׁלֹשָׁה אָבוֹת,
שְׁנֵי לֻחוֹת הַבְּרִית,
אֶחָד אֱלֹהֵינוּ שֶׁבַּשָּׁמַיִם וּבָאָרֶץ.

עֲשָׂרָה מִי יוֹדֵעַ? עֲשָׂרָה אֲנִי יוֹדֵעַ:
עֲשָׂרָה דִבְּרַיָּא, תִּשְׁעָה יַרְחֵי לֵדָה,
שְׁמוֹנָה יְמֵי מִילָה, שִׁבְעָה יְמֵי שַׁבַּתָּא,
שִׁשָּׁה סִדְרֵי מִשְׁנָה, חֲמִשָּׁה חוּמְשֵׁי תוֹרָה,
אַרְבַּע אִמָּהוֹת, שְׁלֹשָׁה אָבוֹת,
שְׁנֵי לֻחוֹת הַבְּרִית,
אֶחָד אֱלֹהֵינוּ שֶׁבַּשָּׁמַיִם וּבָאָרֶץ.

אַחַד עָשָׂר מִי יוֹדֵעַ? אַחַד עָשָׂר אֲנִי יוֹדֵעַ:
אַחַד עָשָׂר כּוֹכְבַיָּא, עֲשָׂרָה דִבְּרַיָּא,
תִּשְׁעָה יַרְחֵי לֵדָה, שְׁמוֹנָה יְמֵי מִילָה,
שִׁבְעָה יְמֵי שַׁבַּתָּא, שִׁשָּׁה סִדְרֵי מִשְׁנָה,
חֲמִשָּׁה חוּמְשֵׁי תוֹרָה, אַרְבַּע אִמָּהוֹת,
שְׁלֹשָׁה אָבוֹת, שְׁנֵי לֻחוֹת הַבְּרִית,
אֶחָד אֱלֹהֵינוּ שֶׁבַּשָּׁמַיִם וּבָאָרֶץ.

Who knows nine? I know nine:
nine are the months of pregnancy;
eight are the days to circumcision;
seven are the days of the week;
six are the Orders of the Mishnah;
five are the Books of the Torah;
four are the Matriarchs;
three are the Patriarchs;
two are the Tablets of the Covenant;
One is our God, who is in Heaven and on Earth.

Who knows ten? I know ten:
ten are the Ten Commandments;
nine are the months of pregnancy;
eight are the days to circumcision;
seven are the days of the week;
six are the Orders of the Mishnah;
five are the Books of the Torah;
four are the Matriarchs;
three are the Patriarchs;
two are the Tablets of the Covenant;
One is our God, who is in Heaven and on Earth.

Who knows eleven? I know eleven:
eleven are the stars [in Joseph's dream];
ten are the Ten Commandments;
nine are the months of pregnancy;
eight are the days to circumcision;
seven are the days of the week;
six are the Orders of the Mishnah;
five are the Books of the Torah;
four are the Matriarchs;
three are the Patriarchs;
two are the Tablets of the Covenant;
One is our God, who is in Heaven and on Earth.

שְׁנֵים עָשָׂר מִי יוֹדֵעַ? שְׁנֵים עָשָׂר אֲנִי יוֹדֵעַ:
שְׁנֵים עָשָׂר שִׁבְטַיָּא, אַחַד עָשָׂר כּוֹכְבַיָּא,
עֲשָׂרָה דִבְּרַיָּא, תִּשְׁעָה יַרְחֵי לֵדָה,
שְׁמוֹנָה יְמֵי מִילָה, שִׁבְעָה יְמֵי שַׁבַּתָּא,
שִׁשָּׁה סִדְרֵי מִשְׁנָה, חֲמִשָּׁה חוּמְשֵׁי תוֹרָה,
אַרְבַּע אִמָּהוֹת, שְׁלֹשָׁה אָבוֹת,
שְׁנֵי לֻחוֹת הַבְּרִית,
אֶחָד אֱלֹהֵינוּ שֶׁבַּשָּׁמַיִם וּבָאָרֶץ.

שְׁלֹשָׁה עָשָׂר מִי יוֹדֵעַ? שְׁלֹשָׁה עָשָׂר אֲנִי יוֹדֵעַ:
שְׁלֹשָׁה עָשָׂר מִדַּיָּא, שְׁנֵים עָשָׂר שִׁבְטַיָּא,
אַחַד עָשָׂר כּוֹכְבַיָּא, עֲשָׂרָה דִבְּרַיָּא,
תִּשְׁעָה יַרְחֵי לֵדָה, שְׁמוֹנָה יְמֵי מִילָה,
שִׁבְעָה יְמֵי שַׁבַּתָּא, שִׁשָּׁה סִדְרֵי מִשְׁנָה,
חֲמִשָּׁה חוּמְשֵׁי תוֹרָה, אַרְבַּע אִמָּהוֹת,
שְׁלֹשָׁה אָבוֹת, שְׁנֵי לֻחוֹת הַבְּרִית,
אֶחָד אֱלֹהֵינוּ שֶׁבַּשָּׁמַיִם וּבָאָרֶץ.

Who knows twelve? I know twelve:
twelve are the tribes [of Israel];
eleven are the stars [in Joseph's dream];
ten are the Ten Commandments;
nine are the months of pregnancy;
eight are the days to circumcision;
seven are the days of the week;
six are the Orders of the Mishnah;
five are the Books of the Torah;
four are the Matriarchs;
three are the Patriarchs;
two are the Tablets of the Covenant;
One is our God, who is in Heaven and on Earth.

Who knows thirteen? I know thirteen:
thirteen are the attributes of God;
twelve are the tribes [of Israel];
eleven are the stars [in Joseph's dream];
ten are the Ten Commandments;
nine are the months of pregnancy;
eight are the days to circumcision;
seven are the days of the week;
six are the Orders of the Mishnah;
five are the Books of the Torah;
four are the Matriarchs;
three are the Patriarchs;
two are the Tablets of the Covenant;
One is our God, who is in Heaven and on Earth.

My parents-in-law have a tradition to assign sounds to each of the characters in the following song as they are mentioned – "baaaa" for the goat, "meow" for the cat, and so on.

חַד גַּדְיָא, חַד גַּדְיָא,
דְּזַבִּין אַבָּא בִּתְרֵי זוּזֵי,
חַד גַּדְיָא, חַד גַּדְיָא.

וְאָתָא שׁוּנְרָא,
וְאָכְלָה לְגַדְיָא,
דְּזַבִּין אַבָּא בִּתְרֵי זוּזֵי,
חַד גַּדְיָא, חַד גַּדְיָא.

וְאָתָא כַלְבָּא, וְנָשַׁךְ לְשׁוּנְרָא,
דְּאָכְלָה לְגַדְיָא,
דְּזַבִּין אַבָּא בִּתְרֵי זוּזֵי,
חַד גַּדְיָא חַד גַּדְיָא,

וְאָתָא חוּטְרָא, וְהִכָּה לְכַלְבָּא,
דְּנָשַׁךְ לְשׁוּנְרָא, דְּאָכְלָה לְגַדְיָא,
דְּזַבִּין אַבָּא בִּתְרֵי זוּזֵי,
חַד גַּדְיָא, חַד גַּדְיָא.

וְאָתָא נוּרָא, וְשָׂרַף לְחוּטְרָא,
דְּהִכָּה לְכַלְבָּא, דְּנָשַׁךְ לְשׁוּנְרָא,
דְּאָכְלָה לְגַדְיָא,
דְּזַבִּין אַבָּא בִּתְרֵי זוּזֵי,
חַד גַּדְיָא, חַד גַּדְיָא.

וְאָתָא מַיָּא, וְכָבָה לְנוּרָא,
דְּשָׂרַף לְחוּטְרָא, דְּהִכָּה לְכַלְבָּא,
דְּנָשַׁךְ לְשׁוּנְרָא, דְּאָכְלָה לְגַדְיָא,
דְּזַבִּין אַבָּא בִּתְרֵי זוּזֵי,
חַד גַּדְיָא, חַד גַּדְיָא.

A26

My parents-in-law have a tradition to assign sounds to each of the characters in the following song as they are mentioned – "baaaa" for the goat, "meow" for the cat, and so on.

Ḥad Gadya – One Little Goat

One little goat, one little goat, that father bought for two zuzim – one little goat, one little goat.

And then came a cat and ate that goat that father bought for two zuzim – one little goat, one little goat.

And then came a dog and bit the cat, that ate the goat that father bought for two zuzim – one little goat, one little goat.

And then came a stick and beat the dog, that bit the cat, that ate the goat that father bought for two zuzim – one little goat, one little goat.

And then came a fire and burnt the stick, that beat the dog, that bit the cat, that ate the goat that father bought for two zuzim – one little goat, one little goat.

And then came some water and put out the fire, that burnt the stick, that beat the dog, that bit the cat, that ate the goat that father bought for two zuzim – one little goat, one little goat.

וְאָתָא תוֹרָא, וְשָׁתָה לְמַיָּא,
דְּכָבָה לְנוּרָא, דְּשָׂרַף לְחוּטְרָא,
דְּהִכָּה לְכַלְבָּא, דְּנָשַׁךְ לְשׁוּנְרָא,
דְּאָכְלָה לְגַדְיָא,
דְּזַבִּין אַבָּא בִּתְרֵי זוּזֵי,
חַד גַּדְיָא, חַד גַּדְיָא.

וְאָתָא הַשּׁוֹחֵט, וְשָׁחַט לְתוֹרָא,
דְּשָׁתָה לְמַיָּא, דְּכָבָה לְנוּרָא,
דְּשָׂרַף לְחוּטְרָא, דְּהִכָּה לְכַלְבָּא,
דְּנָשַׁךְ לְשׁוּנְרָא, דְּאָכְלָה לְגַדְיָא,
דְּזַבִּין אַבָּא בִּתְרֵי זוּזֵי,
חַד גַּדְיָא, חַד גַּדְיָא.

וְאָתָא מַלְאַךְ הַמָּוֶת, וְשָׁחַט לְשׁוֹחֵט,
דְּשָׁחַט לְתוֹרָא, דְּשָׁתָה לְמַיָּא,
דְּכָבָה לְנוּרָא, דְּשָׂרַף לְחוּטְרָא,
דְּהִכָּה לְכַלְבָּא, דְּנָשַׁךְ לְשׁוּנְרָא,
דְּאָכְלָא לְגַדְיָא,
דְּזַבִּין אַבָּא בִּתְרֵי זוּזֵי,
חַד גַּדְיָא, חַד גַּדְיָא.

וְאָתָא הַקָּדוֹשׁ בָּרוּךְ הוּא,
וְשָׁחַט לְמַלְאַךְ הַמָּוֶת,
דְּשָׁחַט לְשׁוֹחֵט, דְּשָׁחַט לְתוֹרָא,
דְּשָׁתָה לְמַיָּא, דְּכָבָה לְנוּרָא,
דְּשָׂרַף לְחוּטְרָא, דְּהִכָּה לְכַלְבָּא,
דְּנָשַׁךְ לְשׁוּנְרָא, דְּאָכְלָא לְגַדְיָא,
דְּזַבִּין אַבָּא בִּתְרֵי זוּזֵי,
חַד גַּדְיָא, חַד גַּדְיָא.

There is a tradition at this point to read or chant Shir HaShirim–Song of Songs – the Love Song between the Creator and Her Creation.

And then came an ox and drank the water, that put out the fire, that burnt the stick, that beat the dog, that bit the cat, that ate the goat that father bought for two zuzim – one little goat, one little goat.

And then came a slaughterer and slaughtered the ox, that drank the water, that put out the fire, that burnt the stick, that beat the dog, that bit the cat, that ate the goat that father bought for two zuzim – one little goat, one little goat.

And then came the angel of death and slew the slaughterer, who slaughtered the ox, that drank the water, that put out the fire, that burnt the stick, that beat the dog, that bit the cat, that ate the goat that father bought for two zuzim – one little goat, one little goat.

And then came the Holy One, blessed be He, and killed the angel of death, who slew the slaughterer, who slaughtered the ox, that drank the water, that put out the fire, that burnt the stick, that beat the dog, that bit the cat, that ate the goat that father bought for two zuzim – one little goat, one little goat.

There is a tradition at this point to read or chant Shir HaShirim–Song of Songs – the Love Song between the Creator and Her Creation.

ספירת העומר

For those making a second Seder, whoever did not count the Omer after *Maariv* on the second night of Pesaḥ should do so now. The counting of the remaining 49 days is tabled below.

הִנְנִי מוּכָן וּמְזֻמָּן לְקַיֵּם מִצְוַת עֲשֵׂה שֶׁל סְפִירַת הָעֹמֶר לְשֵׁם יִחוּד קוּדְשָׁא בְּרִיךְ הוּא וּשְׁכִינְתֵּיהּ עַל יְדֵי הַהוּא טָמִיר וְנֶעְלָם בְּשֵׁם כָּל יִשְׂרָאֵל:

בָּרוּךְ אַתָּה יהוה אֱלֹהֵינוּ מֶלֶךְ הָעוֹלָם,
אֲשֶׁר קִדְּשָׁנוּ בְּמִצְוֹתָיו וְצִוָּנוּ עַל סְפִירַת הָעוֹמֶר:

הַיּוֹם יוֹם **אֶחָד** לָעוֹמֶר.

הָרַחֲמָן הוּא יַחֲזִיר לָנוּ עֲבוֹדַת בֵּית הַמִּקְדָּשׁ לִמְקוֹמָהּ,
בִּמְהֵרָה בְיָמֵינוּ אָמֵן סֶלָה:

❧ Counting the Omer ❧

For those making a second Seder, whoever did not count the Omer after *Maariv* on the second night of Pesah should do so now. The counting of the remaining 49 days is tabled below.

Here I am right now, ready and mindful to participate in the unification of the Transcendent Holy One with the Immanent Shekhinah through the Counting of the Omer.

Blessed are You, Lord our God, King of the Universe, who has sanctified us with His commandments and commanded us to count the Omer.

*Today is the **first** day of the Omer.*

May the Compassionate One return us to the heights and depths of service that existed at the time of the Holy Temple, speedily in our days, Amen.

לַמְנַצֵּחַ בִּנְגִינֹת, מִזְמוֹר שִׁיר.

אֱלֹהִים, יְחָנֵּנוּ וִיבָרְכֵנוּ; יָאֵר פָּנָיו אִתָּנוּ סֶלָה.

לָדַעַת בָּאָרֶץ דַּרְכֶּךָ; בְּכָל-גּוֹיִם, יְשׁוּעָתֶךָ.

יוֹדוּךָ עַמִּים אֱלֹהִים: יוֹדוּךָ, עַמִּים כֻּלָּם.

יִשְׂמְחוּ וִירַנְּנוּ, לְאֻמִּים:

כִּי-תִשְׁפֹּט עַמִּים מִישֹׁר; וּלְאֻמִּים,

בָּאָרֶץ תַּנְחֵם סֶלָה.

יוֹדוּךָ עַמִּים אֱלֹהִים: יוֹדוּךָ, עַמִּים כֻּלָּם.

אֶרֶץ, נָתְנָה יְבוּלָהּ; יְבָרְכֵנוּ, אֱלֹהִים אֱלֹהֵינוּ.

יְבָרְכֵנוּ אֱלֹהִים;

וְיִירְאוּ אוֹתוֹ, כָּל-אַפְסֵי-אָרֶץ.

A Psalm for All the Peoples of the Planet

God, bless us with grace!
Let Your loving Face shine on us!
We want to get to know Your way
here on Earth,
Seeing how Your help is given
to every group of people.

Oh, how the various peoples will thank You,
All of them will sing and be grateful.

Many people will be joyous and sing
When You will set them right with
forthrightness.
And the peoples, as You direct them, will
cheer You.

Oh, how the various peoples will thank You,
All of them will sing, be grateful.

The Earth will give her harvest.
Such blessings come from God, yes from our
God!

Bless us God,
All the ends of the Earth will esteem You!

(Psalms 67)

The Table of the Omer with *Sefirot*

Today is the (day) ***day which is the*** (week) ***week and*** (day of week) ***of the Omer***.
Today is the (Sefirah of Day) ***that is influencing*** (Sefirah of Week).

Day	Week	Day of Week	*Sefirah* of Week	*Sefirah* of Day
1	-	-	*Ḥesed*	*Ḥesed*
2	-	-	*Ḥesed*	*Gevurah*
3	-	-	*Ḥesed*	*Tiferet*
4	-	-	*Ḥesed*	*Netzaḥ*
5	-	-	*Ḥesed*	*Hod*
6	-	-	*Ḥesed*	*Yesod*
7	-	-	*Ḥesed*	*Malkhut*
8	1	1	*Gevurah*	*Ḥesed*
9	1	2	*Gevurah*	*Gevurah*
10	1	3	*Gevurah*	*Tiferet*
11	1	4	*Gevurah*	*Netzaḥ*
12	1	5	*Gevurah*	*Hod*
13	1	6	*Gevurah*	*Yesod*
14	1	7	*Gevurah*	*Malkhut*
15	2	1	*Tiferet*	*Ḥesed*
16	2	2	*Tiferet*	*Gevurah*
17	2	3	*Tiferet*	*Tiferet*
18	2	4	*Tiferet*	*Netzaḥ*
19	2	5	*Tiferet*	*Hod*
20	2	6	*Tiferet*	*Yesod*
21	2	7	*Tiferet*	*Malkhut*
22	3	1	*Netzaḥ*	*Ḥesed*
23	3	2	*Netzaḥ*	*Gevurah*
24	3	3	*Netzaḥ*	*Tiferet*
25	3	4	*Netzaḥ*	*Netzaḥ*
26	3	5	*Netzaḥ*	*Hod*
27	3	6	*Netzaḥ*	*Yesod*
28	3	7	*Netzaḥ*	*Malkhut*

Day	Week	Day of Week	*Sefirah* of Week	*Sefirah* of Day
29	4	1	*Hod*	*Ḥesed*
30	4	2	*Hod*	*Gevurah*
31	4	3	*Hod*	*Tiferet*
32	4	4	*Hod*	*Netzaḥ*
33	4	5	*Hod*	*Hod*
34	4	6	*Hod*	*Yesod*
35	4	7	*Hod*	*Malkhut*
36	5	1	*Yesod*	*Ḥesed*
37	5	2	*Yesod*	*Gevurah*
38	5	3	*Yesod*	*Tiferet*
39	5	4	*Yesod*	*Netzaḥ*
40	5	5	*Yesod*	*Hod*
41	5	6	*Yesod*	*Yesod*
42	5	7	*Yesod*	*Malkhut*
43	6	1	*Malkhut*	*Ḥesed*
44	6	2	*Malkhut*	*Gevurah*
45	6	3	*Malkhut*	*Tiferet*
46	6	4	*Malkhut*	*Netzaḥ*
47	6	5	*Malkhut*	*Hod*
48	6	6	*Malkhut*	*Yesod*
49	6	7	*Malkhut*	*Malkhut*

An Introduction to the *Sefirot*

The counting of the Omer starts on the second night of Pesaḥ and lasts for seven times seven days. That is seven full weeks or 49 days. This corresponds to the period of time it took for the Children of Israel to leave Mitzraim, reach mount Sinai and receive the Torah. On the fiftieth day the festival of Shavuot is celebrated. Kabbalah has long identified this period of seven times seven as a mystical journey through the lower seven branches of the Tree of Life. Each week corresponds to another branch or *sefirah* in the order: *Ḥesed, Gevurah, Tiferet, Netzaḥ, Hod, Yesod, Malkhut*. Each day of each week also corresponds to an equivalent *sefirah* in the same order. Thus the first day of the first week is the day

of *Ḥesed* that is in *Ḥesed* and the third day of the fifth week is the day of *Tiferet* that is in *Hod*. This continues until we arrive at *Malkhut* that is in *Malkhut*. In this way all of the *Sefirot* are progressively connected to all of the other *Sefirot*.

But what does all of this mean?

Without going into deep Kabbalah it is sufficient to say that each *sefirah* represents an attribute or energy of God that permeates the Creation. It should always be understood that the *Sefirot* are not God but rather emanations extending out of God's Allness. As a simple analogy, they are the step-down transformers from the almost infinate power of a nuclear reactor down to the manageable outlets in our houses. In the introduction we discussed the concept of the Four Worlds: the World of *Atzilut* – Emanation; the World of *Beriah* – Creation; the World of *Yetzirah* – Formation; and the World of *Assiyah* – Making. These Worlds are comparable to sets of such step-down transformers. Thus within each World there is the Tree of Ten *Sefirot* that pertains to that World, with each particular Tree being interlaced with the one above and below it.

A further principle concerning the Four Worlds and the Tree of Life is that they are all-pervasive and fractal, like a cauliflower.* This is concisely expressed in the phrase, "As above, so below." Thus the ten stages or "step-down transformers" that extend from the infinite to the finite and allow the cosmic process of Creation to unfold also exist on all levels of the unfolding Creation.

The order of the *Sefirot* are illustrated on the following page:

* Within each *sefirah* there is an entire Tree of Ten *Sefirot* and within each of those ten, entire Trees of Ten, etc. A cauliflower consists of smaller and smaller flowerets that look exactly like the parent.

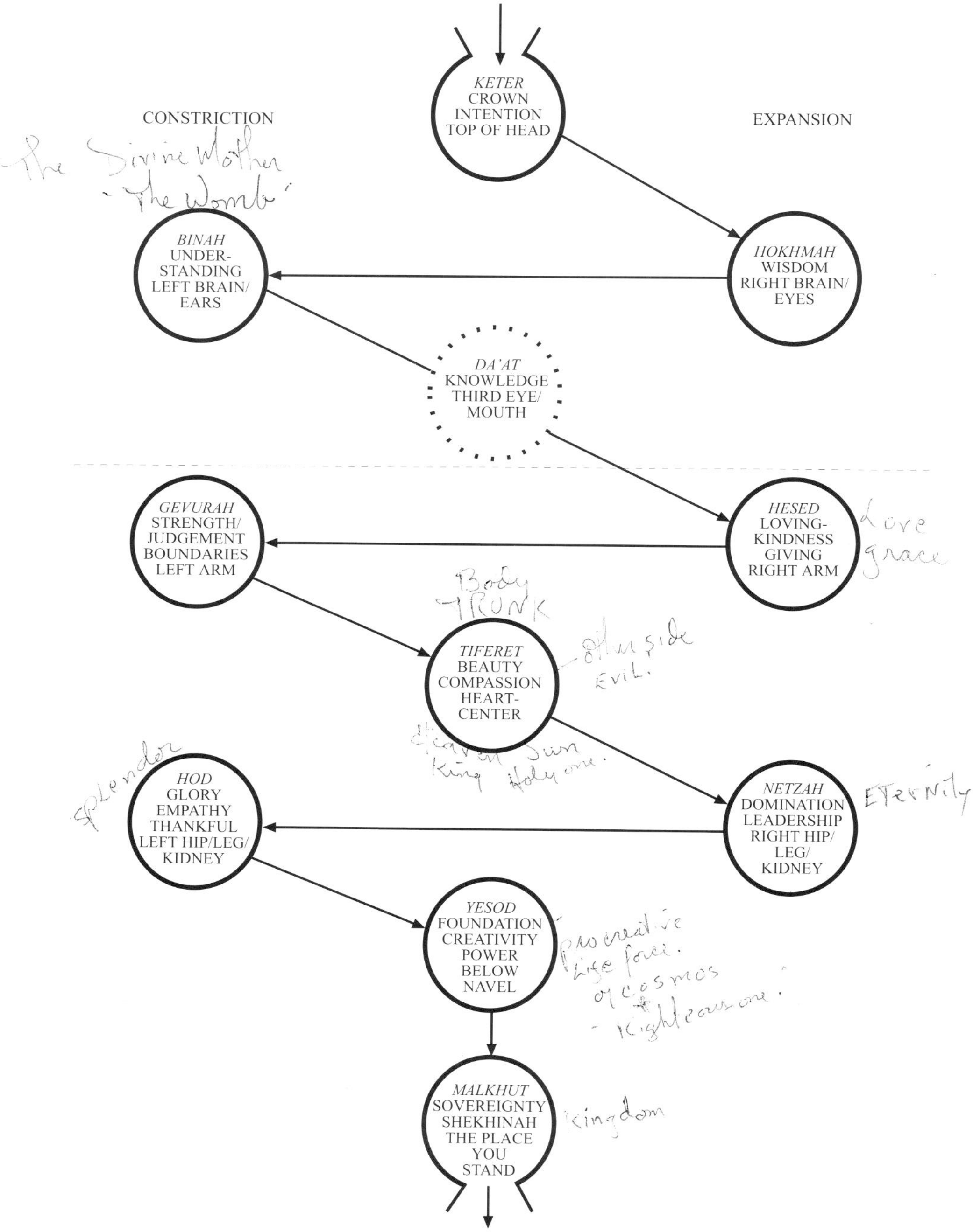
CONSTRICTION
EXPANSION
KETER
CROWN
INTENTION
TOP OF HEAD
BINAH
UNDER-
STANDING
LEFT BRAIN/
EARS
HOKHMAH
WISDOM
RIGHT BRAIN/
EYES
DA'AT
KNOWLEDGE
THIRD EYE/
MOUTH
GEVURAH
STRENGTH/
JUDGEMENT
BOUNDARIES
LEFT ARM
HESED
LOVING-
KINDNESS
GIVING
RIGHT ARM
TIFERET
BEAUTY
COMPASSION
HEART-
CENTER
HOD
GLORY
EMPATHY
THANKFUL
LEFT HIP/LEG/
KIDNEY
NETZAH
DOMINATION
LEADERSHIP
RIGHT HIP/
LEG/
KIDNEY
YESOD
FOUNDATION
CREATIVITY
POWER
BELOW
NAVEL
MALKHUT
SOVEREIGNTY
SHEKHINAH
THE PLACE
YOU
STAND
The Divine Mother
"The Womb"
Love
grace
Body
TRUNK
Other side
EVIL
Heaven Sun
King Holy one.
Splendor
Eternity
procreative
Life force.
orgasmos
Righteous one.
Kingdom

Keter is the Divine Will that flows through all of existence. At all times our *Kavannah* (intention) should be to align our will to that of the Divine. Thus we focus our intention before every action, especially those involving blessings.

Ḥokhmah is the non-dualistic conception of the will. It is the ability to rise above the situation and see the whole, which is associated with wisdom, expansiveness and insight. So the *Kavannah* is to be able to see with God's eyes.

Binah is the differentiation of the thinking process that comes through language and understanding, via the rational mind. It is associated with the ears and so our *Kavannah* is to be able to hear the Divine Will and separate it from the myriad of other voices that continually chat away inside our heads.

A convenient metaphor that one might utilize in order to appreciate these three *Sefirot* is that *Keter* is the will to reproduce, *Ḥokhmah* is the single cellular egg at the moment of conception and *Binah* is the differentiation process in which the single cell begins to divide and differentiate into a fetus. In a similar vein, the next seven *Sefirot* follow the development of the torso and limbs, eventually resulting in birth through the canal in *Malḥut*.

During the Omer we are concerned primarily with the lower seven *Sefirot*.* These are the more tangable of the ten.

Ḥesed is the quality of loving-kindness. It is expansive and generous. It is represented by the archetypal personalities of Abraham and Rebecca. Abraham was known for his love of giving, especially to the passersby. It is said that his tent was open on all four sides so that no one could escape his welcoming hospitality. Rebecca poured water for Eliezer and for all of his camels. Her giving poured like water.

So how is your giving? Are you giving with *Kavannah*, emulating the Divine generosity that gave to you? Do you know how to say "yes" – "*hineni*, here I am"?

Gevurah is the quality of strength needed for maintaining discipline on a spiritual path. It sets boundaries and limits the ego. It is also the known as "*Din*," meaning judgment. It is represented by the archetypes of Isaac,

---

* For a God-centered understanding of the *Sefirot* and their negative elements see: Rebbe Menaḥem Naḥum of Chernobyl, *MeOr Eynayim* (The Light of the Eyes) on *Parshat Miketz* (translation available in the "Classics of Western Spirituality" series).

respect / boundaries

Sarah and Leah.* Isaac was an introverted character who willingly allowed himself to be bound on the altar. He followed in his father's footsteps by re-digging the same wells; he never ventured beyond the boundaries of the Land. Sarah set the rules in the house. She had the strength of character to order her husband to exile Hagar and Ishmael. It is of she that it is written: "*All that Sarah says do*!" (Genesis 21:12). Leah was the unloved sister. She needed tremendous reserves of inner strength in order to stay within the family dynamic and remain in love with Jacob.

So how is your inner strength? How is your discipline dedicated to Holy service? Do you know how to say "no"? Can you open to allow the Divine strength to flow through you?

Tiferet, beauty, is the balance between the right side (*Ḥesed*) and the left side (*Gevurah*), in which discipline is taught from loving-kindness and in which loving-kindness is disciplined. This is compassion. It is also the gateway or ladder between Heaven and Earth, the spiritual and the material. This is Jacob, who transforms from "he who sits in tents" by integrating the "man of the field" (his brother Esau) into Israel (lit.: "straight to God"). It is Ruth, the humble woman of compassion (ruthful as opposed to ruthless). It is the heart center.

How is your heart open to the Divine and to the Creation of the Divine?

Netzaḥ (lit.: victory or eternity) is the attribute of leadership and dominance. It's putting the right foot forward. Moses is the archetypal leader and teacher. He was God's shepherd, guiding the people through the desert. He was the receiver and transmitter of Torah. He gave to all and argued in order to save his brethren, as did Abraham (*Netzaḥ* being below *Ḥesed*). Miriam took affirmative action when she guarded over her brother on the Nile and later when she co-led the people through the Reed Sea and on into the desert. It is said that upon her merit flowed the spring of water known as Miriam's Well.

So how is your leadership? How are you leading your life? Are you walking with God?

Hod (lit.: glory) is the attribute of empathy, of withdrawing the ego to make room for another. Aaron was the High Priest, the one that stepped out of the way to let the Divine blessing flow through to the people. He was the

---

* Leah is also placed in *Binah* because her beauty was not outwardly expressed like her sister Raḥel's, but rather inwardly and was therefore more elevated.

peace- maker, the mediator, the mouthpiece for his brother Moses. He accepted the discipline of the priesthood. Hannah, the mother of Samuel, prayed for a child and then withdrew her own desires by giving the boy up to the High Priest for Divine service.*

So how is your Divine service? How well do you listen to others? Do you know when to follow rather than lead?**

Yesod is the center of power and (pro)creativity. It is the seat of the ego. It is also a gateway between Earth and Heaven while being the balance between the outer work (*Netzaḥ*) and the inner work (*Hod*). It is represented by Joseph, who was a great leader yet cared for his family, who understood that sex without love is like spilling seed, who transformed into the *Tzaddik* (Righteous One) by finally absorbing the lesson that God is in control. Tamar is the female archetype in *Yesod*. She took action that resulted in her giving birth to the progenitor of the line of King David. For her courage and discretion towards her father-in-law (Judah), she too is acknowledged as a righteous woman.

So how is your creativity? Are you using your power for God or for bad? How is your Trust in the Divine hand?

Malkhut is wholeness of all the above. It is the expression of God in the world through our actions. It is the Divine Presence amongst us. It is represented by the line of King David starting from Judah, who learned how to take responsibility in the world. It is Boaz who took in Ruth (Ruth being directly above Boaz in *Tiferet*). It is King David who was the King, warrior, lover and psalmist – all for God. It is Raḥel who was the reflection of the beauty of the *Shekhinah* and lies below Jacob. It is also Queen Esther who went into the inner chamber of the King dressed in the clothes of majesty. It is the energy of the Messiah – the total healing.

---

* Reb Zalman likes to place Sarah in *Hod*, viewing her as a High Priestess initiating Abraham into the Ways of the Spiritual World. Miriam and Rebecca can also switch places: Miriam is connected to water and the flowing of the spring in the desert and can therefore be placed in *Ḥesed*. Rebecca was a manipulator (in both the good and the not-so-good sense) and can therefore be equally at home in *Netzaḥ*.

** Ruth and Hannah can also be swapped. Ruth was willing to give up everything to be with her mother-in-law Naomi. This is a *Hod* modality. Hannah poured out prayer from her heart – this is *Tiferet*. It should be pointed out that all the archetypes could be identified with different emanations. This is true especially of the female entities. The truth is that we are all present in all of the *Sefirot*; the question is – which is dominant now? In this way the *Sefirot* can be compared to the enneagram (see *The Enneagram and Kabbalah* by Rabbi Howard A. Addison, Jewish Lights).

❧ Afterword – ❧
The Journey from Pesaḥ to Shavuot

For almost the whole month between Purim and Pesaḥ, ḥametz (bread) takes on an almost demonic status. Every effort is made to remove every last trace from our presence. The morning before Pesaḥ, the last remnants of ḥametz are burnt. During Pesaḥ no ḥametz is eaten, seen or owned. Shavuot is the culmination of the Pesaḥ experience. It is connected to Pesaḥ through the Counting of the Omer – seven times seven plus one. It is the celebration and reenactment of standing at the Mountain ready to commit to a marriage with God and the living of a Godly life. Surprisingly, though, one of the unique sacrifices that the Torah calls to be offered on Shavuot is none other than ḥametz! In fact it is the only time of the year that ḥametz was allowed in the vicinity of the alter; at all other times the instructions were very clear – no ḥametz could accompany a sacrifice. So how come after having made such an effort to rid ourselves of ḥametz (illusion, pride, inflated ego) during Pesaḥ, we now celebrate it at Shavuot? A parable: when a *Kallah* (bride) and *Ḥatan* (groom) stand under the *Ḥupah* (marriage canopy), we stand in awe of the beauty of the couple and the sanctity of the moment. "She's so beautiful." "He's so handsome." "They look so wonderful together." "How lucky they are to have been brought together!" "Surely this is a match made in Heaven." And we dance before the *Ḥatan* and *Kallah*. And how do they feel? Just a day before they were ordinary people and now they are so special. How happy they feel! How beautiful they feel! They both swell with pride at how blessed they are to have been chosen for each other. And they offer up a prayer of gratitude. This is the good pride that comes in recognition of their uniqueness! This is the bread of Shavuot. But the moment that they should say (God forbid) – "Our wedding was so much better than that wedding," "We are so much more beautiful and blessed than that couple," "We are so much more chosen than they" – then that is arrogance and false pride! That is the ḥametz of Pesaḥ that we need to burn!

Now I understand

Praise G-d! T.Y. Lord.

Through The *Holistic Haggadah*, **Michael Kagan** shares his teachings and holistic approach to Judaism that he has developed through experiential workshops and lectures in Israel and around the world. He moved to Jerusalem in 1977, has a Ph.D. in Chemistry from the Hebrew University of Jerusalem, is married to Ruth Gan Kagan and has five children. He describes himself as an Ortho-practicing, but unorthodox, Jew.
The film, *Seasons of the Soul – The teaching of Reb Zalman and Michael Kagan* – directed by Chuck Davis, extends the theme of *The Holistic Haggadah* to the entire year.

Reb Zalman Schachter-Shalomi is a master of prayer. His great knowledge of the prayer tradition and his sensitivity to language and music allows him great freedom to experiment with sounds and rhythm in order to perfectly determine the appropriate word or phrase in the vernacular that will stir the heart and raise the soul.

Sandra Pond is an artist living and working in Boulder, Colorado. Everything she sets her hands to do is in celebration of her relationship with God. All that she desires is to help create the vessel for the Presence of God to **dwell.** She thus demonstrates, through personal example, how God is the potter and we are the clay. She has been married for three decades and has two sons.